Reading
and Righting

Reading and Righting

the past, present and future of fiction for the young

ROBERT LEESON

Collins

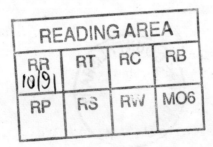

William Collins Sons & Co Ltd
London · Glasgow · Sydney · Auckland
Toronto · Johannesburg

First published 1985
© Robert Leeson 1985
ISBN 0 00 184413-x hardback
0 00 184415-6 paperback

Printed and bound by
Billing and Sons Ltd, Worcester

Contents

Acknowledgements

The arguments and conclusions in this book are my own. But it would not have been possible to write it without much reliance upon the writings of others which I have found valuable, even when, as sometimes happened, I did not share their opinions.

I am grateful for the work of R. D. Altick, John Burnett, Alec Ellis, Brian Simon and James Walvin on education, libraries, literacy and the social life of children; Brian Alderson, F. Harvey Darton, Eric Quayle, and John Rowe Townsend on the general history of children's literature; Gillian Avery, Angela Bull, J. S. Bratton, Nancy Cutt, Stephen Prickett and Isabel Quigly on Victorian/Edwardian children's literature; Mary Cadogan, Patricia Craig, Bob Dixon, Louis James, E. S. Turner, and Martha Vicinus on popular literature past and present; Marcus Crouch, Margaret Meek and colleagues, Sheila Ray, Margery Fisher, Elaine Moss, and Barbara Sherrard Smith on twentieth century children's literature. *Signal* Magazine was a rich source of material on Victorian/Edwardian criticism and *Children's Book Bulletin* provided stimulating theoretical notions on recent fiction for the young. Christine Leeson, Ingrid Selberg, Rosemary Stones and Bobbie Whitcombe offered helpful critical comments during the progress of the work.

The publishers wish to thank Thorpe Hall Primary School, Walthamstow for kind permission to photograph their school bookshop and the pupils for their help and co-operation.

For Jack Lindsay
with affection and respect

Introduction

In this country, fiction for the young has a splendid past, in which high standards were achieved; an unsettling present in which these standards are endangered by controversy; and an uncertain future in which the very foundations of literature are threatened by a surge of rival story-telling technologies. That is the conventional view. It is not a reassuring picture.

This book aims to offer an opposing view – by calling in question some of the splendours of the past, and by arguing that today's disputes and demands arise naturally from the way in which the literature has evolved, and that out of today's conflicts the story-in-the-book can gain a new lease of life, taking its proper place in the multi-media society of the future.

The conventional view sees children's literature as being born in the eighteenth century as part of the developments of the age of print. The earlier oral tradition, the folk tale, it is argued, had no specific place for the child. Children's literature came with the emergence of the modern middle class which (as philosopher James Mill observed) "gave the nation its character". Part of this process, an investment in the future, was the "discovery" of childhood – setting children apart in their own nursery way of life, with their own nursery stories, written especially for them.

To educate and mould the newly discovered child, rationalist and religious thinkers shaped a didactic fiction to "make Tommy a better boy and Polly a better girl". But others pleaded the young reader's need for works of imagination and fantasy. In the end, so the argument runs, imagination won the day. Fairy tales, nonsense, and youthful frolic reigned. Publishers and writers, freed of moral-didactic constraints, combined to produce a flowering of pure creativity, a nineteenth century Golden Age.

Out of this freedom grew our twentieth century literature, flourishing between "ivory tower and market place." By now it had its own landmarks, or classics, against which new work could be matched. And it was fit to be judged alongside all other forms of imaginative writing. As with them, standards of excellence could be established which would outlast momentary considerations of popularity, or suitability for this or that audience. Children's literature came of age in the mid-twentieth century.

Alarmingly, just as the fiction seemed to have reached its point of maturity, the debates of the late eighteenth and early nineteenth century burst out again. Moral and aesthetic values were set against one another, and there was renewed and powerful insistence on the didactic purpose of children's writing and its relevance to the lives of the young reader.

Since this outburst came against the background of a new wave of social and technological change, greatly resembling that of the earlier Industrial Revolution, it appeared to call in question all past achievement, to undermine the very basis of the literature. What hope was there for the future, when simultaneously the storming growth of new entertainment and information media seemed to foreshadow the obsolescence of the Book itself?

To decide whether these fears for the future are justified, or to decide what to do about the future's challenge, one has first of all to decide whether the picture of the past and the present is really as it is painted.

This book will argue from the start that the oral tradition, the folk tale, *did* have a place for all young people, that indeed much of it was of immense value in passing on the community's stored wisdom and values to the next generation. It was because the new class, the cultural elite of the age of print, wished to discard the values of the past, that they accompanied the creation of a new literature for a minority of children with a sustained and sometimes violent attack on the folk tale. Religionists and rationalists joined forces to attack its "vain fantasy" and its "absurdity".

Those who defended fantasy and the imagination had restored the *fairy tale* by mid-nineteenth century. But they did so on the basis of an almost entirely foreign model – French, German, Scandinavian, in a form and with characters alien to native folklore. They replaced the myriad, human-like fantastic creatures of the old *folk tale* with a uniform, diminutive "gauzy-winged" creature out of the eighteenth century *Cabinet des Fées*. They did this so successfully that by the 1890s, anthologist Joseph Jacobs began a rescue operation with the protest: "Who says the English have no fairy tales of their own?"

Discarding, refining, expurgating a tradition deemed unsuitable for the young, the new literature created stories seen as suitable *only* for the young. In place of a story which adult and child believed together, was created a story which the adult did not believe but the youngster was expected to do so.

More was lost than belief. Out of an oral tradition in which all classes and types of people, male, female, young and old, enjoyed in their turn the centre of the stage, developed a printed fiction in which the writers – and the main characters – were drawn mainly from one social stratum. The rest became culturally invisible.

The inevitable rationalisation of this process of control and exclusion was the notion (still held by some today) that the majority below this cultural Plimsoll Line do not wish to see their own kind at the centre of fiction – unlike their forbears in pre-literate times. Instead they prefer, if they read at all (it is argued), to "escape" into the lives of more fortunate people. Acceptance of the literature by those thus excluded involves for them an often unacceptable denial of their own identity.

Out of this situation develops the paradox: that a literature which claims to be the best of its kind in the world has, after achieving not one but two Golden Ages, failed to win the majority of young people. A fiction which won the battle to be free to entertain the young without moral-didactic restraints does not seem capable of fulfilling its historical mission.

There is another historical paradox. In the eighteenth century, young fiction had the attention of, and was avidly discussed by, some of the most admired brains in the country, from Johnson, Goldsmith and Coleridge, to Erasmus Darwin, Joseph Priestley and the other presiding geniuses of the Industrial Revolution, as well as the philosophical counterparts in England of Jean Jacques Rousseau in France.

But as the literature matured, intellectual interest waned. In 1865 a writer in *Aunt Judy's Christmas Volume* remarked: "Children's literature is nowhere studied in this country at a high academic level as a branch of literature." A century later, C. S. Lewis protested at "the playfully apologetic tone" he had to adopt when discussing his interest in children's books with fellow scholars.

The intellectuals, it seemed, cared more for a crude and primitive literature than for a refined and developed one. From the Second World War, a concerted campaign has been waged in certain quarters to induce academics once again to take children's books seriously.

But the paradoxes do not end there. A literary movement which began by insisting on the need for spontaneous pleasure rather than edifying lessons for the child, once the literature had been brought to respond to this need, then went on, in recent years, to deny the relevance of the child's wishes to the choice and judgement of good fiction for the young. A literature which owed its origins to the impulse to teach new lessons was now to declare that it had no more lessons to teach.

Within this literary development, a combination of commercial enterprise and writing talent, freed from moral and didactic restraint, is said to have produced the Victorian–Edwardian Golden Age, historic pinnacle of achievement. And yet, the same factors, unrestrained, in the four decades that followed, until the 1950s, led to what is now considered to be a low point in the history of children's literature. During this low period, fantasy, said to be the great English contribution to this fiction, not only pervaded the tale of imagination, the fairy story, but also the historical novel, the school novel, the family and the holiday novel. The pervasive influence of fantasy did not, however, elevate the genres it pervaded.

The process of refining the literature by discarding the moral-didactic element, in fact, helped to remove its backbone. It was indeed a case of "de-moralisation". Not until after the Second World War, when the sustained attention of a revitalised school and library network lifted children's publishing out of its pre-war doldrums, did breadth and quality begin to return.

While this specialised, artificial literature, born and nourished within the nursery of the cultural elite, was gradually refining itself out of existence, another process had been moving in the opposite direction.

The descendants of the working majority, excluded from education in the new skills of the age of print and literature, as they had been excluded from their role as popular creators of the story, had fought a sustained battle to win as a right for everyone what had been claimed as a privilege by one social group.

In the second half of the twentieth century, a school and a library system expanding to meet this new demand provided the material basis for an enormous expansion of children's reading, and thus of fiction for the young. The newly discovered "child" was in Brian Jackson's phrase "the child of the common man".

But at first the makers of the fiction were reluctant to realise that this was no blank cheque. A literature evolved out of the needs and concerns of one privileged social group could not simply multiply itself and expect to be accepted without question by the majority. The literature needed to change. It needed, to meet this new opportunity, to recover the social breadth and the creative popularity of the folk tale tradition it had so thoroughly dispensed with in the past.

A change like this does not come automatically or spontaneously. Outside pressure, in the form of demands by a new generation of teachers, librarians and parents, by activists for the rights of working-class, black and female children, or simply from the passive resistance of the wider majority of young people, was bound to come. And it was bound to come also in the shape of new writers whose experience and background was closer to that majority than was the experience and background of established authors.

We are still in the middle of this period and while this literary revolution continues another, massive, change rolls on. As the printed word with its new story-technology once threatened the old tradition of the spoken tale, so the new electronic media appear as the most important vehicle for the story, threatening to displace the book.

The very survival of the literature, at any level, depends upon whether it can develop a broad popular appeal and win the backing of the wider audience. A narrowing audience, no matter how highly it values the book, and no matter how well writers respond to this appreciation, becomes less and less viable, as falling sales erode its economic base.

There is room for optimism, though, as out of the upsets and confusions of recent years, certain forward moves can be seen. The growth of alternative publishing, of black, feminist, and community projects, has helped to create a new audience and to widen the old. The return of writers to the ancient role of story-teller, travelling round the schools, not only telling stories but encouraging the next generation to write their own, extends the life of literature into the future, and gives the written story a new/old outlet.

The rise of the school bookshop, changes in the way libraries are run, the arrival of the paperback, all widen the potential appeal of the book to fresh readers, just as they bring to the fore the demands of the young consumer as a factor in the choice of books to be published.

The possibilities are great, just as are the problems and the perils. But the alternatives are clear. Either we work to guarantee printed fiction, one great achievement of the modern era, a living future in a vastly changed world, or we accept that it is going into the time capsule for the edification of future archaeologists.

Discussing all these questions with many of the thousands of teachers, librarians, parents and children whom I have met, in meetings, conferences, story-telling evenings and workshops over the past decade, inclines me towards the optimistic conclusion.

Robert Leeson, July 1984

I

Once upon a time:
Folk Tales and the Young

Once upon a time, there was the story, told by word of mouth, and that was how it was for tens of thousands of years. For most of human history, stories have been wall-painted, danced, acted, but above all, said and sung. Only for a brief part of that history have they been written down, or printed. To think of story, of fiction, only as the book, is to cherish an illusion about the past, and the future.

Yet, literary people do not find it easy to imagine that time when stories were composed and stored in the mind, transmitted by the mouth and received by the ear, all common to human beings. It is that universal aspect of the spoken story which gave it the name "folk" tale. At root this means not just a tale of the working men and women of the countryside, though they did indeed compose most of the stories; it also means a tale of the whole people. Story-teller and audience were very much at one with each other, and so the stories reflected every part of that audience, from whatever level of society they might come. It was, in the true sense of the word, popular.

Over tens of thousands of years, generation after generation of hunter-gatherers, shepherds, farmers and craft workers added their ideas, experiences, the colour and atmosphere of their lives. The story tradition filled up like a deep, enormous pool, fed by long-fallen rains which seeped through many strata of unseen rock.

This pool is the source of all our literature. Stories specially made for children and young people may appear to belong only to the age of print, but the full history of children's literature is closely entwined with the fate of the oral tradition, the folk tale. And entwined in the strangest way. In the eighteenth century, when printed children's literature began to develop, the oral tradition was considered generally unsuitable for the young. Yet, in the nineteenth century, when the folk tale had been transmuted into the "fairy tale", it was considered suitable *only* for the young. Now, in the twentieth century, the folk tale is once again paid the respect it deserves. On the other hand, "adult" literature, the novel, pride of the age of print, is seen as losing its way, and by contrast, stories for the young are praised for having in them the root of the matter. Children's literature, says modern critic John Rowe Townsend, has preserved a "sense of story".

This is entirely as it should be. Story telling is basic to human nature. Story-telling has much to do with the making of human beings. Anthropologist Richard Leakey, in his *People of the Lake*, wrote:

> ". . . who would deny that the facility to share experience, to create a genuine shared consciousness, would be evolutionarily advantageous to creatures whose unusual subsistence economy forced them into uniquely intense social contact?"

If stories have even indirectly some sort of "survival value", then this makes them especially important to the younger members of the community. For children every moment of growth is an education, everything they see or hear teaches them, whether adults wish it or not.

The story has the same meaning for the child as play: it teaches as it pleases, it extends as it relaxes. And it is in games and their related song and dance that the creative capacity of even the youngest has continued to the present day. Iona and Peter Opie remind us of this in their *Lore and Language of Schoolchildren* (1959).

Every children's story is, in the broadest sense of the word, a story about growing up. Stories told by adults to children cannot help but teach, because of the difference in age and experience. The story is the gateway through which the young pass in discovering the difference between facts and the truth, between observation and understanding, which is the essence of all experience and thus all growing up.

Everyone tells stories. A story in dictionary definition is "narrative events in their sequence," and the sequence has to do with both form and content. We dream in narrative. We explain ourselves in the same way. (What is *your* story?) Even journalists professionally committed to the presentation of "things as they happened", can find no higher praise than "that was a good story".

Skill or art in the telling is the guarantee that the audience will listen, will accept and, crucially, will remember. Through thousands of years of story telling, techniques have developed that can be learned and applied, skilfully or not, by everyone. The word *fiction* is derived from the word to form or fashion. From the same root grew the word *feign*, with its suggestion of untruth.

This poses problems for the child, who may one day ask its parents, "Tell us a story", and next day be told by the same people, "Don't tell stories". The linking of the spoken word with lies and the written word with truth ("there it is in black and white") is a thread which runs through the matters discussed in this book.

So story has power, which is why imagination cannot be separated from morality. Attempting to separate the two leads to difficulty, just as the development of the story depends upon the fine balance of the one with the other. To say, "that was a good story" can never mean simply, or only, that it was well done.

Above all, when adults tell "fictions" to children or young people, when the story is the transmission belt for experience and understanding, then considerations of moral and meaning must arise. Moral, meaning, message, or simply the point of the joke, painfully visible, or buried deeply in the flesh and bone of the story, cannot be removed any more than the skeleton can be separated from the body, this side of death.

Modern critic Nicholas Tucker in *The Child and the Book* (1981) remarks that in Beatrix Potter's stories there is no moral except that if you are not careful you may end up making a meal for someone. But if you reflect on it, that is a pretty powerful moral or lesson. Beatrix Potter is tapping a well source as deep as that which children's games draw on – primeval skills in self-preservation. ("What time is it, Mr Wolf?" "Dinner Time!") As with old games, so old stories. Time, repetition, tradition, make the lesson as natural as breathing. It no longer has to be stated, or asserted. It can be assumed. This development, from assertion to assumption, lies at the heart of the development and refinement of the oral story-culture. And it lies at the heart of the development and refinement of the written literature which followed. Looking back from the vantage point of all the stored, taken-for-granted knowledge which writing and print have made available to us, it is not always easy to appreciate the many-layered complexity of social understanding embodied in those stories handed down by our ancestors. Their simplicity is deceptive because they rest upon a deep foundation of common understanding and a shared outlook on the world. Eighteenth and nineteenth century critics mistakenly condemned the folk tale for its apparent lack of moral, just as twentieth century critics sometimes welcome it for the same mistaken reason.

Victorians in the full flush of their mastery over nature and knowledge were inclined to see earlier ages as the infancy of humanity. By mid-nineteenth century the illiterate were already spoken of with contempt. Underestimation of those unable to read or write (or apparently little interested in doing so) led to false assumptions, the effects of which still plague us today.

Modern research into the ways of communities still living in pre-industrial conditions, though, now offers us a clearer and perhaps more respectful understanding of our own distant past. It offers clues to how stories were made, presented and received in the past, and what they meant for those who made and heard them. Thanks, too, to the resilience of the oral tradition, we have through the researches of the modern folklorist a clearer notion of these stories. Paradoxically we may know more today of the oral tradition than did many "educated" people who lived closer to it in time, during the eighteenth and nineteenth centuries.

We have some idea of the extent of story heritage. Even in 1946, pioneers of modern folklore studies in Finland had assembled some 50,000 stories. So vast is the store that the tales have been classified into some 2,500 types. The stories themselves are as diverse as the peoples who made them and as universal as humanity itself. Take for example the 300 versions of the *Cinderella* story, from Europe and the Far East.

Storage of spoken stories entirely by memory involves an incredible achievement. In ancient Greece the 15,000 verses of the *Iliad* and 12,000 of the *Odyssey* were preserved by the memory, not of an individual composer, but the collective memory of traditional "guilds" of vernacular story tellers. At the other end of the time scale the Khirghis poet Jamboul, who died in 1945, had composed some half a million verses, which he could recall without a written text. Twentieth century Irish story-tellers are credited with a memory bank of stories equal to ten novels.

Thus even in modern times the capacity of human memory is still impressive. We never quite forget the stories we are told, though few of us can recall them in the way we first heard them – even the briefest anecdotes – and we must re-create them, altering them as we re-tell them. But to be recalled or recreated the spoken story requires a series of linked acts binding audience and story teller together. Neither can do without the other. The story-telling technique involves composition, transmission and storage. And the technique expresses itself in a similar way around the world and through time. There is an account of a "heroic" story-teller in the epic poem *Beowulf*, set down in England over 1,000 years ago. His technique combines re-call, re-creation and the addition of new material based upon real happenings, which he then blends with historical and mythical "events".

In the massive study *The Growth of Literature* (1940) H. M. and N. K. Chadwick note how similar this is to the technique used by Yugoslav minstrels in modern times. As Arne and Thompson (*The Types of the Folk Tale*, 1961) remark, the teller could not recite the same story twice over. Yet, no matter how many retellings there were, or how much material added, the relationship between teller and audience ensured that the new versions were faithful to the essence and spirit of the old.

Audience participation was essential. It might be the *Mitdichtung des Hörers* of the Germanic tradition – the audience joining in the composition; or it might be the verse and chorus of English ballad tradition. The chorus not only held the audience's attention and maintained mood and tension, it also provided breathing space to improvise and add new ideas and elements. (Ballads, of course, had traditionally other functions than entertainment. In the seventeenth century, John Aubrey knew a servant who could give a complete history of English monarchs in ballad form.)

The spoken story was open to every reach of society and reflected all social strata. There was the story-telling of the minstrel who served chief or king and might be rewarded with gifts (or have them taken away and given to a rival as in the sad case of the Old English poem *Deor's Lament*). And there was the story-telling of the peasant fireside. But there was an interchange between the two. The epic, with its mixture of heroic deeds and wider lore and custom, and the later medieval romance became part of the cottage repertoire, and the peasant story found its way into the hall.

There was a flow between audience and story-teller, between audience and audience, and between the different modes of telling a story – from the drama of fireside recitation to that of the morality play and the seasonal festival. There was no artificial gap between media: Robin Hood's story might be cottage ballad, May Day Festival or castle masque. Robin appears as primeval Green Man, a yeoman farmer and as wronged knight, according to version, before being recruited to fight in the Crusades. (The ultimate fate of many fictional heroes and rebels was to fight abroad for king and country.) Yet Robin Hood's essentially rebel message was never completely digestible, and from time to time in the sixteenth century, it was forbidden in various places to portray "Robert Hude" or "Mayde Marian" on May Day.

Different audiences involved different story-tellers. The skald who sang for the chief, the minstrel who sang for baron or king, was often a professional. The amateur of the cottage trade might well be a local. (Caedmon, the Saxon hymn-writer, sneaked away to see to the communal pigs to avoid having to say or sing his piece when the harp was passed round the tavern.) Or he might be a wanderer. And wanderers have played an important part. The Russian oral story was evolved to great length and complexity in the nineteenth century, partly through the habit of tramps prolonging the narrative by various devices to ensure supper and a night's lodging. Wanderers from farm to farm in twentieth century Australia, developed the "tall story" to an art form.

In the Middle Ages, the English Minstrel's Guild, like the French, was for the professionals. It tried to protect them from the amateurs, from "rude husbandmen and artificers of diverse trades", who invaded the craft. It punished any professional who "stole another's castle from him". It had royal patronage right into the age of print, and English kings of the day watched carefully both amateur and professional. Henry I threatened satirists with the loss of a hand. Richard III threatened anyone who "told stories to the discredit of the king and his ministers."

But institutional censorship was very much a matter for those at the top. Further down the social scale, audience and story teller between them were the censors just as they were writer, publisher, bookseller, librarian and critic combined.

It was an art with its specialists, but it was a non-specialised art. What Malinowski noted about the New Hebrides (quoted in Jack Lindsay's *A Short History of Culture*, 1969) – "One . . . may be a better carver, dancer or story-teller but no one is unable to . . . carve, dance or tell stories" – could apply to any pre-literate society or community. The difference between story teller and audience was that of degree not kind.

It was a social art and that was its strength – and its limitation. The ever-present audience, its willingness to listen and accept, the physical endurance of both teller and hearer, and the interplay between the two meant that the tale could evolve only at a snail's pace.

The story must proceed in a straight line, avoiding the need to re-cap, beyond the ritual repetition of what happened to, say, three brothers or sisters attempting the same task in succession. Digression must be limited and as few people appear in each scene as possible. Character, in broad bands of good and bad, stupid and cunning, generous and greedy, was made plain in action, rather than described in detail. However, the darker complexities of the human spirit *are* reflected – the deep misery of the excluded Grendel in *Beowulf,* the strange brother-sister relationship of Robin Hood and the Abbess, or that between the king and his daughter in some of the versions of *Cinderella.*

Modern judgements on the folk tale sometimes use the term "unsophisticated", seeing the pagan notion of fate as being more primitive than the Christian notion of God's grace or the modern notion of coincidence. But these judgements should not be made hastily. The folk tale concept of the Other or Faery World with its relative time scales – a night spent in a fairy mound is seven years or a hundred years in everyday life – is more akin to the thought of Einstein than is that of the nineteenth century scientific enthusiast.

The oral tradition contained everything which a pre-literate society thought worthy of notice and worth passing on. And so it was especially important to the young generation. Just how important we can only guess. Did the spoken story have a special part within itself for children, or did they simply take their share of what was there? A good story would appeal to the old as to the child, wrote Sir Philip Sidney, the Elizabethan poet. Old and young would pass the night in story telling, says another account. How young? Tom Thumb and his doings were "carolled", by "shepherd and ploughboy", according to the first known chapbook version of the story, published in 1621. And you could be a ploughboy then long before they will let you do a newspaper round these days.

If children's literature was an innovation in the eighteenth century, that implies the existing oral tradition had no tales specifically for the young. This notion fits in with the argument that childhood has been recognised only in the past 300–400 years. It depends, of course, what you mean by childhood. Childhood is a relative thing. It varies from person to person, from group to group, from one era to another. But its natural frontier is the age of puberty. That most certainly has been recognised throughout human history and marked by many ceremonies, as have birth and death. In recent years, post-Freudian thinkers have been probing the sexual significance of the simplest of folk tales. They clearly have a great deal to do with people passing from childhood to adulthood, from innocence to knowledge. But one does not have to psycho-analyse the oral tradition to see that *Quest* and *Test*, the two fundamental elements in folk tale, are both of particular meaning for the growing human being.

Folk heroes and heroines are often young. And the younger, the more heroic. None is more successful than the youngest. And if like Jack of the Beanstalk, or Jack Hickathrift, or the vanquisher of the Lambton Worm, they are apparently useless, idle and despised when young, so much the greater will be their maturity and success. Stories are often about going out into the world in

22

symbol and reality. Twelve was the age at which Elidor the Welsh boy ran away from his harsh teacher. Tom Thumb was on the road within a short time of his birth, and he so small. Tom Thumb with his pranks, born to a couple so old they had given up hoping for children, is a story cunningly constructed to appeal to all ages. It was one of the most popular of folk tales and most often attacked by eighteenth and nineteenth century critics of the old story tradition.

One might guess that as the young grew into the work their parents did, which was one part of their education, and into the games which were another part of their learning, so they grew into the stories which were the third part of their life's teaching. There are matters in all folk tales which a child can understand; there are often others which require maturity of mind and body fully to appreciate.

> Little Robin Redbreast, sat upon a pole,
> Niddle noddle went his head, poop went his hole,

can be understood and enjoyed by the smallest.

> The huntsmen went a-riding, in red coats so gay,
> Little John had no coat to wear, at home he must stay.
> With the fur of my tabby cat, I will make him a little hat
> See my John ride away

can be savoured much more when the passing of puberty makes mysteries plain.

Stories already known to older people are heard for the first time by children. Thus they are always new to someone. They may be grasped only after further tellings, or even with added clarifications or "morals". Automatically, then, they are special for the young.

What values did the young draw from the oral tradition?

They were the values of the hunter-gatherer, the shepherd, overlaid by those of the farmer, touched on by those of the merchant, noble and monarch at further and further remove.

They are pagan. Christian notions come into them through the pens of those who set them down, as the Early English recorder of

Beowulf infused the epic with Christian spirit while leaving many pagan parts untouched. They came via the typesetter, as when Caxton in the fifteenth century turned Hercules into a "Good Crysten Knight" or when the old story of the Cheshire Cheese (a classic tale of abundance, sharing and greed) was given an added pair of welcoming angels to make the cheese's self-sacrifice acceptable.

The told story is basically about the relationship of humans with the natural world, and humans with humans, but very much more about the first than the second. It is full of spirits, which inhabit trees, water, rocks and animals, wild or domestic. Nothing is inanimate. They give warning or advice: a sheep helps Cinderella in one, Scots, version.

The other world is not elevated or distanced and divided into heaven and hell. It is ever present and near at hand. It may be entered by accident, or deliberately under the impulse of greed, folly or self-sacrifice to rescue loved ones, this being done by women as well as by men. In eighteenth century popular chapbooks, folk tales of people who had gone to the other world and returned safely were transformed into "true" accounts of people who had "been to Heaven" and returned.

The oral tradition is part of culture of a subsistence economy, of communities living mainly on what they can produce themselves. And so it is full of want and abundance and the virtues of sharing. It is bad manners among the hunter-gatherers of the Kalahari today not to share something you found in the bush. And in folk tale it is the youngest child sharing a crust with the old hag at the cross-roads who learns the secret of the treasure. Selfishness and greed among the villagers makes the Dun Cow, with its endless supply of milk, abandon the village.

Yet at the same time in folktales there is much winning of treasure, much gaining of kingdoms or half kingdoms, marrying of princes and princesses. The story had a vital function – readjusting in illusion the imbalance of wealth in the real world.

"When Adam delved and Eve span, who was then the gentleman?", the slogan of the Peasants' Revolt of 1381, emphasises that poverty and work are the human condition, riches the exception. Labouring in the fields, below the walls of the castle, in a world bounded by the horizon, you did not have to be a genius to know where wealth came from, or where it went. It came from the labour of the poor, which was why they were poor and the rich were rich. The notion of labour as the source of wealth drawn from the earth was common to peasant and medieval thinkers like Sir Thomas More. Not until the triumph of "political economy" in the nineteenth century was this notion dismissed as "madness" by Utilitarian thinkers.

Still, the high-born had the wealth and the low-born did not. The question was, did they deserve it? Robin Hood stole only from the undeserving rich. The notion of the deserving or un-deserving poor was one which came with eighteenth and nineteenth century middle-class morality. For the tellers of folk tales the poor automatically deserved. Poverty itself guaranteed virtue. Money was the root of all evil. Virtuous poor and wicked rich abound in the oral tradition.

Wealth tended to undermine virtue. Those who had rank and wealth were required by custom to prove they still had virtue as human beings. And the best way for the rich and powerful to prove that, was by suffering hardship or deprivation. The anonymous author of *The Land of Cockaygne*, one of many medieval ballads and stories about paradise on earth, said that any noble who wanted to reach that happy land would have to wade through muck for seven years.

Rank was recognised – chief, duke or prince. The blacksmith's son got the kingdom, he did not establish a republic. Kings – Alfred, Arthur, Edgar, Athelstan, John – they all appear in folk tale, perhaps suggesting the age of the tradition. But rank must be justified. Status must be measured against standing. Jack the Giant Killer agreed to serve the king's son, when he had seen him beggar himself to rescue a man unjustly imprisoned. Tom Thumb was born in the days when an "unguarded" (unarmed) ploughman might meet and advise the king, not as "today" when the court is full of "embroidered fools".

Poverty and work were virtue. But you needed cunning to retain the fruits of labour. This is shown by many contests between farmers and the Devil. Powerful adversaries are always ready to rob you. If you can rob in your turn, as Jack of the Beanstalk robbed the Giant, then good luck.

The "work ethic" did not begin with Protestantism. There are innumerable stories of brownies and boggarts and other household spirits, to emphasise the point made by modern scholar Katherine M. Briggs, whose work spans folk tale and children's literature, that people of the other world reward the "cheerful giver, the cheerful wayfarer, the cheerful worker". These spirits would punish idle servants and desert mean masters. Blue Cap who lived down the mines wanted the rate for the job. Cutty Soames, another mine-goblin, was only unpleasant to unpopular overmen. But it was the ethic of those who worked together, master and servant, rather than that of those who watched at a distance to make sure others worked for them – which might be more accurately designated "profit motive".

In these stories everyone has their place – men and women, boys and girls, farmers, tailors, beggars, kings, queens, because everyone as audience was involved in the making, hearing, judging, storing, passing on and re-making of the tale. It was part of the culture of a seemingly fixed and rooted society, renewing itself as did the natural world around it, a world held in awe and respect.

Stories transmitted by word of mouth were fated to disappear in mid-nineteenth century England, as the ancient way of life based on farm and village was swallowed up by industrial society. But the spoken story was in danger long before the way of life that sustained it was undermined. It faced a challenge from the moment a single spoken word was written down.

That which recorded and preserved could also destroy.

2

Writing is Power:
The Manuscript Age 500–1500

Of all inventions, that of the alphabet has best claim to have changed the world. There is magic in writing. To change spoken words into a code so that they may be understood when the speaker has gone, or is even dead, gives them an inhuman power. And the code, unlike speech, is not common to everyone, but belongs only to those who are taught it. Those who can teach it belong from the start to a new elite, closely linked with secular and religious power. Those who can read, and even more those who can write, smaller in number and closer to the source of command, form a fellowship with people like themselves anywhere. They know what the community around them does not. They are free from its ignorance and its prejudices. As Ernst Fischer, the twentieth century Austrian scholar put it, they are the voice taken from the chorus, the first individualists. And to pass on this vital skill to the next generation requires an early start, so the young of the "book people" become the conduit for that influence and power. Three thousand years ago, an Egyptian scribe advised his son to master writing to avoid a life spent in manual labour.

Those Near Eastern societies which brought alphabets into use recognised their power and potential for disruption. They undermined the power of memory – that collective act which bound early communities together – while they increased the power to think privately, to speculate, by lifting from the mind some of the burden of storage. Writing and reading were employed first in the temple, the storeroom and the palace. Only later did they intrude into the world of the story. But they did so first as an act of power. The setting down of the ancient Greek epics was the deliberate work of rulers like Solon and Peisistratos.

By fixing the texts, confining them to manuscript, they drew to themselves all the magical power of the people's past life and helped to confirm their own right to command.

Thus a contradiction enters the process of writing and reading, which has been with humanity since the invention of the alphabet. The influence of letters reaches out and gradually transforms society. But the power given causes those who have it to restrict the spread of the ability to read and write. First they seek to pass it on only to their own kind, through children or chosen pupils. Then they try to hinder others in their attempts to learn. Yet this conflicts with the basic human impulse to share, and share in new discoveries, an impulse with great survival value for the species. So the struggle over the right to learn reading and writing is a central part of the history of our society and still, in England, an intensely political matter.

The manuscript age in England lasted around a thousand years, from AD 500 to 1500. For the first 800 of those years it was confined to monks and priests and the spread of written texts only began to quicken in the last two centuries, 1300–1500, when the pace of social change began to increase.

The inroads made by writing into the world of the spoken story were thus slow at first, like the spread into a lake of rushes and reeds around it. There were economic reasons. The basic material, parchment, was immensely costly; for example, a bible consumed 300 sheepskins. There were also technical factors. Manuscripts were at first prepared for reading aloud to the largely non-reading audience. Until the late Middle Ages the true test of poetry was that of recitation. Anyone whose verse did not stand up to that test was a failure.

Writing down a story "slows down" the rhythms. That is an observation of folklorists. The truth of this can be easily tested.

I know myself that to read a story from the page is not half as effective as to tell it from memory (which inevitably involves recreation). Roberto Lagnado, a story-teller at work in schools today, has refused to write down his stories which he insists must come afresh from each telling.

"Listen to the voice of the pages" was the instruction to student monks in the Middle Ages. Silent reading was an innovation and regarded as a curiosity. Yet silent reading gives a power to learn beyond that of the listener – as anyone taking notes in a lecture can testify. Silent reading however, is an un-social act, a mark of the individualist. And in a world where each monastery might have only enough manuscripts for one book per monk per year, it was not easily practised.

Those old English manuscripts written down in the early years, are a mixture of the religious and the secular. They stand at the frontier of the oral and the written tale and because the art of writing in England is linked with the arrival of Christianity, they stand at the frontier of the pagan and the Christian, where one was expected to give way to another. In any case the impulse to record a "heathen" oral tradition was limited. In the eighth century, Alcuin told the monks on Lindisfarne: "In your house the voices of those who read should be heard, not a rabble of those who make merry in the streets. In the refectory the Bible should be read, the lector heard, not the harper, patristic sermons rather than pagan songs. For what has Ingeld to do with Christ?"

This is the first known shot in the long war between religious scholars and the pagan "superstitious" oral tradition. In the fourteenth century the Wife of Bath in Chaucer's *Canterbury Tales* declared that the "friars" have long since driven away the fairies. Three hundred years later Bishop Corbet laid this crime at the door of the Puritans. By mid-nineteenth century children's writer Jean Ingelow was blaming the Industrial Revolution.

It is difficult to say how much of the oral tradition was recorded in early medieval times. The devastation of war and invasion destroyed much manuscript. But the total volume of written work was increasing. By the thirteenth century in Europe a sort of mass production was being carried out in "scriptoria", the early ancestors of the publishing house, where monkly specialists in writing and illustration were employed.

All this activity was confined to a minority of population and at first its effect on the majority was limited and indirect. But, through the churches Bible stories, derived from the oral tradition of the Near East, found their way into the folk lore of these islands. ("When Adam delved and Eve span . . .") In the York morality play, for instance, the Shepherds of the Nativity are transformed into local characters.

But only after the arrival of the Normans in late eleventh century, with their brutal seizure of land, meadow, wood, stream, pond, mill and barn, and their obsessive recording of who owned what – details which the local population had always "known" – did writing really begin to invade the way of life of everyone. From around 1300 onwards a written deed of ownership became the key to any legal dispute about property. The "word" of your neighbours about boundaries, "unwritten" law, became secondary to parchment deeds. From this time on, secular scribes appear alongside the monks as the volume of written work multiplied. And, as M. T. Clancy observes in his *From Memory to Written Record* (1979), inside the scriptoria a new art form flourished. When not illuminating priceless scriptures, the monks were busy forging deeds of ownership, to ensure the wealth of the abbey beyond the lifetime, or the memory, of the patron.

Other documents were to make their inroads into the oral tradition. Chroniclers like Jean Froissart, political servants of monarchs, used "oral history" techniques. Other chronicles recorded not just the "actual" recollections of old battles, but tales like "Elidor" or "Cap O'Rushes" an English version of "Cinderella". Stories we now treat as "fiction" were written down as "what people say". Froissart and his like, though, while making their contribution to history, were hired for propaganda purposes just as the minstrel was paid to sing praises.

To the association of writing with received truth, power and wealth, was to be added its association with pleasure. The thirteenth and fourteenth centuries were to see the growth of a luxury trade in manuscripts for light reading among those laymen – lawyers and merchants or nobles – who had learnt to read or could hire someone to read for them. For this market the oral store of various countries was tapped for strange and appealing stories. *The Gesta Romanorum*, garnered from classical history and mythology, came into English via Latin, translated and set down along with native legends of Sir Gawain and other heroes. The old legends of Celtic Britain and France around the figure of Arthur were woven together as medieval romance, to make Anglo-French rulers feel at home in their new cultural setting.

In Chaucer's late fourteenth century *Canterbury Tales* we see these elements come together – English tales mixed with others

30

which seem home-grown but are drawn from the Arab world via the Italy of the *Decameron*. Chaucer skilfully uses the device of a pilgrimage and thus transforms a series of noted down tales into something that foreshadows the novel. Since he is writing, not speaking, he can create scenes in which several people converse together and are yet differentiated from one another. This was something most word of mouth story-tellers would have found difficult if not impossible.

The main market for such manuscript stories was among those engaged in "trade and manufacture". Though they represented but one in 20 of the population and their centre, London, was then smaller than present-day Luton, yet the market grew. In various cities secular scribes organised themselves into guilds.

Gradually they ousted the monks from all but directly religious work. The beginnings of commercial book production were laid. Rag paper, which came from the East via the Arabs, was far cheaper than vellum. This impelled further change. Commercial booksellers – and even a system of commercial loans of manuscripts – appeared in the London of Chaucer's day, the 1380s. By the fifteenth century the technology of manuscript was under severe strain. Scriptoria with teams of scribes could produce "editions" of 50 books, but they could not keep pace with the combined demand for legal, administrative and other documents as well as the fiction market.

Outside the towns the influence of writing had seeped down among the poor, though few of them could read or write. Plague, civil war and the breakdown of serfdom had set peasants, craftsmen, discharged soldiers on the roads. If they were to find employment, or avoid whipping by town beadles, then they must carry a certificate signed by a "prudhomme" of their neighbourhood. With these changes the basic way of life which sustained the oral tradition was going through the first stages of its historic decline. Its people were more and more subject to the rule of written words whose meaning they could only know if those above them chose to reveal it.

3

Stories for Sale:
The Age of Print 1500–

Printing arrived in England in the late fifteenth century as the manuscript age was at its height. The written word had taken a thousand years to impose itself on the society of the spoken word. Print made itself felt within a century. The impact was rapid first of all within that part of society where manuscripts flourished. Though a *de luxe* manuscript trade for the private libraries of the rich continued and though legal documents and apprentice indentures were handwritten for centuries to come, the scribe was on the way out. Within decades there are stories of scribes claiming relief from tax because of lack of employment.

Just as earlier the manuscript had conformed to the needs of a pre-literate society, so for a time printed books imitated manuscripts in word and decoration. Soon enough, though, print developed its own style. It already had its own momentum, producing as many letters a day as a scribe could produce in a year. Though editions of books no bigger than a present-day pamphlet might be small they were still ten to 20 times the normal edition of a manuscript. More books, and cheaper. The potential market widened; the demand grew.

But it could be no wider than the number who could read and write. The pressure to have children taught the new skills was bound to grow. The working family which had always taught its members what they needed to know could not cope with this new demand. Only the richest could afford a home tutor, cleric or layman. Teaching in the new skills, first in church schools, later in secular "grammar" schools, brought a new element into the lives of all involved.

"Learning" was no longer training in this or that trade or profession, but meant knowledge of a new kind, defined by reading and writing. It was a new distinction between those who were "taught" or "educated" and those who were not. The rich and powerful might employ someone to read and write for them, but eventually you do not command those who have powers you have not. Education, in terms of the ability to read and write, filled the area of power and influence, religious or secular. It became one of the chief distinctions, together with rank and wealth, between those who had influence and those who did not.

During the first century of print, nearly half the printed books went into the grammar schools to be used by young people. The book was a means to an end and an end in itself. It taught the young to read, and through reading it could teach them how to conduct themselves. Books of Nurture, Books of Conversation, appeared in the fifteenth and sixteenth centuries. The overriding use of books was didactic. The new medium was too important and costly to be lightly used. But the forms employed for teaching – the verse and the fable – are what we now associate with fiction. Telling a tale had traditionally been the best way of passing on something in a way it might be remembered. So today's sharp distinction between reading for learning or for pleasure was not appropriate. The power of the new medium brought its own pleasure.

The power was well understood at the top. Edward IV, patron of the Minstrels' Guild, was also patron of Caxton the first printer. The Church which had seen the secular scribe invade its manuscript monopoly, was swift to assert its claim to control print. Under royal sanction and clerical supervision, the number of printing presses was limited to twenty. It was held at this level from the fifteenth to the seventeenth century. This small group of commercial printers remained dependent upon the goodwill of the church.

Thus the three elements crucial to the development of printed fiction for the young – church, school and the printer-bookseller, were already in place.

As the new arrived, the old departed. Manuscripts began to vanish from reading use, save by printers who plundered them for saleable material. The Minstrels' Guild had gradually faded away by Queen Elizabeth's time. The scribes who had taken the minstrels' place were now at the service of the machine. They did

33

not "make" the book any longer, but prepared texts as raw material for the press. They copied from old manuscripts, cobbling together two or three tales to make a longer book, cutting to make the whole fit. They adapted the content of old stories to meet the demands of a new audience. And eventually, when the supply of old manuscripts was to run out, they would begin to write, or compose, stories to satisfy the growing demand for the new.

A ballad monger might make his own songs and sell them door to door. But in the main trade, the writer was not the same as the original story-teller. For the story was also undergoing a change. In the old days the story had been a service rendered to rich patron or popular audience, in return for patronage or supper. In the new days, the story was taken for cash payment, even stolen, and sold as an item on its own to other people whom the author might never meet. The service had been changed into a commodity, something made in solitude, eventually to be read in solitude. It was to be an essential part of the culture of the age of commerce, the age of individualism.

And between the story-teller and the audience appeared a succession of intermediaries – bookseller–printer, librarian, teacher and eventually, critic.

Print, of course, made much faster inroads into the oral tradition. If the effect of the manuscript age could be compared with the growth of rushes and reeds around a pool then that of print was the over-running of the pool by vegetation, until the water almost vanished and the area of the lake was only marked by the shape of the water meadow.

The Elizabethan writers of poetry and prose, Spenser, Herrick, Drayton and others, drew heavily on folk themes. The Elizabethan playwrights, such as Shakespeare, Peele, Lyly and Dekker, peppered their plays with folk allusions. But they belonged mainly to an urban world even if their memories were of the countryside. They and their successors were appealing to a city audience. London trebled in size during their century. Tudor land enclosures drove more thousands off the land, and the wanderers reached London, often to form part of an unskilled population excluded from membership of the crafts. Their lives in slum and suburb fostered a kind of urban folk lore. A prurient curiosity among the educated about "low life" was supplied by the writings of Nashe and Greene. But for those who could read but a little or had only a little to spend, opportunist bookseller–printers had the answer. They produced 16- or 32-page "chap-books", so-called because they were carried in the bags of chapmen or pedlars, who roved the country sleeping in barns and making a living as best they could.

In chapbook story versions the folk heroes from the greenwood were urbanised and lost something of their primeval force and virtue. The outlaw archers Adam Bell and Clim of the Clough were pardoned and made peace-keepers. Long Meg, the fighting barmaid of Westminster, was tamed by marriage. Moore Carew the beggar carried on robbing and cheating, but strictly on his own account. From Robin Hood to the cutpurses and highwaymen of Newgate is a winding road which reflects above all the detachment of story-teller from audience, one of the effects of the age of print.

Print was to have yet another diminishing effect upon the oral tradition. Print needed a wider market for each of its products. Its texts had to be understood around the country. Caxton made clear the problem from the start. Too many dialects, almost like separate languages, stood in the way. He and his successor Wynkyn de Worde set themselves the task of filtering out all expressions they considered obscure.

Basing themselves on the English of the Home Counties, they imposed this on the market. The development of the "King's English" went along with those developments that were turning England into a single nation and bringing it under secure central governments, a government which was to impose itself upon Scots, Welsh and Irish neighbours. Some of its negative effects still plague us today: the widening of the gap between written and spoken word, and the reducing of all tongues and dialects spoken outside the favoured counties to the status of a "patois", to quote H. J. Chaytor in *From Script to Print* (1945). The King's English and, later, Standard English came to dominate not only other ways of writing, but other ways of speaking. Out of the elitism of the book came the convention that there is only one "correct" manner of speech and that others are quaint or crude. The reviewer of a children's book in *The Times* (10 March, 1976) who thought it a nice conceit to make a fictional cat a Cockney because neither can pronounce the vowel "O" properly, was perhaps not aware of what a monstrous assumption this was.

Yet for the development of the story, print had its virtues. It solved the problem of limits on length and complexity imposed by audience and story-teller fatigue. It solved the problem of multiple character action. It helped the writer, in silent communion with the unseen reader, to consider in detail motive and the psychological aspects of character. It enabled writers over two centuries to draw together the devices of the story and of the theatre to create a new art form, the novel, or as Henry Fielding the eighteenth century playwright-novelist called it, the "comic, epic poem in prose".

Poetry, separated from recitation, could become deeper, more philosophical, exploring experience and emotion in solitude. It did not entirely lose its audience, but a hierarchy of poetry for quiet reflection above that for public performance was created.

Print and all that went with it led inexorably from the age in which verse ballads and plays were important forms of popular story-telling to modern times, when poetry has often been seen as a minority "educated" taste.

Print and writing placed the essential means not only of education, but also of creative story making, within the way of life and control of one stratum of the population – the "educated". And print was a crucial factor leading to the creation of a children's literature, along with the novel, during the eighteenth century.

Some of these effects sprang directly from the nature of print. But as with other technological changes, the effects of print were aggravated, made more radical, and speeded on their way by deeper social changes of which they were but a part.

The period of three centuries and a half, from 1500 to 1850, during which print overwhelmed the oral tradition in England was also the period in which that part of the population who engaged in trade and manufacture swelled from five to nearly 50 per cent, in which the country was changed utterly from agricultural to industrial nation.

Within that change and within that part of the population, the role of the "book people" or, as they called themselves, first the "middling sort" and, later, the "middle class", is vital.

4

The "Middling Sort": The People of the Book 1500–1850

They called themselves the "middling sort" – merchant, craft master, scrivener, lawyer. Cunning, courageous, never idle, they were as able to fire a cannon as to invent it. The Spaniards called them "Protestant Pirates", and they mastered the Grandee abroad in the sixteenth century, as they mastered the Cavaliers at home in the seventeenth. Restless and reckless, sober and cautious, their eyes on the future, in this world or the next, they were above all individualists, a cloud of atoms held together by the conviction that they were of a special kind ("Men of high degree are vanity, men of low degree are a lie", said the 63rd Psalm). Always a minority, balanced between the poor and the rich, they were ready to turn to one or another in time of crisis: ready to lead movements of protest, able to detach themselves to make deals with the powers that be. Endlessly seeking more freedoms, more rights, they were endlessly anxious that those rights should not be dispensed too widely. Their ranks thus contained the noblest of liberators and the worst of hypocrites, religious bigots and enlightened educators.

Their quest for influence and power went on over three centuries, along with their quest for understanding of themselves and their world. And in that quest their chief means was the book, from the Bible (their guarantee of knowing what God said without taking the word of the priest for it) to the novel (the "guarantee that the individual will always be more than one billionth part of a billion", as William Golding told the Nobel Prize Jury in December 1983).

For them the book, print and trade were linked from the start. Caxton's stated reason for working out a uniform English text was the difficulties which dialect differences placed in the way of merchants as they bought and sold around the country. Freedom to trade (against the court monopolists of Charles I), freedom to print, sell, read and comment on the Bible and other books (against the edicts of his bishops): these were the aims which brought the middling sort with their servants and journeymen on to the battlefields of the Civil War in the 1640s. The notion of Cromwell's soldiers, marching with Bibles in their knapsacks, is a myth, but a powerful one.

Hard core of this army and clearest single voice among the middling sort were the Puritans. They were in fact as diverse themselves as the middling sort, and much misunderstood today, when "Puritan" often refers to the critic and the censor. Originally, in the sixteenth century, it stood for a purifying force in religious and social life. It was indeed a force for revolutionary social change. Only if one sees the Puritans' actions as part of a long struggle to change society, can one throw light on this strange mixture of the liberating and the repressive.

The Puritans opened their assault on the bishops' control of the printing presses in 1640 by complaining of "lascivious, idle and unprofitable ballads" selling in London. The bishops, they alleged, were not truly interested in morality but only wanted to suppress reforming, Puritan ideas. In 1641, the Star Chamber was abolished and with it went Crown–Church control over the presses. During the Civil War and the short-lived Commonwealth Government that followed, the number of presses trebled to 60. From them came a flood of pamphlets and books on almost every topic. For some Puritans, the Presbyterians, there was too much freedom. But Milton, Cromwell's foreign secretary for a while, defended free publication in his *Areopagitica* – "Give me the liberty to know, to utter and to argue freely".

Strict control of the presses was clamped down again, when the Monarchy was restored in 1660. Charles II and his restored bishops, by insisting that they sign the 39 Articles of the Church of England, which they refused to do, drove many of their Puritan opponents out of the church, university and the grammar schools which the church controlled. These people, the Dissenters, or as they were later known the Nonconformists, formed the most active element in a social opposition which as before found its expression in literature, in writing and teaching. The Rule of the Saints for which they had fought was postponed, but they had faith, they could work and wait for the future – if not they, then their children would reach the Promised Land. Their contribution to a new, printed literature for the young was to be crucial in the next century and a half.

New ideas were in the air. A new class of well-to-do people wanted education – in book terms – for their children. They wanted books that would teach, not the "feigned fables" and "vain fantasies" of the oral tradition. But the teachings must appeal to the growing mind. There was a demand for new editions of books like *Aesop's Fables* – entertaining tales with the moral made clear. Even Charles I's unpopular censor, L'Estrange, in private a man with enlightened views on education, produced an edition of *Aesop*.

In this new era censorship in its old form could not last. The undertow of the movement towards free trade, beneath all the political and religious battles, was too strong. And in the 1690s the presses were going full blast again, not just in London and the university towns, but throughout the country. Some printers served the didactic trade, some the frivolous; some, opportunistically, served both. As Harvey Darton says in his *Children's Books in England* (1932), "Penny Merriments and Penny Godlinesses" poured from the presses. There were books for those who could afford them (a book cost a good deal more than a pair of breeches), chapbooks or instalment "parts" of books, or ballad sheets, for those who could not. Those who could not read, the majority in farm, village or town, would turn to someone else who could, to read for them. The process by which the reader would replace the story-teller had begun.

The Puritan-Dissenters' part in the making of the new literature is a remarkable one. It is said, with some truth, that they aimed above all with their writing to teach truth, Godliness and morality to the young. It is also said that they were against fiction, against fantasy and the imagination, that they frowned on enjoyment in the young, preferring to concentrate children's minds on approaching death and repentance to avoid damnation. They introduced the touching death-bed/conversion scene, the climax of many a children's (and adults') story for two centuries to come.

39

But all these aspects of their work need closer examination, because they are not what they seem.

Preoccupation with death and death-beds is not surprising in writers like John Bunyan, Thomas White, James Janeway, Thomas Willis and other Puritans who had experienced war, fire and plague; who lived at a time when, even in peacetime, life was short. But the Puritan interest in the gateway between this life and the next is at one with their interest in childhood, in nurture, conduct and morality, honesty and industry. It is an interest in the future; and in a future, different, better society. The wickedness of this world is not simply a complaint about the human condition, but also a critique of the way things are run. God, said Hugh Peters, Cromwell's chaplain, did not want the Saints to stand around with their hands in their pockets waiting for his Kingdom to come on earth.

Janeway, who published his *Token For Children* in 1671, is noted for his grim insistence on life's end. But his promise to his child readers that "in heaven they shall never be beat any more, they shall never be sick or in pain any more" breathes a quite contrary spirit of warmth – of better life in a different order. Like Bunyan, Janeway lived "in two worlds at once", says Harvey Darton (*Children's Books in England*). In modern terms we recognise, through the religious language and talk of the next world, the revolutionary import of what they were saying.

It is interesting, too, that in making their sober, didactic points, these writers, from the lesser-known right up to the great Bunyan, were far from unimaginative. Willis uses vivid imagery in his *The Key to Knowledge* (1682), White indulges in comic exaggeration in *A Little Book For Little Children* (1660). In striving to produce a body of reading matter which would convey a message to the young different from the ancient store of folk tales with their giants, ghosts and goblins, the "Godly" book led on towards a new fiction, despite all the protestations of those who produced it.

The process is contradictory and fascinating. On the surface it is a battle between "fiction" or "vain fantasy", and "truth", between the didactic and the fantastic, between morality and entertainment. But underneath it runs the struggle between an old way of life and scale of values, and a new. The new, to gain an

40

audience, turned constantly, perhaps often unconsciously, to the forms and conventions of the old, with its still powerful and enduring appeal.

John Foxe's *The Book of Martyrs* (1563) was a Puritan manifesto, a kind of counter-attack to the saints' lives published by the Catholic Church. Both were, in their way, religious versions of the old folk-heroes, half human, half spirit. But the saints' lives had compromised themselves in the battle with the pagan tale by including miracles, giving dubious authority to tales of magic. For its readers, Foxe's book was not like either saints' tale or folk tale. It was *true*. It was about real people, about events in current times. It was about the heroes of a social group under pressure. Their stories were more violent and horrific than any of the folk tales of the sixteenth century, which the Puritan Reginald Scot declared "servants have affrighted us with since we were children." Foxe's *Book of Martyrs* was to rob generations of children of sleep just as effectively. But because its purpose was acceptable, it was given as a Sunday School prize right until the twentieth century. As the real events which inspired it vanished into the past, it became like the tales of old, a part of the folk lore of a new society, a new class, ready for fictional appeal, not instruction.

One can see this complex process working itself out in three books published between the 1670s and the 1720s. All best-sellers, all written at first for adults, all became immensely popular with children. They are John Bunyan's *Pilgrim's Progress* (1678), Johnathan Swift's *Gulliver's Travels* (1726) and *Robinson Crusoe* by Daniel Defoe (1719). Two are written by Dissenters, Bunyan and Defoe, the other by an unorthodox Minister of the Church, Swift.

Like all the folk tales before them, they are about a quest, a test for the hero and an eventual reward. They all convey lessons and messages through the use of vivid imagery. The authors were all propagandists. They had all written pamphlets for wide distribution using clear and simple English. But all three books are "fictions". The characters are invented people (though Defoe used a real-life castaway, Selkirk, as the model for his Crusoe). All three stories were accepted as true by those who read them, just as audiences had accepted folk tales as true. They were accepted by those who condemned the stories of the oral tradition as "abominable absurdities", "occult and inexplicable causes" or "fantastic visions". These new stories were in their way fantasies, but unlike the old, they were not "vain" – their purpose was clear, it was asserted, not assumed like that of the folk tale.

In his journey towards the celestial city Christian (*Pilgrim's Progress*) leaves his family behind. But they are not forgotten as are the families of the departing folk hero or heroine. Eventually they follow him. Like the folk hero, Christian meets dragons, giants, enchantments, visions, and he wins a kingdom. Bunyan and his readers knew such victories to be denied them here and now. So they must win them in the spirit.

Giant Despair of Doubting Castle is a real figure of folk tale and can be accepted as such by children even today. He is also a psychological experience – symbolising the personal doubt and depression that can come to an individual, or the social despair that can overcome a frustrated and persecuted group. By inventing Christian, by making him as recognisable as any real life martyr, *Pilgrim's Progress* carries the reality of Foxe's book over into fiction. Blending the substance of a religious allegory with the structure and conventions of the folk tale, Bunyan points the way forward to the novel. Bunyan had served in the army, been tried in court and kept in prison. But his book, unlike Foxe's, was not an imaginative reconstruction of actual happenings, it was a truthful imagining of the way the world goes, created in Bunyan's mind, aided by his own experience.

The folk tale had human beings and non-human spirits, which disturbed the Puritans. Bunyan resolves the problem by locating them all in the human mind. Human attitudes and moral outlooks are also implicit in the struggles of the old folk tale. But these have journeyed so far from their origins that by now the attitudes are buried almost invisibly within the story. Thus the fantasy appears to be vain (modern commentators sometimes assume the folk tale has no moral because they cannot discern it). Bunyan in his tale makes the Giants and Dragons openly display and represent moral (or immoral) qualities. His attitude, his outlook is asserted and proclaimed, whereas in the long re-told, developed and stylised folk tale, all attitudes are assumed.

Bunyan thus took one of the crucial steps in the creation of the fiction of the printed word. First the new content, the new message, the new meaning must be declared, asserted. For the middling sort, this book said where they stood. It also declared that they existed. If you do not appear in the stories of your society's culture, you do not exist. You are "invisible", culturally. Christian, the hero, typical Puritan craftsman like John Bunyan, was proof that his kind of people existed. And they had to go on asserting their values until these became so much a part of the whole society's way of life that they could be taken for granted, assumed. Thus the development of printed fiction is a journey from assertion to assumption. Until Bunyan's Pilgrim made his *real* journey, the new book story could not escape from the old oral tale. It had to be true, before it could become fiction again. Without the new morality the tale would not be worth telling. Without the authority of age-old forms of story-telling, the new story could not win the audience and thus survive.

Gulliver's journey is like the folk journey, in that it takes him into different kingdoms. These seem unlike the real world. They have their own rules, though, and Swift was well versed in lore about alternative fairy worlds. And they reflect that world in which we live. Among the tiny people, the giants, the graceful horses and the grotesque humanoids, we meet again all the faults and follies of humanity.

Again, as with Bunyan, the young can read what they like from *Gulliver's Travels*, taking it as a fantastic adventure among imaginary people. In maturity they can read it as a satire on the rich and great. At a distance, now, we can see, perhaps more faintly, these same two levels of understanding operating in the story-culture of the oral tradition. With the new literature, expressing the known experience of the modern world, we see these things more clearly.

Crusoe's journey is that of *explorer*, like Gulliver's. But Crusoe's journey is also that of *conqueror*. Crusoe is human, and superhuman. He makes engaging mistakes, but he triumphs over incredible difficulties. He stands in for the reader, doing what the reader would wish to be able to do, to survive in danger and a hostile environment. And, for the eighteenth century English of the middling sort, he does more. He takes over a native population, after rescuing them from more "savage" enemies. His phrase "my people perfectly subjected" is significant. For in the real England in which he lived, Defoe looked in vain among the competing merchants and craft masters and rebellious journeymen, for what he called the "Great Principle of Subordination", that social order in which all would willingly accept their place.

Then, as later, the finding and making of Empire were seen as the solution to never-ending social trouble at home. Crusoe was to provide the model for hundreds of similar and worse adventures abroad, written specifically for the young in the next two hundred years, as England set out to subject the world. As the King, in *Gulliver's Travels*, put it:

> A crew of pirates . . . see a harmless people, are entertained with kindness, they give the country a new name, they take formal possession of it for the King, they set up a rotten plank or a stone for memorial, they murder two or three dozen of the natives, bring away a couple more by force for a sample, return home and get their pardon. Here commences a new Dominion acquired with a title by Divine Right.

The new literature, the new era for society, were launched. The means to wealth and power for the middling sort were coming to hand. Where they had invested faith in the future, they were to invest in more material things. But their greatest investment, for the future, was in their own children.

5

The Discovery of the "Child"
1540–1789

There are three signposts on the way to a children's literature, coming at intervals of a century. They are Roger Ascham's *The Scholemaster* (1545, but published later), John Locke's *Thoughts Concerning Education* (1693) and Thomas Day's *Sandford and Merton* (1783–1789).

They have a number of common features. They all show the middling sort at work trying to influence the ruling class, in which they were tireless. (They preferred to advise monarchs, only cutting their heads off under extreme pressure of necessity.) Roger Ascham managed to be tutor to both Queen Mary the Catholic and Queen Elizabeth the Protestant: a very skilful Puritan he. Locke, though only seventeen when King Charles lost his head, was a Puritan who, though tolerant of other people's beliefs, defended the Cromwellian Revolution of 1649 and lost his position when involved in political action under King James II. His treatise, though intended for the home tutoring of a high born boy, was of a broad and general character. Thomas Day, enlightened landowner and rationalist, aimed his book at the education or re-education of the spoilt Tommy Merton, son of a rich family. As Day put it: "distinctions of rank may indeed be necessary to the government of a populous country but it is for the good of the whole not of individuals that they have any just claim to be admitted." Those at the top should show by their manners, "that they lament the necessity of their elevation and that they would willingly descend nearer to an equality with their fellow creatures."

We sense in all of them the masked impatience of a social group, conscious of its own moral and intellectual superiority, with those whom the system has placed over them ("Men of high degree are a vanity"). It is interesting that the reform of the rich and aristocratic, particularly the young and spoiled, is a continuous concern of children's fiction.

It runs from Georgian moral tales, through Thackeray's *Rose and the Ring*, Kipling's *Captains Courageous*, to Edith Nesbit's *The House of Arden*. Though it must be said that the middling sort, as fits their middling station, have always been equally concerned to correct the lower orders ("Men of low degree are a lie").

Power, or access to power, through the education of the child is a common and constant theme and as we see from Ascham, Locke and Day, it is education by the book. All are concerned about what the privileged child should not read or hear. Ascham warned against the jottings of "lascivious monks" and the "lewd rude rhymes" of London. Locke urged wide reading, but excluded the "perfectly useless trumpery" of the old tradition. Day with his rational mind objected from another standpoint to the "fantastic visions" of old folk tales.

Ascham is concerned that godly books should be read. A century and more later, Locke had to hand a much wider range of literature, with various editions of fables and similar entertaining and enlightening literature, and is much concerned about *how* the child can learn to read. It is fascinating to read his advice about the use of picture books and to compare it with a quotation from Margaret Meek's *Learning to Read* (1982):

> And if those about him will talk to him often about the stories he has read and hear him tell them, it will, besides other advantages add incouragement and delight to his reading . . .(*On Education*, 1695)

> To learn to read children need the attention of one patient adult or older child for long enough to read something that pleases them both. (*Learning to Read*, 1982)

Another century later, with Thomas Day's *Sandford and Merton*, the book of instruction has become a piece of fiction about the pupil. Day says that while describing everything "according to the order of nature", he has used the most "unbounded licence". So his book is something of a landmark in the development of the new fiction as well as the philosophy of education.

Locke argued that the child's mind was open, waiting to be written on like a new sheet of paper. This was common to middling sort of thinking. His seventeenth century contemporary, L'Estrange, editing *Aesop's Fables*, speaks of the child's mind as "blank paper ready indifferently for any impression."

The link between the idea of a child's mind as a blank sheet and the wish for a fresh start in society is clear, and clearer as with Thomas Day we approach the age of the French Revolution. A twentieth century French writer, J. Pons, has declared that Day's book was full of the spirit of the Revolution, and Day did admire France's Jean Jacques Rousseau. There is indeed much similarity between the French idea of the "child of nature" and the "blank sheet", as there was much in common between the aspirations of the middling sort under an increasingly effete aristocracy in both England and France in the eighteenth century.

The eighteenth century was for the middling sort very much the age of the child. There were a lot of children about. After taking three centuries to double (between 1400–1700), the population then doubled again between 1700 and 1800. It was to double and double again before 1900, and for most of those two centuries children under the age of fourteen made up nearly 40 per cent of the population. Today the proportion is less than 15 per cent.

It has been said that the young in the eighteenth century were being treated more and more as children, rather than as small adults. They were being dressed as children, a practice that was general in Western Europe. Just when the process of recognising "childhood" began is difficult to say. Philip Aries, in his *Centuries of Childhood* (1962), traces it as far back as the late Middle Ages. Certainly the English *Babee's Book*, in the fifteenth century, with its "Child, when thou goest out to play", is very suggestive. John Locke is credited by Penelope Mortimer (in an essay in the volume *Only Connect*, S. Egoff and others, 1969) with having invented childhood. And J. S. Bratton, in her fascinating study, *The Impact of Victorian Children's Fiction* (1981) reminds us that Victor Hugo claimed to have discovered the child.

The invention or discovery of childhood is then seen as leading to the creation of children's literature. "Before there could be children's books, there had to be children," argues John Rowe Townsend in *Written for Children* (1974).

I would be inclined to put it the other way round and say that this concept of the "child" or "childhood" depended upon the book and upon education being seen exclusively in book terms. The book thus defined the "child", and such "childhood" was the privilege of a social minority. Harvey Darton says that eighteenth century children's literature was directed towards those who would "remain children for some years." He is talking about a special kind of childhood, restricted in two ways, restricted to the offspring of the well-to-do, and a childhood confined to the nursery.

This privileged "childhood" guaranteed no rights to the child. Not until the 1850s were children recognised as children in the courts. Children could be sentenced to death or transported. In 1789, William Blake penned his mournful cry about the little chimney sweep. Not until 1875 was this kind of labour, or the harsh gang system in rural areas, employing children as young as five under threat of whipping, outlawed. As is well known, a national society to protect *children* was founded half a century *after* one to protect animals, and then did not get Royal Patronage.

There was, indeed, no protection for the child in childhood other than the economic security of its family. Childhood existed only for those who could afford it. Freedom to trade and to make a profit out of others' labour was dominant among the "Liberties of the Subject", much written of in the eighteenth century. This "liberty" unleashed a storm of change to which tens of thousands of child industrial workers were to fall victim. For the middling sort, the best shelter for their children was confinement in the nursery. There, by the book, they would learn the skills needed to succeed in the world. It was a privilege, for there could be no rights. Hannah More, dramatist, Sunday School pioneer, writer of religious tracts and other little books for children, whose work spanned the crucial years of 1780 to the 1830s, summed up the situation in her *Strictures on the Modern System of Female Education* (1799). "Rights of Man?" she asked sarcastically. *Then* what: "rights of women, of youth, of babies?"

The emergence of the child was part of a wider process of transforming the family among the middling sort, a "domestication" process as Harvey Darton neatly describes it. It took place roughly between the time of Roger Ascham in the sixteenth century, and Thomas Day in the eighteenth. It was in fact the domestication of women and children only. The change from working family (master, mistress, children, journeymen and servants under one roof) to "domestic" family, began during the first historic periods of unemployment in mid-sixteenth century, when craft companies began to exclude any "mayde or woman-kind" from jobs that might employ a male head of family. This exclusion was accompanied in the late sixteenth and early seven-teenth century by a veritable pamphlet war over the merits of men versus women. "Let her rule the roast – if you rule the roost", wrote one author. Shakespeare's *The Taming of the Shrew* is a pale reflection of the battle of words. At this time too, the critique of the oral tradition took on a particular form, with attacks on "Prophane and Old Wives' Tales", tales of an "affected, tattling nurse", or worse still, the "chit chat of an old nurse or madman."

The catastrophic Plague and Fire of London in the 1660s speeded up the exodus of well-to-do craft masters from the city. They shifted home, wife and children to the suburbs. The workshop, now separated from the employers' home, was looked after by a poorer craft master, or "garret captain", what we would now call foreman or manager. The social contact between the middling sort and their "poorer brethren", which had been close since the fourteenth century, was weakened.

The children of these "domesticated" families were separated now from other children, whose working lives began at five, six or seven years of age. The child of the nursery was privileged, but it was a child without independence, a child under house arrest.

In the story *Summer Rambles* (1801), little Harry asks:

> ... Mamma, what can I do that I may not be idle? I cannot dig, you
> know I am not strong enough.
>
> MAMMA: Nor is it needful you should: your papa has money
> enough to pay people to work for him and a great many poor
> labourers live by what they get from him.
>
> HARRY: Then I may be as idle as I please.
>
> MAMMA: Indeed you may not; there are many other ways of
> employing your time besides digging or planting ... all you can

now do is to attend to the instructions of your papa and your masters and learn against you are older . . .

Protection from outside influences of course also meant, if possible, insulation against the old folk tales, either published in garish cheap books or told from memory by maidservants or nurses.

From the 1780s onwards the process of replacing these stories, of banning them from the nursery, was accompanied by a cleaning up process by which a minority of tales were made suitable. This began in a small way by removing vulgar verses about Cock Robin from Tom Thumb books, brought propriety to Robin Hood and Jack the Giant Killer, then swept on like a cleansing wind through *Gulliver's Travels* and *Robinson Crusoe*, and did not even stop short of Shakespeare and the Bible.

If the children of the old days had no stories *of* their own, the children of the middling sort in the days of the book were to have no stories *other* than their own. Whereas the sixteenth century Books of Nurture and Books of Conversation were intended for children *and* servants, as both were part of the same working family, by the eighteenth and nineteenth centuries the family was seen as excluding the servant.

The child was not to be influenced by the servant. In 1783, Lady Eleanor Fenn published her book *The Rational Dame*, with its hints on supplying "prattle". Eric Quayle, author of *Early Children's Books* (1983), rightly regards this book as significant of the times, and quotes extensively from its preface in which Lady Fenn sets out her ideas on how children should be brought up. Above all, they should not receive "their first notions from the most illiterate persons".

Lady Fenn, and many others, were ready to provide the books which would replace the maidservant as the bringer of tales.

6

New Readers, New Writers
1760–1800

By the end of the eighteenth century the nursery trade was being served by a growing number of specialist publishers. The term *publisher* was now in general use. Booksellers had expanded their old calling and taken over from the printer the job of "supplying the trade". These firms saw themselves as selling books to both "mother and tutor". Some had scores of juvenile titles on their lists, which they promoted in familiar ways, with gifts of balls or pin-cushions. And there was a growing body of children's writers, both amateur and professional.

This was no little cultural enclave though. These writers were known to each other, but were also known widely beyond their own circle. Sarah Trimmer, author and editor of the famous critical journal *The Guardian of Education* (1802–1806) is mentioned as universally known in Byron's poem *Don Juan*; Maria Edgeworth, the novelist, knew Walter Scott, and she also knew Erasmus Darwin, grandfather of the famous Charles; William Roscoe, writer of charming nursery verse (*The Butterfly's Ball*, 1807) was also Member of Parliament, friend of Whitbread the brewer, Godwin the radical bookseller and Mary Wollstonecraft, woman's rights champion and herself a writer for children.

Indeed there has probably never been a time, even in the Victorian heyday, when people who wrote for the entertainment and instruction of children were more a part of intellectual and political life, than in this period of ferment, of political revolution abroad in France and America, and industrial revolution at home. They were confident, enthusiastic and, for a time, tolerant, generous and sceptical, determined to get to the truth and write it large on the blank sheet of the young mind. When Samuel Wilberforce, leader of the Evangelical movement, said "Whoever educates a child undertakes the most important duty of society," he spoke for them all.

The river of children's literature swelled, fed by two streams, one from religious – ideological, the other from commercial– literary sources. There were the enthusiasts like Thomas Day, and there were the professional writers like Oliver Goldsmith who, now that the day of the aristocratic "patron" was passing, appealed direct to the public.

Since the book was a commodity, a thing for sale, this meant an appeal first of all to the publisher/bookseller. The scribe had been transformed into the hack. And that term could apply to a Goldsmith as well as to an unknown.

As an article in *The London Tradesman* (1747) put it, the writer was "treated to an abundance of slights". The trade would "depreciate his performance . . . with no other intention but to beat down his price."

John Newbery, pioneer of the children's book trade, who launched his *Little Pretty Pocket Book* in 1744, was alleged to accommodate his hacks three in a bed. Samuel Johnson, who knew him well, said he "made his authors pay dear for the plank he thrust out to them." Newbery, like publishers who came after him, Marshall, Catnach and others, was out to make money. His motto, says Harvey Darton, was "Trade and Plumb Cake".

He was both opportunistic and shrewd in weighing up the potential market for books which would "infallibly make Tommy a good boy and Polly a good girl", and in finding the writers with the skills to produce them. Like Goldsmith, who worked for him, Newbery's attitude towards the oral tradition was ambivalent. More typical of the mid-eighteenth century was the hostile attitude of the writer of a guide to London who declared:

> Tom Thumb shall now be thrown away
> And he that did the giant slay
> Such ill-consorted, artless lies,
> Our British youth shall now despise.

Newbery argued that his character Tom Tripp was better than Tom Thumb, though no bigger, because he was a great scholar. He did not mind using Jack the Giant Killer in his advertisements for his *Pocket Book* which he was selling to "parents, guardians, governesses" with didactic intent.

Goldsmith, who had used folk lore in his *Vicar of Wakefield* (1766), was ready, for a consideration, to edit out the cat from *Dick Whittington*, the cat being magical, and thus suspect.

Goldsmith is believed to be the author of *Goody Two Shoes*, the first novel for children, which Newbery published in 1765, and which is now regarded as the first classic of the literature. This book contains a powerful attack on people who "stuff children's heads with stories of ghosts, fairies, witches and such nonsense when they are young". Those brought up on this diet would "remain fools all their lives."

Goldsmith's friend, Samuel Johnson who, like Boswell, was an admirer of Jack the Giant Killer and the other chapbook heroes, made a famous and spirited defence of giants and wizards and enchantments, though when he suggested that "babies" did not need books about babies he crossed swords with the redoubtable teacher and writer Richard Lovell Edgeworth, Maria's father.

But there is no sign that Johnson made any real move (and certainly not in his own fiction writing) to preserve the essence and style of the folk tale. Boswell had ambitions to write for children and it is a pity he never did. For his *London Journal* suggests he had the heart of the matter in him:

> It will not be an easy task for me . . . it will require much nature and simplicity and a great acquaintance with the humours and traditions of the English people.

But there were a number of factors working against the preservation of these "humours and traditions".

There was, as stated earlier, the exclusive nature of writing as a minority skill. There was also the eighteenth century drive towards the development of "style", in the newly founded literary journals. Richard Dodsley aimed in his 1761 version of *Aesop's Fables* to exclude all "coarse and provincial terms" and "obsolete" expressions. Much more pervasive, first in the nursery, then beyond it, was the influence of the imported French "fairy tales". The term is first used in mid-eighteenth century. Perrault's tales, re-told with the contrived charm of the court and bourgeois household (his Cinderella is the daughter of a "gentilhomme") came into English as *Tales of Past Times* (1729), preceded in the early years of the century by Countess D'Aulnoy's *Contes des Fées*. Her "fairy tales" were not edited nor retold, but completely invented. From these fashionable models the printed fairy tale began steadily to overwhelm the weakening native tradition of the folk tale.

But there were deeper changes at work to undermine the old. Introducing the 1856 edition of his *Popular Tales*, Wilhelm Grimm sets out what conditions are needed for the folk tale to survive:

> Wherever assured and well established order and usages prevail, wherever the connection between human sentiment and surrounding nature is felt and the past not torn asunder from the present these tales are still to be found.

In England, however, the past *was* being torn asunder from the present, in a time of social and economic upheaval as the country changed from offshore island to world power. Information and opinion, knowledge, discovery and invention multiplied, notably among the middling sort. Every home, claimed Samuel Johnson, now had "its chest of knowledge". This was a rhetorical claim, of course, but when Johnson said "literature pervaded the nation", he was nearer the mark.

Among the minority likely to have their "chest of knowledge" were the Dissenters. Excluded for the past century from grammar school, university and Established Church, they had made their own churches, Quaker, Unitarian, Methodist. They created their own Sunday and Day Schools and even their Dissenting Academies, to rival the more hidebound, Church-dominated universities. In the North West and Midlands areas, where manufacture now began to flourish, minds were at work which were non-conformist in every sense. The world of children's writers like Richard and Maria Edgeworth, Anna Letitia Barbauld and William Roscoe was linked through the Dissenter network with pioneers of the Industrial Revolution like Priestley and Wedgwood.

Teaching in the Dissenting Academies, a generous, but not

always smooth mixture of strict Non-conformist Christianity and scientific rationalism, made an immense impact. Warrington, one of their centres, where young William Roscoe studied nature in the Botanical Gardens, was known as "The Athens of the North". The tide of new ideas swept everyone along. It affected all the new writers for children, even when, like Mrs Sarah Trimmer, they belonged to the orthodox wing of the Church of England and were hostile to radical, rationalist politics. In her most famous work, *Fabulous Histories* or *The Robins* (1786) she felt obliged to explain that robins could not really talk. Her friend, Mary Kilner, in her *Memoirs of a Peg Top* (c.1781), took care to tell her readers that peg tops were inanimate objects. In order to create a new fiction, the new writers had to find their foothold in reality. Their inventions must not be "vain" or "fantastic".

Dissenters forced the pace in writing for the wider public. John Wesley urged that Methodists should produce tracts for the poor, written "simply and nakedly". When he died, the work was carried on by the Religious Tract Society (RTS). Though the Church of England with its Society for the Propagation of Christian Knowledge (SPCK) had both official approval and had been at work already for more than a century, the Dissenters had the drive to make up for that. They were linked with trade and manufacture and that was the way of the future.

Both Dissenters and Church of England had their Sunday Schools to give religious instruction to the poor. Commercial publishers like John Marshall supplied them with "godly" books and other customers with chapbook romances and translations from *The Arabian Nights*, though he rejected the "prejudicial nonsense" of the oral tradition.

Altogether it was a motley but formidable gathering of talents and motives. There was the scientific-rationalist reformer trying to educate the torpid pleasure-loving upper class into new ways of industry. There was the Dissenting Church of England reformer with a mission to save souls. And there was the publisher with his hacks in Grub Street. The missionaries of God and Science learned market skills to spread their gospel. The capitalist publisher studied the market thus created. It was a fruitful clash between those who were prepared to be as entertaining as the success of their message required, and those who could be as didactic or as amusing as the market demanded.

Their common ground was the outlook of the middling sort on the threshold of a new world. In the making of a new literature they were both hostile to and exploitive of the old story traditions. In place of the old notion of fate, they brought either a conviction of the will of God or a rational attitude to nature and coincidence. Both might be combined in the same person. Lady Eleanor Fenn, writer and Sunday School patron, urged that children should be surprised with "real wonders". Erasmus Darwin's poetic effusions about the invented wonders of the new age offered the excitement of understanding nature. It is closer in spirit to William Roscoe's much more accomplished verse than some critics will allow.

The rational view of the world allowed human beings to detach themselves from nature making them explorers and exploiters rather than fearers or believers. It also underlay a criticism of the rich and praise for the virtues of the poor. The villains of Newbery's, Maria Edgeworth's, and Thomas Day's writings are grasping squires, enclosing landlords, greedy lawyers. How much better, Tommy Merton discovers, "it is to be useful than rich and fine; how much more amiable to be good than great." Thus far they absorbed the old folk tradition of virtuous poverty. But not too far. For little Tommy goes on to ask: "Are all the poor better than all the rich?" And he is told that the wickedness lies not so much in being rich as in being idle. The "wealthy luxurious man . . . without business or profession, arts sciences or exercises" is a "miserable animal".

A theme that unites Day, Trimmer, Edgeworth and other children's writers is kindness to animals, the furry creatures stoned by the rough boy, the hare hunted by the squire. Though not, it seems, the "poor little robins", which Matthew Boulton told James Watt he was killing with "fixable air" in home experiments. We do not know what Mrs Trimmer would have said about that.

Nothing in these generous attitudes to the poor, to the slave, to animals, nor in the intolerance to fatalism, waste and idleness, may be taken at its face value. Underlying it all is a desire to see the old way of life banished and to usher in the new.

That does not mean to say the old cannot be re-cycled. *Goody Two Shoes* (1765) which survives in pantomime form today, is close to folk tale. But Margery Meanwell, the heroine of this story, like Day's heroes Harry Sandford and Tommy Merton, is domesticated. All have surnames, unlike the folk-type. Margery is less dependent than the others, but she, like the others, is bound to a real and local scene. She makes her fortune not by good luck, but by visible virtue and diligence. Her brother ventures abroad (as though the folk hero/heroine were split in two) and returns, Crusoe-style, with a bag of gold. Margery resists the oppressions of farmer and squire, but does not defeat and plunder them: instead she forgives and reforms them. She takes her place among the middling sort at the end, as a schoolteacher. And her story is commended to all:

> Who from a state of rags and care
> And having shoes but half a pair
> Their fortune and their fame would fix
> And travel in a coach and six.

These new heroes and heroines, like the robins, cats, dogs and mice, peg tops, and pin cushions which abound in eighteenth and early nineteenth century stories, belong at home, within the recognisable, respectable family. They are creatures of fantasy like those of the old tales, but unlike those stories, the authors "know" these are fictions and say so openly. They expect to be excused the offence of the old story-teller, because their intention is so Godly, so rational, so unreservedly good for their select audience.

7

Starting up the "Moral Steam Engine"
1790–1830

At the dawn of the 1800s, the scene was set for a dramatic surge in
the production of fiction for the young that would match the surge
of the middling sort towards the promised land of economic and
political influence and power. It came in the form of the Tract
movement. Tracts were pamphlet-sized books for the young and
unlettered of any age. Using story to convey the moral message,
these flooded the country between the 1790s and the 1840s.
Tracts had already existed for two centuries and more, both
religious and political, but now the number was to swell from the
hundred or the thousand to the million as advanced print
technology, now shod in iron and powered by steam, answered
the needs of the religious reformers (known as the Evangelicals)
and the social economic reformers (the Utilitarians). It was
altogether, as Coleridge remarked, "a vast moral steam engine at
work".

It began in the West Country, where the talented writer
Hannah More, turning from the attractions of writing for the
London stage, set to work to save the minds and souls of ragged
miners' and farm labourers' children. To do this she launched
her Cheap Repository Tracts.

They began as an accompaniment to the Sunday School
movement, which had its origins in nearby Gloucester, where
Robert Raikes the founder had concerned himself with occupy-
ing the young on their one day of leisure. In the closing decades of
the eighteenth century, the poor had multiplied. The population
in the manufacturing areas doubled and trebled. And it was, so a
Government agent told the Home Secretary, "a new race of
beings". These "beings" were at work by the time they were five
years old – no nursery for them. Their moral welfare, if not their

58

physical well being, was of great concern to the respectable. The aim of the Sunday Schools, whether run by Dissenters or Church of England patrons, was to teach the children of the poor to read the Bible. This raised a problem. Would they use the newly acquired skill of reading to study the scriptures or other improving works, or would they read the unsuitable – old romances, tales of violence and superstition, full of the coarse jests which made the Tom Thumb chapbooks so popular?

Or, even more dangerous, would they read one of the many political pamphlets which had begun to circulate in town and village, some of which appeared to attack the roots of religion and social order?

Hannah More summed up the problem. "Vulgar and indecent books were always common. But speculative infidelity brought down to the pockets and capacities of the poor, forms a new era in our history." Among the chapbooks and ballad sheets in the packs of the wandering pedlars, in town and village, were copies of the revolutionary pamphlet *The Rights of Man*. Far, far worse than Tom Thumb, was Tom Paine. Thomas Paine's pamphlet was a defence of the ideas of liberty, equality and fraternity, expressed so alarmingly in the French Revolution. Hawked along with copies of *Jack the Giant Killer* and the *Seven Champions of Christendom*, it is said to have sold nearly a million copies in ten years. With a population of ten million, if this figure were even half true, the impact must have been enormous.

Bad harvests, industrial disruption, the economically exhausting war with Napoleon, meant widespread discontent. There was a fruitful market, among former pupils of Sunday Schools or of the cheap village day schools run by a local dame, for radical pamphlets, for editions of poems by Byron and Shelley.

Shelley's words,

> Shake your chains to earth like dew
> Ye are many, they are few

had a message that neither the hand loom weaver nor the framework knitter made idle by new machinery could ignore. Nor could the ruling class, nor the middling sort. Shelley was an atheist. Thomas Paine was not. Most radicals of the time were also religious. So Hannah More's charge of "infidelity" is pure polemic. But the Establishment, both political and religious, felt threatened. They were convinced, as William Hone the radical bookseller wrote, that the "little books" hawked around the country were

> . . . full of blasphemies and libels
> And people love them better than their bibles.

The menace did not end there. There was also the so-called "Newgate" literature, which had grown in quantity since the early 1700s. There was the tale of the "London Apprentice" who, sentenced to death for a minor crime, escaped the gallows three times. These tales of violence, robbery, repentance and death were sold at public executions along with religious tracts. The highwayman rebel-rogue was no Robin Hood, but with scant respect for property was still a bogeyman for the respectable. Already in the 1760s, fairy tales had been linked with "stories of theft and murders, of imprisonments and executions", as being bad for the young. Even the expurgated Robin Hood tales were suspected of encouraging "vice and crime".

Suppose, too, that among the twopenny broadsides, the penny ballad sheets and chapbooks read aloud in cottage or slum, the folk hero should reappear with his equalising mission still intact? Like King Ludd marching at the head of his machine breakers, with "Great Enoch", his hammer, in hand:

> Great Enoch now shall lead the van
> Stop him who dares, stop him who can.

There was widespread fear among the middling sort that an upsurge from below might plunge society into anarchy, "worse than the overwhelming deluge of Huns and Tartars", in the words of philosopher James Mill. This was a tone of anxiety about the "poor" in stark contrast to the genial enthusiasm of Thomas Day and his contemporaries.

Some were quite sure that the danger lay in actually teaching the poor to read – even for an hour or two on Sundays. As one cynic put it – why teach them to become "more scientific machine breakers"?

Hannah More took the opposite view. Teach the poor to read and provide them with the *right* reading matter, one that would speak of their lives, of the virtues of honest toil, of acceptance of their place in society. Her Cheap Repository Tracts with their tales of young farm servants, postillions, miners, though much more often servants than industrial workers, streamed out to combat the "flood of mischief".

She left little to chance. She had the help of the enlightened local gentry. Rich patrons could subsidise the Cheap Repository Tracts and make them as inexpensive as Tom Thumb. The local lady or lord of the manor could force village shopkeepers to stock tracts rather than Thomas Paine's work. Volunteer gents and ladies rode or walked round, using their influence to get local young people to read the tracts. In his anthology *Destiny Obscure* (1983), John Burnett quotes the recollection of a young shepherd of those days. A gentleman called at his cottage: "Do you like reading, I will leave this tract with you and when I come again, I shall know how you like it."

The tracts, said Hannah More, were "sheep in wolves' clothing". They were disguised to look like chapbooks, just as their heroes and heroines were vaguely like those of folk tales – though their message that spiritual rewards were better than earthly ones, though even these might be won by "exertion", was directly counter to that of the old story. They had a mixed reception. Many were read. Many were thrown away or used in rural privies. The notorious barber in Thomas Prest's *Sweeney Todd* in the 1840s offers tracts to the children of his victims. Dickens and other popular writers, and even more refined High Church writers of children's books in mid-century, poked fun at the "tractarians".

But the tracts moved with the tide of social change. Simple and easy to read, they helped young and old to master the new skill. Some tract writers like the Rev. Legh Richmond, sincerely devoted to the poor, recorded their spiritual experience with realism and dignity. Richmond was popular enough with Sunday School children to be anxious about the corrupting effect upon him of this popularity.

Where Cheap Repository Tracts led the way, the Dissenters' RTS and the Church of England SPCK publishing companies followed. They not only produced and distributed millions of tracts but, using their organisation, capital and experience, produced more full-blown works of semi-fiction, then pure fiction, as the tract writers served their apprenticeships and went on to more sophisticated fiction writing. Authors like Mrs Sherwood and her sister Mrs Cameron (admired by Thomas Arnold, the famous Head of Rugby School) learned their trade in the tract movement. They wrote both for the cottage and the nursery, and became quite skilled in distinguishing between the two markets.

There were subtle differences between two sorts of deference, that owed by nursery children to their parents, and that owed by servants to their employers. Gillian Avery, modern writer and critic, in her *Nineteenth Century Children* (1965) points out ironically how differently the tale of religious conversion, mainstay of the tracts, developed in the nursery and the cottage novel. Children of the nursery were not allowed to convert their parents (who were after all God's Viceroy on earth), though they might say, convert an aunt or uncle. Cottage children, however, were freely allowed to warn their parents of the dangers of vice and folly.

The nursery novel of the time was stern. Mrs Sherwood's famous Fairchild children (*History of the Fairchild Family*, 1818) were beaten to make them love one another. But sternness was tempered, Gillian Avery points out, by little naughtinesses, like a fondness for food, and occasional disobedience (to governess, not parent). Such indulgence was never allowed little servants.

Using, consciously or unconsciously, the conventions of the romance or folk tale, the tract-trained writer could develop a new narrative style on a strong moral framework. If a servant in these books found a treasure, it would not be, as in folk tale, the end of their troubles, but the beginning. For they would certainly be accused of stealing it. All would be well in the end, but there would be no reward or compensation. Virtue was indeed its own reward.

The complex relationship between new literature and old, between respectable and popular, is seen most clearly in the mainly religious magazines for young people which now appear, encouraged by new printing techniques. The *Evangelical Miscellany* (1816) with its mixture of adventure, moral fiction and useful information, has in its way the same basic contents of children's comics of later ages.

All the new magazines were a combination of commercial drive and religious caution. A good example is the magazine *The Excitement* (1830), whose story is told by Eric Quayle in his *Early Children's Books* (1983). The editor, Rev. Adam Keys, skilfully used tales of missionary adventures, deep sea yarns, horror stories like the Black Hole of Calcutta and the French Reign of Terror, to excite and interest his readers. He felt it enough that the stories should "contain something of a religious nature". What was important was that they should "enter with the deepest interest into all the various feelings" of the reader. His fellow clergymen disagreed, and he was dismissed for diluting the religious message. But his was the approach of the future.

Busy in the magazine field along with the Evangelicals were publicists of the parallel secular movement, the Utilitarians. The Society for the Diffusion of Useful Knowledge (a rationalist comment on the title of the Church of England publishing house) put out a *Penny Magazine* in the 1820s which grew rapidly for a decade, then dwindled. A Library of Useful Knowledge was begun, and an ill-fated Encyclopedia. Writers like Harriet Martineau were engaged to write not only popular treatises on political economy for young and old, but also little novels, like *The Turnout* (1829) which claimed to show the ineffectiveness of striking.

The message of political economy was, in the words of Charles Knight, editor of the *Penny Magazine*, "labour plentiful, price low, labour scarce, price high . . . a law of nature against which it was vain to contend." The message was put over with much useful general and scientific information in pamphlets and lectures.

This "utilitarian" and rationalist message was not always to the taste of religious reformers. Sarah Trimmer feared the "pride of human reason". Equally, many rationalist thinkers thought it wrong or unwise to force orthodox religion down the throats of the young.

There was, however, still a great deal of common ground between the religious and secular wings of the middling sort or, as they now began to call themselves, the middle class. They were as sure of their own fitness as ever. As James Mill wrote in the *Westminster Review* in 1826: "The middle classes . . . have long been spoken of, and not grudgingly, by their superiors, themselves, as the glory of England".

United and on the side of the angels, the glory of England were irresistible. Led by Evangelist Samuel Wilberforce, Josiah Wedgwood the industrialist and the like, the campaign to end slavery, closely identified with the old order, succeeded in its main aims by the 1830s. When it came to reducing working hours for the "white slaves" in the factories at home or legalising the trade unions, then neither Wilberforce nor Wedgwood could muster the same enthusiasm. The attitude to the poor at home was changing. The answers to questions about poor and rich and equality, once given so confidently by Thomas Day, found a more ambivalent response in the verse of Ann and Jane Taylor or the later writings of Esther Copley. The middle class was reaching out for wealth and power, like the father in Emily Ospringe's story *Punctuality* in the 1820s, who is "anxious to improve his children's principles and render them truly good and great as well as ingenious and rich."

The question was how could one develop a system of education which would do that for the children of the middle class, while simultaneously teaching the children of the poor *not* to aspire to the same things? How to induce the poor to pay "willing honour" to their superiors, in the words of Hannah More; or help them to "bear with patience the evils they suffer", as Malthus the economist put it?

Given these middle class attitudes and the total hostility of the ruling class, education for the poor barely developed. Dissenters and Church of England had, by 1812, not only rival publishing houses, but rival day school systems. As rivalry grew more intense they strove to raise money to increase their school networks. But to reassure suspicious sponsors they insisted that their aim was to teach *only* reading, and not writing. Even the more enlightened felt a limit must be put on the education of the working classes. As James Mill put it: "There are degrees of intelligence which must be reserved to those who are not obliged to labour." Several attempts before the 1820s to get Parliament to vote public money for the education of working-class children, including one by

William Roscoe the children's writer, were defeated. Nothing more was done on this front till the 1830s.

Meanwhile the middling sort had grander objectives. With victory in the anti-slavery campaign, reflected in children's titles like *The Enlightened African* and *The Grateful Negro*, the Evangelical movement was strongly diverted into missionary work in India and, later, Africa. Mrs Sherwood's famous book *Little Henry and His Bearer Boosy* (1814) about a boy who converts his Indian servant, is a foretaste of many stories to come about admirable young Englishmen and devoted "native followers".

Wilberforce and Hannah More died in the 1830s. The Evangelicals, having heeded his call to reform the nation, were set to reform the world, as Nancy Cutt (*Ministering Angels*, 1979) notes. She quotes an impressive comment by Isaac Taylor, brother of poets Jane and Ann, in 1830:

> May the Commerce of the British realm long flourish, especially as it is becoming by the favour of Divine Providence the means of conveying the Bible with the temporal, spiritual and eternal blessing of the Gospels.

At home the stage was set not only for moral but for political reform. The campaign to change the franchise reached a new peak in the 1830s, with mass demonstrations for "The Bill, the whole Bill and nothing but the Bill". With the aid of the working class, who were also demanding the vote, the middling sort were able to force the hands of the landowner-majority in the House of Commons. And with the aid of Lord Russell ("Finality Jack") they were able to secure a very limited voting system based on property that included just one in six of adult males. It was, as *The Poor Man's Guardian* journal said, a "humbug" bill.

Now the middling sort, if their hands were not yet on the reins of power, were riding pillion. The laws enacted by the new Parliament give a sense of the direction in which they wanted the horse to move. A ban was placed on young people under nine working in the textile industry. Those from nine to thirteen, in the mills, were to attend some sort of school, *after* they had done eight hours' work. Church of England and Dissenting school organisations were to share £20,000 of Government money. And with the new Poor Law those in need were to go into the workhouse, men to one building, women and children to another.

Thus the ambivalent attitude to "childhood" and the sanctity of the family was underlined.

8

The "Fruitful Plain of Youth"
1832–1851

Between the Reform Act of 1832 and the Great Exhibition of 1851, the middle class became "almost a ruling class" (Harvey Darton – *Children's Books in England*). A ruling class they could never be. There was not enough room for them all at the top of the ladder. But they were of the ruling order. Trade and manufacture was now the way of life. With the repeal of the Corn Laws in 1846, the power of the "landed interest" waned, agriculture was relegated to the back of the economic stage, while cheap food imported from abroad to feed the swelling city populations was paid for by hugely increased exports of machinery and manufactured goods (more than the exports of France, Germany and Italy put together).

The city poor were not fed too lavishly, however. Trade and manufacture brought boom and slump. Mass unemployment came in the "Hungry Forties". The contrast between richer and poorer grew with the economy. By 1850 the average middle class income was between two and five times that of even the most skilled worker.

As Thomas Hood wrote, in a comic epic in one of the "annuals" which were now popular family reading:

> The yearly cost of her golden toys
> Would have given half London's charity boys
> And charity girls the annual joys
> Of a Holiday dinner at Highbury.

Hunger and unemployment in the cities sharpened working class anger at the "humbug" of the Reform Act, which had denied them the vote they had helped the middle class to win.

This blatant injustice led not a few middle class people to support the movement for the People's Charter which grew to enormous size between 1838 and 1848. Though it must be said that more typical of middle class opinion were those who turned out as special constables when the Chartists' Great Petition for the vote was brought to Westminster – and rejected.

There was a growing feeling of achievement and complacency, which was strengthened with the establishment of Queen Victoria's reign. Here was a ruler with none of the unacceptable features of earlier monarchs, the "stupid excess and gross extravagance contemptible affectation folly and self pretence". Respectable people could now settle down "seeking our reward in approving conscience and the peace of well-ordered happy homes . . . like our liege lady." (H. Keddie, *Three Generations*, quoted in Nancy Cutt's *Ministering Angels*, 1979).

For the middle class, the ruling and employing classes were more and more themselves writ large. More and more they were employers themselves – in the home. By 1851, more than one million women and girls, ten per cent of all females over the age of ten, were domestic servants. Here was a section of the working class young under close observation by the writers of nursery fiction. Though as Nancy Cutt points out, these writers knew little of other working children – the "piecers" in the mills, the trap-openers in the mines or the six-year-old slaves under the whip in the field gangs.

Ignorance of what was known as the "million", was still the rule. Thackeray the novelist noted that the respectable knew as much about people of the London slums as they did about the people of Alaska. This ignorance was still mixed with some apprehension. But in Victoria's time, it had turned from concern about what might happen if the poor were educated, to concern at what might happen if they were *not*, if they got messages from the wrong quarter. In Charles Dickens' *A Christmas Carol* (1843), the Spirit of Christmas Present summons up a girl ("Want") and a boy ("Ignorance"). The promise of the boy is "doom".

But even enlightened self interest or concern was still not strong enough to overcome the deep-seated reluctance of the well-to-do to spend on public education. Money voted by Parliament was still confined to the private network of church run schools. The Church of England still got about three quarters of the allocation, the Dissenters the rest, though in 1847 Catholic schools were given a share. And even in the 1850s the total amount of Government money spent on education was only one per cent of the Budget.

Schools were mostly poorly run and over-crowded, and relied heavily on physical discipline, with beatings "round the class" and a ready made "sin-bin" in the form of a cage holding the reluctant pupil, hoisted to the ceiling. One estimate is that of those educated, the most achieved was an average of five hours' schooling a week over an average of four years. And of course, hundreds of thousands still got no schooling at all.

There was outside the schools, however, a large and varied voluntary effort to educate the poor. It came from middle class and working class organisations. The Society for the Diffusion of Useful Knowledge sought to "diffuse the best information", and thus "easily allure all classes even the humblest into the paths of general knowledge". The Society and its backers launched Mechanics' Institutes to draw in "industrious individuals listening with mute admiration to the sublime truths of philosophy." The pompous tone, the message "go out and become yourselves capitalists", drew derision or indifference from industrial workers. The Mechanics' Institutes, and to a large extent what followed them in mid-century, the Working Men's Clubs, organised by the "Christian Socialists", were gradually deserted by workers and taken over by middle class leisure students, "persons in easy circumstances".

The Society's *Penny Magazine*, soaring to 200,000 circulation, slumped and was out of business by 1845.

Many people with good intentions, like children's writers William and Mary Howitt, talented and broad minded Quakers, sought to understand and help working class children and adults. They were frustrated at the lack of interest in the message of enlightenment they offered.

As Brian Simon in his wide-ranging survey of education in this period points out, many of the self-appointed enlighteners did not realise that the problem of education was bound up with that of poverty, of long working hours and, above all, the democratic rights denied to working class people. A delegate to a congress of the fast-growing co-operative movement said of the SDUK that it was "all very well and useful", but that people like himself "felt degraded in the land of their birth having no participation in their political and social rights."

Bronterre O'Brien, former star pupil of the school run by the Edgeworth family, brought to the Chartist movement an increased emphasis on education. "Education will follow suffrage as sure as day succeeds night", he declared. Noting that most working class children got their education after a day's or a week's work, *The Northern Star*, the Chartist newspaper, said: "The need that exists for Sunday Schools at all is a strong condemnation of all our fiscal political and social arrangements. The Sabbath should be a day of rest. But there is no rest for the children of the poor."

Chartist groups, Co-operatives and other working class organisations in the cities organised day schools and, where that was not possible, Sunday schools, where the teaching was secular. In some cases the co-operatives sponsored existing private schools, inspecting them and guaranteeing religious teaching at the request of parents. The stress was on grammar, mathematics, science. There were even examinations and festivals where children recited Chartist poems as well as works by Byron and Shelley. At the high point of the movement there were enough schools for a delegate conference, and radical publicist George Jacob Holyoake produced textbooks, while Rev. William Hill, first editor of *The Northern Star*, wrote a *Rational Grammar and Entertaining Class Book*.

If a copy of this work still exists it must indeed be a collector's item. For this is as far as the Chartist movement was able to go in producing its own children's literature. In the long run they could not compete with the state-backed religious schools. As R. D. Altick in *The English Common Reader* (1951) points out, "the lower classes were largely at the mercy of religious and utilitarian educational and publishing agencies." Not only were these Chartist and Co-operative schools difficult to keep going in times of "bad trade". There was also a sustained campaign by the church and by local priests and vicars who did what they could, from legal action to door to door visits warning parents they would go to hell, to eliminate the competition.

But above all there was the growing conviction among working class people that the state should provide a non-sectarian free education for all. In 1837, William Lovett, a toolcutter, and John Collins, a cabinet maker, while serving political prison sentences, produced a programme for a "system of common schools" for all up to the age of 14, with a broad curriculum, including physical training. Education, they said, "is not a boon", but a right. "If the low wages and inadequate means of parents be such as prevent them educating their children, it is the duty of those parties who profit by their labour to provide the necessary education."

During these two decades through religious Sunday and day schools, workhouse schools, hours snatched from work in factory schools, mutual improvement groups (adults learning with painful slowness alongside speedier children), the ability to read began to spread among the working class.

How fast it spread is difficult to say. The official mark of literacy, a signature on the marriage register, does not give much indication. Nor does the customary school test, the reading of a verse in the Bible. But a poll of some 1,400 East Enders in the 1840s shows nearly half of them regularly reading a Sunday newspaper.

The Church of England SPCK publishing house, reviewing its own propaganda campaign in the early 1830s, noted that "the population of this country ... for the first time is becoming a reading population actuated by tastes and habits unknown to preceding generations ... there are many among the working classes willing to spend small sums in the purchase of works."

Reading matter became cheaper and more colourful with the steam press, stereotyping, less expensive paper and binding, the use of colour. While at the up-market end the three-decker novel costing a week's wages for a craftsman might sell as little as 500 copies, at the down-market end, sales of "part" novels or penny periodicals, fortnightly or weekly, might reach tens of thousands. At either end of the social spectrum stories might be read aloud "in the family way on the Sabbath", or at "penny readings" run by the local Co-op, thus spreading the desire to read among wider circles.

In the bulk production of fiction small publishers, printing and selling in back streets, led the way. In their hands over several decades, the chapbook, broadside or ballad sheet was transformed first into the "part" publication then into the weekly journal, of which there were at least 80 by the 1850s.

In this process, as one contemporary saw it, the "highly poetical" oral tradition, with its "harmless superstitions" was replaced by the "vilest trash". "Trash" is the universal description. The highly successful *Chambers Magazine* was intended to "wean people from trash". It was a word much used by people who did not intend to endanger their morals by reading it, as Edward Viles, author of the sensational, long-running magazine serial *Black Bess*, said in defending his work.

Viles ridiculed the charge that such popular literature encouraged crime. As he pointed out, all the stories made it clear that crime brought retribution. Retribution was the saving clause which enabled stirring tales of crime to be sold at public executions, where hawkers competed with tract sellers. As one seller remarked, comic stories and "low life" tales were popular, but "nothing beats a stunning murder". The ghost of Robin Hood lived on in Dick Turpin, Claude Duval and the renowned apprentice boy Jack Sheppard. Successive re-writings removed most of the Robin Hood elements, leaving what Eric Quayle (*Early Children's Books*) wittily calls the "laissez faire" aspect. "Vile trash", though, was one of the few areas in which the spirit of the folk tale lingered on. Martha Vicinus (*The Industrial Muse*, 1974) has shown how ballads and tales of "factory boys" and apprentices, of weaver and cabin boy heroes, were sold in the cities and how a number of the broadside publishers tried to preserve the folk tradition. Louis James' *Fiction for the Working Man* (1974), describes how in the hands of talented hacks and editors, like the radicals G. M. W. Reynolds and Edward Lloyd, Thomas Prest, James Malcolm Rymer and Edward Viles, populist notions of poor virtue and rich wickedness were preserved in the cheap magazines while they were vanishing in respectable literature. The wrong done by some wealthy squire, mayor or lawyer, was as essential to the story of the highwayman as is the ritual punishment/redemption on the gallows.

The heroines of these serial stories which gripped readers as a TV serial grips viewers (with characters written out for lack of appeal just as ruthlessly) were often made of sterner stuff than the fainting ladies of the parlour novel. Prest, of *Sweeney Todd* fame, praises "woman's high mental fortitude".

Alongside these periodicals was a thriving theatre with its pantomime and melodrama. The "tie-in" was the order of the day, whether the original author liked it or not, as Dickens for one found out to his cost, when pirated stage versions of *Pickwick* almost beat the book on to the streets. The writing of many such serials bears a strong resemblance to theatrical dialogue with stage directions. Short sentences and plenty of conversation are a perennial element in popular appeal. The hacks stole from anywhere and anyone, much in the manner of the oral tradition, although now the consequences were more serious. Both Dickens and Harrison Ainsworth found their novels, *The Pickwick Papers* (1836), *Oliver Twist* (1837), *Rookwood* (1834), *Old St Paul's* (1841), were plagiarised and travestied without mercy.

But it is also true to say that Dickens and Ainsworth and others profited well from their reading of the *Newgate Calendar* and *Terrific Register*. Ainsworth's highly successful *Rookwood* feeds off Defoe's early eighteenth century pamphlet about the London Apprentice. Many respectable writers for children drew consciously or unconsciously from the same well.

Unrestrained by the considerations of the religious and philanthropic magazines, or the more directly political journals, the cheap fiction periodicals were free to develop and so set their mark on the basic plot of romance, adventure or horror story. Many authors of later children's literature, from R. L. Stevenson to Geoffrey Trease, have acknowledged the basic and unforgettable impression upon their young minds of the penny dreadful, just as the poet Coleridge once fed his feverish imagination on chapbook tales.

It can be argued that much of the popular literature, wandering further and further from the folk sources of its stories, was trash. But its role in maintaining (even in vitiated form) the ideas of the old story, and its influence, often unacknowledged, on the rest of the literature which affected to despise it, must also be recognised.

Much hostility arose from its popularity with the young, whether middle class or working class – "low papers which found their way into the servants' hall" might find their way upstairs into the nursery. Although the cheap periodicals were intended for adult reading, they could not help, in a period of increasing literacy, drifting down the age scale. We learn how far this process had gone in a much quoted statement from a popular magazine editor in the 1840s, that since the magazines were read by

> ... a class so different in education and social position from the readers of three volume novels ... we sometimes mistrust our judgement and place the manuscript in the hands of an illiterate person, a servant or machine boy for instance. If they pronounce favourably upon it, we think it will do.

The statement is full of meaning. It shows how far the penny dreadful had become fiction for the young. It shows too that the people producing it regarded themselves as belonging to a higher cultural level. And it shows how the word "illiterate" had speedily acquired a broader meaning, full of social condescension. Yet more does it show how remote, even with popular literature, the author of the tale was from its audience. No popular story-tellers of old would need second-hand evidence of their own appeal. But the "folk" story was now passing out of the hands of the folk into the hands of professionals belonging to another social stratum. Their attempts to retain popular appeal at a distance were bound to become more and more tinged with cynicism. James Malcolm Rymer, one of the most skilled of these writers, had become alienated enough to declare that the would-be author must "study the animals for whom he has to cater."

Politically active workers, like those in the Chartist movement, were bitter about the way the working classes were often portrayed in fiction, the butts of "so-called humorists". Even in popular fiction, noted William Thompson, the "humble hero always turned out to be the long lost son of a lord". But the search for an alternative approach was a hard one.

Working class writers were drawn to imitate classic models or respectable middle class writers. Robert Story was much influenced by Isaac C. Watts and Anna Barbauld. Over-seriousness was another problem: "I do not see," wrote Chartist author Ernest Jones, "why truth should always be dressed in stern and

74

repulsive garb. The more attractive you make her, the more easily she will progress."

Jones, Thomas Cooper (himself the model for Charles Kingsley's hero *Alton Locke*, 1850), Reynolds and Linton, all Chartist writers, did make their contribution to nineteenth century literature. Reynolds, in particular, skilfully made use of popular forms like melodrama, blending them with powerful radical content. As he spiced his serials with the wicked doings of the rich, he insistently demanded – "Is this just?"

The Chartists tried in an organised way to encourage working class and radical writing through *The Northern Star*, Cooper's *Journal*, and other publications, printing poems, serialising novels. Cooper particularly urged the young Chartists, to "join hands and heads to create a literature of your own."

But the publishing resources of the radical working class movement, their journals which fluctuated in demand and success with changes in the economic and political situation, and their general lack of funds could not match the output of their opponents. R. D. Altick (*The English Common Reader*) has shown how the Evangelicals and to a lesser extent the Utilitarians, through their control over institute, day and Sunday school, with their developing book and magazine publishing apparatus and the lending libraries they organised, dominated the field.

T. W. Wheeler, whose novel *Sunshine and Shadow* was serialised in the *Northern Star*, remarked bitterly that "the opponents of our principles have been allowed to wield the power of imagination over the youth of our party without any effort on our part to occupy this wide and fruitful plain."

To occupy the plain, religious publishing houses were now prepared to widen their appeal as they developed their expertise. The SPCK, for example, appointed a special committee to deal with aspiring authors, and were ready to be less dogmatic in putting over their message in order that it should get a hearing among the increasing circle of working class readers.

At first much of their effort, in the words of J. S. Bratton (*The Impact of Victorian Children's Fiction*, 1981), was aimed at producing "expanded versions of the kind of tract that concentrated all inventive effort on representing the poor child's interests as coinciding with what their employers required of them". These books were often bought by ladies to pass on to the working class children who were their maids of all work.

Increasingly important was the up-market or nursery end of this religious publishing which now began to bring into view familiar names – Harriet Mozeley, Charlotte Yonge, Elizabeth Sewell. Lower printing costs enabled longer and more complex works to be written. The desire for broader appeal is clear in Harriet Mozeley's aim to show children "as they are" rather than "moral portraiture for unreserved imitation or avoidance." Logically such portrayal would be more successful with children of the nursery rather than those of the servants' hall or the streets outside.

Thus, in striving for a broader appeal, slowly secularising their message, the religious publishers were giving greater scope to creative invention. There was competition, not just from Utilitarian journals like *The Penny Magazine*, but others more steadily successful like the independent *Chambers Magazine*, which mixed fiction with "healthful, useful and agreeable mental instruction".

And there were commercial publishers like Nisbet, Nelson, Constable, feeding off the market created by the secular and religious campaigners, or Longman earning its pennies from the expanding school market. They used some of their profits to create their own sphere of influence, developing relationships with writers in which the moral impetus, though never absent, had to co-exist with the commercial.

The contemporary historical and adventure writers like Mayne Reid, Dickens, Ainsworth, Captain Marryat were all undoubtedly people of moral purpose. Marryat, who was keen to have his books bound and presented to appeal to the young, launched his Juvenile Library to "excite, amuse and instruct". But they were working from a different end of the spectrum from the moralists. They could develop literary skills in which the moral was bound to become less obtrusive.

And as the middle class settled down in their new situation there was a reaction against the obtrusive and assertive. F. D. Maurice, the Christian Socialist, wanted God to appear in children's books as reassurance for the child, not an awful warning. He complained that "The Evangelicals preach to sinners as though they were heathen" (a remark whose ambivalence is more evident now than it would have been then). Dickens, launching his *Household Words* magazine in 1850, stressed that there would be "no utilitarian spirit".

There were other developments assisting this trend. In the school network the newly appointed Government inspectors began to cast a critical eye over the existing tract-type reading matter offered to pupils, asking whether it would actually induce the child to read.

Then in 1850 a bill struggled through Parliament, which permitted towns of a certain size to spend a halfpenny rate on setting up free public libraries. These could now slowly begin to provide an alternative to the religious society library, the expensive commercial library and the penny lending service of the back street newsagent.

9

Triumph of the Fairy Tale
1850–1870

The two decades between the Great Exhibition of 1851, which demonstrated Britain's lead over commercial and industrial rivals, and the 1867 Paris Exhibition, which warned that France, Germany, the United States, were catching up, were a time of consolidation and confidence. Everything seemed to work to a plan at the centre of which were the respectable English. Abroad – so it seemed to W. H. G. Kingston, enthusiastic and popular boys' adventure writer – "savages exist to employ the energies of Christian men." At home, in the increasingly successful novels of writers like Charlotte Yonge, "the poor existed for spiritual benefit of the middle and upper classes." (Mary Cadogan and Patricia Craig – *You're A Brick, Angela*, 1976).

If only everyone else would accept the rightness of things. Presenting itself to the reading public in the 1850s, the Religious Tract Society magazine *Leisure Hour* made clear how wide its net was cast, to catch the "masses" as well as the young nursery reader spending a Victorian Sunday in "painful vacuity". "Are we not one people, one great Commonwealth . . . with sentiments recognisably popular, ideas actually shared?" the editor asked.

It seemed this might be the case. Across the social divide, union leaders now spoke of their organisations as "respectable and respected". Whereas in the 1830s, Thomas Arnold, who was to become headmaster of Rugby School, thought trade unions were a "fearful engine of mischief", by the 1850s, his admirer Thomas Hughes was writing articles in up-market journals explaining and justifying working class organisations. Hughes was also running improving lectures for working men, giving them lessons in the manly art of boxing. (Though according to Isabel Quigly – *The Heirs of Tom Brown*, 1982 – they were under strict instruction not to knock him down). Skilled workers and the now million-strong social group of doctors, teachers and other professionals, could read the same entertaining and improving magazines, or enjoy books from the new Parlour and Railway Libraries.

As the Chartist movement retreated from the centre of public life, and settled in the main cities to become the focus of a renewed campaign for the vote in the 1860s, some former radicals retreated from their convictions. Charles Kingsley, who had made a Chartist the hero of one of his novels, repented and became Chaplain to the Queen in 1859. Edwin Brett, eager to put behind him the times when he had spoken on radical platforms, turned to launching the magazine *Boys of England* (1866) to combat the back-street magazine. Edward Lloyd who once launched serials like *Sweeney Todd*, with its violence, its cynical contempt for lawyers and tract-distributors, was moving towards the editorship of the *Daily Chronicle* and membership of the Reform Club. As E. S. Turner points out (*Boys Will Be Boys*, 1975) Lloyd's obituary diplomatically did not mention the Demon Barber.

England's centre of gravity now firmly lay in the respectable family modelled on a respectable monarch. "Mother wanted us to call her Mother Dear, because the magazines said the Royal Family did", says one memoir quoted in John Burnett's *Destiny Obscure* (1982).

The respectable family was now thoroughly domesticated. The father, source of the family's means of living, the "breadwinner", was elevated and remote. In domestic novels from the pens of Charlotte Yonge, Emma Jane Warboise, Elizabeth Sewell and others, "disobeying Papa was like disobeying God". The mother had a special role and status midway between father and children. While as Patricia Cadogan and Mary Craig point out, wives were "legally equated with mental defectives and criminals", yet because of the social position of their family, some power might rub off on them:

> Every class teaches the one immediately below it and if the highest class be ignorant, uneducated, loving display, luxurious and idle, the same spirit will prevail in humbler life. How great then is the

responsibility of those who "guide the house". (*How To Be A Lady*, 1850)

This involved a division not merely of social responsibility but of human qualities. As Thomas Hughes' popular school novel *Tom Brown's Schooldays* (1857) spelt out, there was on the one hand, the "strength and courage and wisdom of fathers and brothers and teachers", and on the other, "the love, tenderness and purity of mothers and sisters and wives."

John Stuart Mill, son of James Mill, when he came to write his classic work in 1869 saw it as the *Subjection of Women*. Respectable children's writers were conscious of this, but conscious of it as a sacrifice to be borne. Thus, when Elizabeth Sewell brooded over her vanity and irritability as a child, or Charlotte Yonge urged that "the most disagreeable" course "is always the safest", one has the feeling that their words were written to convince themselves as well as their readers.

Yet many of these women, the backbone of nineteenth century children's literature, Mary Pilkington, Agnes Strickland, Barbara Hofland, Emma Marshall, Frances Browne, Elizabeth Sewell, Hesba Stretton, Frances Hodgson Burnett, wrote partly or wholly to maintain families, as breadwinners. The injustice of the situation cannot have wholly escaped them. Charlotte Yonge took the orthodox view that Eve had brought the burden on herself, that the respect of men could only be earned by the subjection of women. Compensation would come with the feminine role in "renovating" the world. The behaviour of subjection, carefully enforced in early childhood, would be self-regulating in later life. These were things "children of gentle birth learn . . . they hardly know how . . ." perhaps, "through the unanimous consent of their story books". Lower class children lacked this training and self-training.

But for them, too, books could play a part. This no longer meant tracts alone but suitable novels given as prizes for attendance and good behaviour in the network of church day schools, now numbering some 30,000 or the even larger network of Sunday Schools. The number of domestic servants was still growing, outstripping the growth of population and exceeding the numbers in the textile industry. Many little servants still came from the village, leaving home at eight or nine, travelling long distances, seeing their own families perhaps once or twice a year. Their employers' anxiety about their social training expressed in the earlier tracts has now diminished with the new mood of complacency. Perhaps with generations "born" into service, the need for such "training" was less.

One can see assertion passing into assumption in the enormous success of a novel like *The Basket of Flowers*, translated from the German and selling a million copies from 1855 onwards. This time it is a gardener's daughter who is unjustly accused and then vindicated (the sub-title is "Piety and Truth Triumphant").

The folk notion of humble virtue is maintained. The servant reader can identify and the nursery reader sympathise with the good servant wronged. The basic relationship between mistress and servant is left undisturbed. The old assertive tract message of goodness manifested in loyal service is subsumed into the fabric of the story.

The old elements of folk melodrama are neatly transformed in Mrs Charlesworth's *Ministering Children* (1854), where a bad squire is balanced with a good one, and there is a benevolent middle class family on hand to rescue the unfortunate. Mrs Charlesworth was sincere in her concern for country people thrown into the "current market of towns and cities". Her wish for the old order stemmed from deeper feelings than those of wanting working class people to know their place. But this was a vanishing world.

By the thousand they were deserting the cottage for the "current market". They crowded into the city slums where, as Sir Edwin Chadwick commented in 1843, "in this one room they are born, live and die" (quoted in James Walvin, *A Child's World*, 1982). And eventually from the midst of this new urban population came a new character to add to the stock of young fiction. Along with the virtuous cottager and the faithful servant appeared the figure of the waif – the "street arab".

Mid-century social surveys of London's backstreets had disclosed a whole teeming world of children, who literally fought for their lives; though Henry Mayhew, that acute observer, noted, these young people had "few childlike qualities". Their poverty made it possible to pity them. They were no threat. Their ingenuity and courage in staying alive made them ideal subjects for what Gillian Avery (*Nineteenth Century Children*, 1965) calls "sensational stories of ragged London depravity". Chief exponent of this kind of writing was Hesba Stretton, pen name of Sara Smith, Non-conformist postmaster's daughter from Staffordshire. She was talented, independent, aware of the struggles of the poor and the condescension of the rich. Her novels vividly depicted the outsiders of children's literature, describing working life with assurance, but above all with sympathy for the worker. Fame came to her as chronicler of the urban waif with *Jessica's First Prayer* (1868). She is credited with launching the "street arab" school of writing, though George Sargent, with *Roland Leigh, The Story of A City Arab* (1857) came earlier. But Hesba Stretton, with her talent for the sensational and the sentimental (the essential talents of contemporary popular literature), brought this novel to a pitch of popularity which would inspire imitations for decades to come.

Like some of the penny dreadful writers, she had radical convictions which stiffened sentiment with jabs at the conscience of the rich. She invested her waif characters with the kind of independence not seen in nursery literature since *Goody Two Shoes*. Like Sargent's hero Roland Leigh, Jessica is too ragged to be welcomed in a place of worship. (This gave the lie to Charles Kingsley's hearty claim in *The Water Babies*, 1863, that in England, church doors were never closed to the poor.)

With her convictions, Hesba Stretton, like her fellow Dissenter Elizabeth Sewell, had to do more than write. She campaigned actively against the neglect of the poor city child, helped launch the NSPCC in the 1860s and parted company with it when she thought charity money was misspent.

To some extent her attitudes were shared by Charlotte Maria Tucker ("A Lady of England" or ALOE) with her appeal in *Rambles of a Rat* (1857): "Were all the children of the middle classes in England to give each but one penny a week, no wretched boy need wander about desolate in London."

But it contrasted with the condescension in Charlotte Yonge's Sunday School magazine, *The Monthly Packet* (1851–1898), towards factory girls and "their tendency to lie down and go to sleep" on Sundays, when they ought to be out walking in the country. Condescension, complacency, pity, replaced the strident anxiety of earlier writing. And with this change came a further dilution in the religion/didactic content.

Charlotte Yonge was deliberately "less directly religious" than past Church of England stalwarts, like Mrs Sherwood. Her aim was a "delicate aroma" of Christianity. Fellow Christian, Thomas Hughes, acknowledged that he wrote *Tom Brown's Schooldays* (1857) for "the chance of preaching". But he also wanted "a real novel for boys . . . not didactic like *Sandford and Merton*". The new magazine *Boys of England* (1866) promised a "moral and healthy tone", but "no sermons in disguise" would be mixed in its programme of "the boldest fiction."

Others were trying to reconcile God with a new more scientific understanding of nature. Another Darwin, Charles, the grandson of Erasmus, was having his indirect effect upon children's books with *The Origin of Species* (1859). Kingsley's writing tried to embrace both evolutionary science and an underlying "miraculous and divine" element. Mrs Gatty and ALOE showed ingenuity in blending general knowledge, fantasy and religion. As Nancy Cutt (*Ministering Angels*) puts it, ALOE, 40 years a Sunday School Teacher and missionary, was skilful in her efforts to "filter religion out" of her stories.

John Ruskin, art historian and writer of a Victorian children's classic *King of the Golden River* (1851), thought a great deal about how children should be approached. In his 1868 introduction to *German Popular Stories*, he spelt it out. The child "should not need to choose between right and wrong . . . it should not conceive of wrong . . . through daily entreating of gentleness and honorable trusts", it should grow strong, "not in bitter and doubtful contest with temptation but in peace of heart and armour of habitual right from which temptation falls like thawing hail . . . self commanding, not in sick restraint."

It is in this atmosphere of teaching by assumption rather than assertion that the "fairy tale" completes its triumphant return to the English nursery. It had been a long journey.

In the early nineteenth century, the hey-day of the Evangelicals, strong measures had been employed against what was thought disagreeable in the folk tale tradition. The unsuitable, advised Robert Bloomfield "could be used for lighting the fire", or "a pair of scissors will soon rectify" (Mrs Trimmer). Less violent, but equally thorough, was the "refining" process employed by editors. No longer would the beggar "fart for very fear" when Tom Thumb spoke to him out of nowhere.

As part of the refining process the cleaned-up Tom Thumb was published along with the imported French stories of Charles Perrault and Madame D'Aulnoy, which were refinement itself. When Tabart published his collection of tales in 1818, imported stories made up more than half the contents. Powerful reinforcement came from abroad in 1823 with the first English translation of *Grimm's Popular Tales*. To the changes brought about in the originals, by Wilhelm Grimm's editing, were added even greater changes by the translators. Hans Andersen's folk-style stories, first in English in 1846, were even more "refined" by translators, as Brian Alderson makes us aware (*Hans Andersen and His Eventyr in England*, 1982).

With the arrival of Andersen, says Harvey Darton (*Children's Books in England*) the fairy tale "came into its own." The new, artificial, mainly imported and refined product gave Victorian writers the opportunity to re-shape the moral tale. Sir Henry Cole, adviser at the Great Exhibition to Prince Albert, launched his *Home Treasury* in 1843. He claimed that this volume was a counter-attack on the fashion for moral-didactic tales which had caused "the many tales said and sung from time immemorial", to go "almost out of fashion". Francis Paget, author of the German style fairy tale *Hope of the Katzekopfs* (1844) made a similar claim. With them begins the presentation of the mid-century fairy tale as the restoring of liberated fantasy and imagination to the nursery.

It is far from being as simple as that. If one considers the above two books, or Ruskin's *King of the Golden River* (1851) Frances Browne's *Granny's Wonderful Chair* (1857), Thackeray's *The Rose and the Ring* (1857), ALOE's *Fairy Know a Bit* (1866) Kingsley's *The Water Babies* (1863), Jean Ingelow's *Mopsa the Fairy* (1869), or even the *Alice* books by Lewis Carroll (1865 and 1871), there can be no doubt that these are for the moral cultivation of the Victorian child of the nursery. Kingsley was honest. He wanted the "pill swallowed by a generation" which was not believing in God as they ought.

Ruskin, Thackeray and ALOE especially urge, in their tales,

the redeeming qualities of hard work for the luxurious idle. When in her *Story of a Needle*, ALOE tells lazy children that they shall be punished – "seven long years you shall toil in humble estate" she assumes the non-humble status of her readers. Why those already "humble" should be punished is not made clear. But in *The Water Babies* Kingsley feels the poor need to be redeemed and cleansed ready to enter paradise alongside the already clean and respectable. For Carroll's Alice, the worst thing that can happen is that she should wake up and find herself living in a poor child's home. Through the artificially contrived "fairy tale" criticism of the rich is distanced in space and time from contemporary industrial England. Though ALOE allowed her fairy valley to be industrialised, and the Mayhew brothers made a parable of *Industry, the good genius that turns everything gold* (1847), there is generally, as Gillian Avery (*Nineteenth Century Children*) says of Jean Ingelow's *Mopsa the Fairy*, an "impulse to escape into a dream world leaving poverty stricken, wet, factory-ridden England behind."

The distancing from actual reality, which might complicate the moral lesson, is achieved in two ways. The models for these (and most subsequent fairy tales) are generally foreign – with perhaps the exception of Frances Browne and Jean Ingelow. In the process of creating fantasies for the nursery, the English Tales "became a *mélange confus* of Perrault and the Grimms" (Joseph Jacobs, *English Fairy Tales*, 1898 edition).

Then, as modern scholar Katherine Briggs in her writings on the folk and fairy tales has shown, with the use of the diminutive "gauzy-winged" creatures from the eighteenth century collection, *Le Cabinet Des Fées*, the *folk* tale was re-styled the *fairy* tale. Puck, Brownies, Boggarts and all were gradually diminished in size until they reached a size convenient for the Christmas Tree and the "childish" imagination.

So casually was the native oral tradition discarded that when preparing the story of *Rumpelstiltskin* (from the Grimms) for English publication in the 1820s, Edward Taylor "remembered" that he had once met this story in an Irish version (*Trit a Trot*). It also existed in English (*Tom Tit Tot*) and in Scots versions. But, as Joseph Jacobs commented regretfully when he published his own rescued collection of English tales in the 1890s, the "rude vigour" of the native versions had been discarded for the "superior elegance" of the continental.

These changes in the tale overcame the barrier the middling sort had erected between the child and the "lies" of the folk tale. In place of a tale told by "illiterate" maidservants who believed it, we have the honest "lie" of the fiction made specially for children by adults who knew it was not real. "You are not to believe a word of it even if it is true", writes Kingsley of the "tomfooleries" of his *Water Babies*. Thackeray in his *Fireside Pantomime* (1847) recalled his being reconciled to Red Riding Hood, on discovering it was not true. The Rev. F. E. Paget urged, aggressively, the "palpable, fantastic absurdities, the utter impossibilities of a tale of Enchantment." *Aunt Judy's Magazine* (1866) went into raptures over the "impossible" Lewis Carroll's stories. The underlying moral assumptions made acceptable the deception involved in asking children to believe what you might not believe yourself.

On the other hand, however, certain fictions, whose larger than life heroes and heroines appealed to the young, were met with implacable hostility. The cheap illustrated penny weeklies for the newly literate adult had by the 1860s, in the words of R. D. Altick (*The English Common Reader*), "branched downwards", to become "ostensibly a juvenile literature". What was worse, in the view of James Greenwood (1873), was "the gradual spread upwards in what is called the social scale of this sort of trash". In his study *Boys Will be Boys* (1975), E. S. Turner describes how the penny dreadful with its adventures of Charley Wag, the boy burglar, Joe the Ferret, The Wild Boys of London, the Outsiders (a kind of early Cockney Rejects) was read not only by the errand boy, but penetrated beyond the tradesman's entrance. Charlotte Yonge had noticed and deplored this contamination. But Charley Wag with his "sex, scandal and a crude form of Socialism" (E. S. Turner) together with the other penny dreadful characters, served a strange and contrary purpose. They provoked a loosening of talent and purse strings among religious and commercial bodies to put up an answering barrage. Within a decade scores of new magazines for the young were on the market. *Boys of England* (1866): "wild and wonderful but healthy stories"; *The Penny Magazine* (1863) "never suggested anything unworthy of an English gentleman". *Chatterbox* (1866) was launched by Rev. J.

Erskine Clarke of Derby, who aimed to wean working class lads off penny dreadfuls with exciting stories "without splashing blood on every page". There was *Good Words for the Young*, Christian but open minded, and Beeton's *Boys' Own Magazine* (1855) which, with its serials and its watch and pencil case prizes, rivalled the downmarket Newsagents' Company with its pistols and stilettos.

To beat you must join, and the respectable *Boys' Miscellany* ran a Sixteen-String Jack serial alongside "How Little Boys Become Great Men." This was risky since the boy might believe he could become a great man by following the example of Jack, or the many riders of Black Bess. That was the trouble. Charley Wag's salacity might bother the respectable, but it was his way of earning a living, however impossible, which outraged them. Compare the self-pitying whine of Sam the cab driver in Anna Sewell's *Black Beauty* (1877) with the defiant cynicism of *Joe The Ferret*: " . . . the honest cove slaves for half a bellyful of grub all that he may be called a good boy and have a clear conscience. I ain't got a conscience and I don't want one." Or the "Wild Boys of London", with their cry of "One law for the rich, another for the poor".

In this war between magazines acceptable and unacceptable, frontiers were often crossed. But the acceptable had the advantage of official approval and greater capital input. For now some publishers were rapidly making their fortunes.

There was Routledge with his Shilling Railway Library and his 1,000 "juvenile" titles, including Marryat and Ainsworth, Mudie with his circulating library, W. H. Smith, John Murray, Nelson; Nisbet and Blackie with their religious background; Collins and Longman expanding along with the growing school business. As the commercial and "reward" suppliers moved into territory which had been opened up by the RTS and SPCK, they took up some at least of the moral responsibility implied. Mudie and W. H. Smith saw themselves as moral watchdogs. John Murray promised "heads of families, clergymen, school teachers, employers of labour" that they would find "nothing offensive to moral or good taste" on his list. Nelson's and Blackie's "cheap but gorgeous" fiction steadily won the approval of the Sunday and day school prize givers.

Cheap publication was then, as now, sometimes achieved at the expense of the author. ALOE thought she needed "no earthly remuneration", but the market had become the deciding factor. Hesba Stretton did need her remuneration. She threatened to leave the RTS when she found her religious publisher lying and cheating. Harriet Martineau, author of the little books for children on "political economy", found herself, with poetic justice, exploited by the Utilitarians' Library of Useful Knowledge. The Society of Authors, newly formed, stepped in to save the "handmaidens" of God and Mammon alike from being underpaid.

As said, the school market expanded, but very unevenly. Between 1849 and 1861, the amount of state money paid to church schools rose from £125,000 a year to £800,000, though even then it was still less than one thirtieth of the defence budget. And in 1861, Palmerston called for "a little free trade" in education (a familiar cry for those living in the 1980s) and cut the budget by a quarter. With monetarist "efficiency" the New Education Code introduced "payment by results". School finance and teachers' salaries were tied to the end product rigidly assessed.

The result, to the despair of the HMIs, led by Thomas Arnold's famous son Matthew, was "drill, drill, drill upon a single book." As school experts had predicted, the education of working class children suffered a setback. Matthew Arnold, however, strove to raise the quality of the "feeble, incorrect and colourless" books supplied to schools. Another inspector, more forthright, condemned the "twaddle, false moral and degraded sentimentality" offered to the working class pupils.

Even by the end of the 1860s perhaps only 40 per cent of the 6–10 year olds and 33 per cent of the 10–12s were actually getting education, in the mixture of Church of England, Dissenting, Ragged, Workhouse, Dame and other schools. Some were supported by the state, some not. Some were inspected, many more were not.

Working class resentment grew fast. In 1850, Richard Cobden had warned the House of Commons that people were "sick to death of the obstacles you throw in their way." A year later *The Times* blamed "bitter dispute and fierce animosity" among the churches for the failure to advance education. State action was "paralysed". The Working Men's Association in London declared: "We cannot consent that our children shall be apportioned among the religious sects."

The demand for a national secular or non-denominational schooling was put forward again by the newly formed Trades Union Congress in the late 1860s. A pamphlet on these lines by carpenters' leader Robert Applegarth sold half a million copies.

The Reform Bill of 1867 added one million male skilled workers to the town voting lists, doubling the electorate. So an Act to reform education could not long be deferred. It came in 1870, and with it a turning point not only for the nation's schools, but for the whole range of fiction for the young.

10

School and Empire:
From Boy's Own Paper to Greyfriars

In 1875 Alexander Strahan, editor and publisher, offered guidelines for the production of good fiction which would win the adolescent reader from the "flood of bad literature."

> It must be full of incident and pictures, its motif must be will and feeling rather than ideas. It must not be goody goody and it must certainly not be prudish ... Perfectly pure and modest of course it must be, but it must be gay and fresh. And the spirit of divine obligation and human service must be everywhere present, though nowhere obtruded.

These elements were mixed, well or badly, in thousands of stories in both book and magazine form which came from mainstream publishers in late nineteenth and early twentieth century. Any writer, of whatever reputation, had to be in serial as well as book form. It was, though, above all in the magazine that the genres developed, that ideas were copied and handed on and the recognisable shape of the fiction emerged. There were two basic forms, the school story and the adventure, and they were mainly boys' stories. Girls got a foothold only later. Boys' stories had huge success: at the up-market end, *The Boy's Own Paper* (1879) was to have generations of readers and the admiration of archbishops and prime ministers. At the down-market end, the Amalgamated Press "comics" swamped the back street magazines.

The up-market magazines employed the talent of the time, Robert Louis Stevenson, Rider Haggard, Arthur Conan Doyle, Talbot Baines Reed, Jules Verne; and they expressed the highest ideals. "The strong fellows must look after the weak, the sharp must lend a helping hand to the duffer", Reed told a youth club audience in the 1880s. It was, says Patrick Howarth, author of a study of Henry Newbolt, "a law that you cannot stand by while the weak are bullied by the strong."

Talent, ideals and commercial success produced a kind of fiction for the young which moved rapidly to its peak in the 1880s and 1890s and then as swiftly fell into fantasy and self-parody, surviving in these forms into the 1920s and 1930s. The school story, Frank Eyre noted in his *British Children's Books in the 20th Century* (1971) was brought to a "perfection of unreality". Yet, even in the late nineteenth century, Arnold Lunn, author of *The Harrovians* (1913) had been aware of its "lack of realism".

Cynicism about the genre was already apparent by the early 1900s. P.G.Wodehouse's schoolboy characters were likely to be "seriously ill" if exhorted about the old school. And by early twentieth century, Henry Newbolt, it is reported, was beginning to be nauseated by insistent demands to hear his famous school/ empire poem *Vitae Lampada*, at public lectures.

Why did the School and Empire literature degenerate? It is argued, reasonably, that much repetition by inferior writers debased the original ideal. But the original ideal had the seeds of corruption within it from the start. This literature, though more advanced in its forms, was as much an ideological campaign as was the early nineteenth century tract movement. Thomas Hughes wrote his *Tom Brown's Schooldays*, "just to get the chance of preaching", while Kipling's *Stalky and Co.*(1899), began life as "some tracts or parables on the education of the young". The impulse behind the campaign was to win acceptance for two gigantic acts of acquisition, which set the seal on the new order in Britain and the world in mid-nineteenth century: the Empire abroad and the public school network which provided its cadre force, at home.

By mid-century, the overseas possessions had become vital as markets. Exports exceeded imports by nearly 30 per cent. Outflow of capital multiplied by fourteen times before 1900. Along with the money went human beings, well over half a million emigrants leaving Britain during the early 1880s alone, many to settle in what were known as the "white colonies". The best known adventure writers, W. H. G. Kingston and

R. M. Ballantyne, eagerly promoted emigration, especially by the young.

Ballantyne, who also wrote waif stories for *The Boy's Own Paper*, saw "street arabs" finding a new life abroad. Thousands of orphans were sent to work on colonial farms, many in conditions of forced labour. Kingston, who was active in the Society to Promote Colonisation, said in a lecture on New Year's Day, 1849: "The Anglo Saxon race has been awarded the office of peopling the yet uninhabited parts of the globe, civilising . . . and spreading the faith of Christ." Tasmania, of course, *became* uninhabited when the original population was wiped out by the colonists. But the Maori, Zulu and many other peoples, not least in India, resisted stoutly. They were overcome in no less than 75 colonial wars during Victoria's reign. Each war produced its heroes, each one its justifying "massacres" of British troops or civilians.

Eager lecturers, like Thomas Hughes, helped spread propaganda for the Empire down through the social strata. He foresaw "a chain of English speaking nations which would have little trouble in making their will respected and keeping the world's peace." These sentiments found their expression in the rule book of the Carpenters' Union in 1860. For the "surplus labourers and mechanics" of "the Anglo Saxon race", "emigration is the natural outlet to distant colonies whose inhabitants they are destined to bless." Kingston linked the need to "feed the poor" and "discipline the turbulent" at home with the "civilising mission" abroad. Cecil Rhodes saw the "importance of imperialism" in avoiding a "bloody civil war". The training of those who were to "discipline the turbulent" was crucial. As Robert Lowe told the House of Commons, if the lower classes were to defer, then the "higher classes" needed schooling so they might exhibit "a higher cultivation" to the lower. The new rulers themselves needed civilising. Schools were needed, in Chesterton's phrase, "not for the sons of gentlemen, but for the fathers of gentlemen", or as the head of Radley School put it in 1872, "to confer an aristocracy on boys who did not inherit it."

By mid-century the education system for these social groups was in a poor way. Of the Nine "Great" so-called public schools, only Eton flourished. Others were flagging. Down the scale the old grammar schools were in an unhealthy state. The charitable trusts and foundations which ran them were often badly administered. Such was the concern that in the 1860s, the Taunton Commission was appointed to study the education of those "between the humblest and the highest."

There were two solutions. One was to set up new private schools to meet the new, imperial needs, Cheltenham for "the defenders of Empire", Wellington for the "competent and muscular . . . dashing breed of young officers", Haileybury for the bureaucrats of the Indian Raj. Further down the scale were the Woodard schools, in three grades, for sons of clergymen and gentlemen, sons of substantial tradesmen, and sons of petty shopkeepers.

It must be remembered that in nineteenth century England most people, poor or rich, paid for their education. The New Board Schools, set up after the 1870 Education Act, did not become truly free until the end of the century. But some "poor scholars" did have free places in the public and grammar schools. That was what the charities were for. In Rugby and Harrow, local boys benefited.

The exclusion of these "free scholars", while retaining the benefits of the charities for the schools, was accomplished over a number of years, thanks to a good deal of ingenuity and legal chicanery and often barefaced insolence. Brian Simon, in his three-volume study of educational history, describes the process.

Legal judgements in 1807, 1827 and 1882, with the help of an obliging House of Lords, made it possible for "charitable" schools to take in fee-payers without losing charitable funds. Poor scholars were bullied, segregated in inferior premises and, sometimes against strong local protest, squeezed out. The new breed of headmaster refused to "squander endowments" on those who "do not require such an education and cannot profit by it." Or, to quote a public school history published as recently as 1983, scholars who were "ignorant, unmotivated . . . totally unsuited to a classical education" (TES April 29, 1983).

By the 1880s, the process of clearing out the free scholars was complete. It was marked by a sudden rush on Eton, Harrow and the other schools to establish missions in the East End, clubs for "rough boys and girls", where, in the words of a sermon from the head of Harrow, the upper classes could "exercise their obligation by teaching the lower classes the moral virtues."

The 100 or so new and re-organised "public schools" became in the words of Isabel Quigly (*The Heirs of Tom Brown*, 1982) "training grounds for sahibs". From the 1870s team games were made compulsory. The emphasis was on the cult of the "manly".

"Manliness" has an interesting history. Early educators like Thomas Day and Erasmus Darwin favoured it as a maturing process. Thomas Arnold, saintly head of Rugby in the 1830s, saw it as boys growing up and becoming responsible. These earlier ideals, it is said, were debased by later hearties, not least Hughes with his Tom Brown – "sensual, book-hating man", as one reviewer put it. The public school boy-man became the Kingsley, Ballantyne, Henty hero "a splendid animal . . . generous, healthy English boyhood."

Was an original Arnoldian idea corrupted? Or was the basic assumption corrupt from the beginning? "Idealistic" Arnold helped along the process of squeezing the local boys out of Rugby, by charging double fees for certain services. Nor was he free from "manly" philistinism. Just after he left Rugby for Oxford in the early 1840s, he complained of boys' "childishness", which he attributed to "the great number of exciting books of amusement like Pickwick or Nickleby".

Suspended adolescence is the ambience of the school stories, its heroes forever "on the brink of puberty" as Noel Coward later said, staying 20, 30, 40 years in the fourth form of Greyfriars. The schoolboy *was* the public schoolboy. To have a chance in real life, remarked the head of Uppingham during the controversy over the free scholars in the 1860s, a boy must stay five, six, seven years in secondary school. This "silently decides that none but the monied classes" can benefit. When Tom Brown announced that "all boys are sent to a public school in England", he was saying that those who were not, did not exist.

By adolescence, the working class boy or girl was already at work. Not until the eve of the First World War was raising the school leaving age to 13 officially mooted. Not until the 1940s did the majority of working class children stay on at school after puberty. Thus the school story "on the brink of puberty" could *only* be a private school story, just as in the adventure stories, the army seems to be composed mainly of officers. If a boy should pass from the Sixth form (as he might, and not just in fiction) to command a unit fighting rebels in the Sudan, and the men under his command had by his age already been at work seven or eight years, then he had to be a "man". Hence the cult of the boyish, muscular hero.

Magazines which could through effective popular fiction successfully justify robbery at home and abroad as one all-embracing mission of civilisation, needed special qualities. The most successful of them had a special combination of religious fervour, typographical expertise and business acumen. *The Boy's Own Paper* (1879) had them all, plus a dash of liberal politics. Jack Cox describes it well in *Take A Cold Tub, Sir* (1982), the story of BOP. Talbot Baines Reed, author of *Fifth Form at St. Dominic's* (1887) embodied most of these features in his own person. Like Charles Hamilton (Frank Richards) the twentieth century creator of Greyfriars, Reed was no public schoolboy. This may have helped him to perfect his "unreality". But he had talent, plus a blend of deep, natural moral feeling and amiable self-mockery. The editorial team at BOP, poised between the clergymen of the controlling RTS committee, and the quarter of a million readers, produced work of a remarkable flavour, and spread it through society.

BOP editor George Hutchinson asked Reed to aim his stories at the lower middle class schoolboy. He knew the magazine was read by "schoolboys, office boys, apprentices and cadets". BOP's resident experts were as ready to advise young workers on the evils of striking as young gents on the perils of masturbation.

Still, BOP was relatively expensive at sixpence. So other periodicals were there to fill the gap, in what E.S. Turner (*Boys Will Be Boys*) calls "the scramble for the pennies and half pennies of the New Board school generation".

One such was *Boys of England* (founded 1866) which, in the 1870s, offered its readers the saga of Jack Harkaway, anarchic schoolboy-adventurer. Harkaway is vaguely descended from Fielding's Tom Jones by way of Captain Marryat's famous seafaring hero Jack Easy. Like Easy, Harkaway breaks all the rules. Unlike other famous Victorian schoolboys he shows no remorse for wildness. In the eyes of his creator his role was to win the young reader from the penny dreadful, and restraint was inappropriate. But every excess in Harkaway's behaviour is shown as justified by the villainy of the villains, more often than not foreigners. Harkaway draws on the appeal of the rebel rogue of tradition, but unlike them he is on the *right* side.

Reinforcements in the battle against the penny dreadful were moving up in the shape of the Amalgamated Press comics of the 1890s, owned by the Harmsworth Brothers (later to be Lords Northcliffe and Rothermere, founders of the *Daily Mail* and *Daily Mirror* and proprietors, for a while, of *The Times*).

They launched their comics, not at a penny but at a halfpenny. They promised that "these healthy tales of mystery and adventure will kill stone dead" the opposition. First *Marvel* (1893), then *Union Jack* (1894), *Boys' Herald* (1903) ("Healthy Paper for Manly Boys"), then *Gem* (1907) and *Magnet* (1908) to name but a few, made clear where the Harmsworths drew the line on the rebel rogue of the penny dreadful. "No tales of boys rifling their employers' cash boxes and making off to foreign lands", they promised.

Where earlier publishers dealt in thousands or tens of thousands, Amalgamated Press were to deal in millions. Aided by the latest rotary press and colour printing developments, the Harmsworths did win the field from the back street firms. The penny dreadful was killed, A. A. Milne ironically remarked, by substituting the "ha'penny dreadfuller".

The chief aim was to swing the spirit of violent adventure away from the anti-rich sentiment of earlier popular literature. Not surprisingly then, the closing of the nineteenth century saw the arrival of detective heroes, mostly inspired by Conan Doyle's *Sherlock Holmes* (1891). Sexton Blake and Nelson Lee are the best known. Not short of cash themselves, these detective heroes employed boy assistants from poor circumstances. Being "unofficial" they could employ any means in fighting their chosen foes, while often ridiculing the police. They were at one and the same time outside the law and on the right side.

Unofficial but righteous violence was the rule. In his *Fifth Form at St Dominic's* (1887) Reed laid down that "a pair of well-trained, athletic schoolboys with a plucky youngster to help them . . . are a match any day for twice the number of half tipsy cads". The loyal elements in the lower class could be recruited to fight "lesser breeds without the law" both at home and abroad.

Meanwhile in the real world, in semi-military organisations like the Boys' Brigade, founded by a Non-conformist in 1883, tens of thousands of working-class youngsters were taught "habits of obedience, reverence, discipline, self respect and all that tends towards a true Christian manliness". By 1900 the Boys' Brigade had earned its founder a knighthood.

The literary problem of "lawless adventure" was most easily solved abroad. If for both Cecil Rhodes and Salvation Army leader William Booth the Empire was the "way out" for social problems, so it was for the writer or editor wondering what next to do with the violent but law-abiding hero. When there are no more pranks that Jack Harkaway can legitimately play on the much abused staff of various schools, his creator sends him abroad, where his talent for fighting foul can be used without restraint. What was horseplay with Jack Easy becomes sadism with Jack Harkaway, in which "a touch of the tarbrush" in an opponent justifies a multitude of sins in the hero.

The transition from school to Empire, written into the prospectus of Cheltenham or Wellington, is also written into the school story. As school story writer, Harold Avery, put it, (1895) ". . . in the hard fight to save his goal we see in those grey eyes the first kindling of that light" which will shine when "he stands face to face with danger and even death." From the "breathless hush of the close" to the blood-stained desert sand, where "the voice of a schoolboy rallies the ranks", in Henry Newbolt's poem, is a logical and intended step. It excites the reader without inciting him to break open the cash box.

Outrageous behaviour legitimised calls for an outrageous enemy. As Isabel Quigly points out (*The Heirs of Tom Brown*), stories both up-market and down contain every current "attitude compressed and therefore concentrated, not just snobbery and jingoism . . . but uglier things like anti-Semitism and racism". "A trio of darkies", "a nigger, a genuine nigger", these turn of the century phrases strike the modern reader in the face, but they were written with unconscious ease as the unjustifiable was justified. By contrast, the only place where a Black character might take the popular hero part was in a down-market comic, as with the exceptional iron-fisted Pete of *Marvel*.

For "unconscious" one should not read "natural". The original spirit and letter of the school and adventure story were steadily corrupted. In the 1840s, Mayne Reid, radical republican whose adventure stories were free of religious fanaticism, viewed the non-English world as a Gulliver rather than a Crusoe. Captain Marryat was able in *Masterman Ready* (1841–42) to foresee the time when England would "no longer boast of her possessions all over the world." But as Patrick Howarth (*Play Up and Play the Game*, 1973) tells us, Thomas Hughes, training volunteers at the time of the Crimean War, thought the Empire was to last "for the rest of time." Kingsley in *Westward Ho* (1855) saw the day when "no wind can sweep the earth which does not hear the echoes of an English voice." If Marryat raised moral questions about the treatment of Black people, later writers "organised their stories so as to avoid such questions", writes Howarth.

It is interesting, briefly, as a contrast to consider the most famous of nineteenth century adventure stories, Stevenson's *Treasure Island* (1883). Here is "lawless adventure", superbly described. Harvey Darton (*Children's Books in England*) calls it "the very apotheosis of the penny dreadful which virtuous and healthy magazines had been founded to dethrone".

John Rowe Townsend (*Written for Children*) sees it as written with a "lordly disregard for the moralists". But closer reading of the book shows a supreme quality of moral logic which gives the book its backbone. One has only to think of how a hero, invited, as Jim was, to cut and run from Long John Silver, to whom he has given his word, would have acted in the work of Kingston, Ballantyne, Henty or their lesser imitators. The book is a comment on the greed of its "respectable" adult hero. Jim Hawkins is as much a comment on Victorian rapacity as Carroll's *Alice* is a comment on Victorian hypocrisy. *Treasure Island* is thus the exception that underlines the rule of the genre, and is remembered where the rest are forgotten.

For other writers, the school, where "the headmaster is the God and the public schoolboy the ideal", and the Empire where the Almighty has awarded the task of converting the heathen to the English, are more and more the centre of a belief which supplements and even replaces religion. The imperialism of G. A. Henty is "as simple as a child's faith in God, or father or Santa Claus", says Marcus Crouch (*Treasure Seekers and Borrowers*, 1962). Rider Haggard, speaking in praise of Rudyard Kipling at a meeting in May 1898, said that he did not believe in the Divine Right of Kings but did believe in "The Divine Right of a civilising people". Thus far had the middling sort gone from the Civil War battlefields of Edgehill and Naseby.

There were contemporary objections to the cult of war and Empire from both socialist and church circles. But the shrewdest critique of the Henty/BOP approach came from abroad, from a Dutchman who wrote in the rival *Captain* magazine (May 1908) that, thanks to their efforts, the young Englishman came to believe he was equal to two or more Frenchmen, about four Germans, an indefinite number of Russians and any quantity "you care to mention of the remaining scum of the earth." The writer ridiculed the claims of mutual devotion between England and colonies by citing the tones of condescension in which the English would speak of "colonials".

Not only were there criticisms and contradictions. There were defeats and shocks. As Guy Arnold (*Held Fast For England*, 1980) tells us, Henty burst into tears when he heard of the British military defeat at Majuba Hill, and cried, "this disgrace will never be wiped out." Worse was to come: the discovery that more than one third of the recruits to fight the Boers were not "splendid animals" but undernourished and unfit for military service. The shocks of the Boer War were a foretaste of harsher pressure, as in the early 1900s England felt the competition from its rivals.

BOP, shifting its centre of gravity from the Sunday School to the Scout Troop at the turn of the century, was also under pressure from its competitors. It lost ground steadily until, just before 1914, it had turned into a monthly. It was squeezed between the more sophisticated *Captain* magazine which carried adverts for Players while BOP tried to fight the smoking habit, and *Chums* with serial stories from John Buchan and P.G.Wodehouse, as well as the brasher Amalgamated Press comics.

These now featured the clash between rival imperialist states with stories of invasions of Britain by foreigners "jealous of our progress", and tales of massive airships that could wipe out cities. As the newly established magazines searched for more and more raw material, old favourites were re-hashed. Even the rebel rogue Jack Sheppard reappeared. But now he was the "idle" apprentice.

As the first rank of writers – Stevenson, Henty, T. B. Reed and Rider Haggard – died, their places were taken by lesser imitators. According to Harvey Darton "army and navy officers on retired pay crowded the publishers' lists." In the new atmosphere where fervour and confidence had been replaced by growing anxiety about the state of affairs abroad, where a newly militant working class and newly founded Labour party changed the political map at home, the contradictions in the literature now had freer play.

Talbot Baines Reed had been mildly self-mocking, as in his *Dog With a Bad Name* (1882) where the school needed only two reforms, the sacking of the staff and the expulsion of the pupils. F. Anstey's *Vice Versa* (1882) used fantasy/satire to warn against illusions about schooldays. But Kipling's *Stalky and Co.* (1889) was openly cynical about the cult of games and Empire, above all when the imperial message is delivered by a visiting "jelly-bellied flag-slapper", whose manner suggested the social status of a "bargee". If imperialism were a religion then it was not easily and publicly practised by this new generation of public schoolboys, nor was that "dream of glory that boys do not discuss even with their most intimate equal" really to be shared with the lower orders.

Stalky was openly critical but still privately devoted to the dream. He left school for India, to become "a sort of guru" to his Sikh soldiers. As Isabel Quigly says, he is a forerunner of the real T. E. Lawrence (of Arabia). And, one might add, Greenmantle and the other fictional heroes of John Buchan in the twentieth century. The hearty confidence gives way to wishful thinking on the one hand and parody on the other. By the early 1900s, P.G.Wodehouse's "Mike" is asking "Are you the Bully, the Pride of the School or the Boy who takes to drink?" The heart is no longer to be worn on the old school sleeve.

Humour offered the more lasting solution. Avery's Diggory and Rats stories, in Victorian/Edwardian days, point to the inter-war BOP stories of Gunby Hadath, and they in their turn point to

Buckeridge's Jennings in the 1940s and 1950s. Humour was the essential ingredient of the Amalgamated Press school comics which entertained both the public schoolboy and the many other readers for whom the life of the better off seemed like one long caper interspersed with orgies of tuck. *Gem* (1907) and *Magnet* (1908) and others, served by the indefatigable Charles Hamilton, using as many pen names as there were magazines and sometimes more, with their tales of St Jim's and Greyfriars, were the ultimate comic solution.

There were, of course, those who still played the game the old way, like the schoolboy in the eve of war BOP serial: "Fancy taking part in a war. Better than a house match." And some, like the headmaster in H. A. Vachell's *The Hill*, (1905) believed that "to die young clean, ardent, in perfect health", was a cause for joy. For such, the guns and the mud of Flanders were about to provide the final critique.

II

Moral Fantasies:
The First "Golden Age" 1870–1914

Away from the ritual combats of playing field and battle field, subtler, deeper changes were taking place. Out of a blend of the family story and the fairy story was emerging a modern novel, a model for the sort of writing likely to earn critical acclaim in the century to come. The keynote seems to be the liberation of child and story from the restrictions of Victorian morality. Relieved of the need to set an example, the child seems free to question and answer back in the nursery (there is an interesting dialogue between governess and children about truth and the fairy tale in Kenneth Grahame's *The Golden Age*, 1895). Better still, they are "free" to leave the house and roam the woods beyond the garden in the haze of an endless summer.

This is the First Golden Age, the time of *Alice's Adventures in Wonderland* (1865) and *Through the Looking Glass* (1871), *The Wind in The Willows*, (1908), Edith Nesbit's Bastable family stories (1902–1906), Frances Hodgson Burnett's *The Secret Garden* (1911). This is the time, we are told, when levity and fancy took off, even inhibitions on behaviour were relaxed and a new generation of inspired and talented writers produced the Story, pure entertainment to be enjoyed for its own sake.

On closer examination, however, one sees how carefully circumscribed is the new freedom, and how carefully defined is the child who enjoys it; how fantasy is used more and more to escape or transcend restrictions and limits in real life, the structures of an accepted and assumed way of life. The children of Jefferies' *Bevis, the Story of a Boy* (1882) or Kenneth Grahame's *The Golden Age* can wander, knowing that as they return, the meal (by magic?) will be on the table in dining room or kitchen. Fantasy allows Alice to challenge family authority by providing animals, playing cards, chesspieces, to take the places of adults. Her magic world, in which she can turn everything upside-down and challenge dictates and hypocrisy, is a very careful extension of the nursery to which she will return. Her one moment of real depression and fear is when she begins to question who she is and says:

> "I must be Mabel after all and I shall have to go and live in that poky little house and have next to no toys to play with."

Freedom to roam, to misbehave and contradict is not the freedom to work or starve that exists in that large, vaguely defined and often threatening outer world – the world of the vicious Stoats and Weasels, of Grahame's Wild Wood in *The Wind in the Willows* (1908), or the Goblins underground in George Macdonald's *The Princess and the Goblin* (1872), or the London where people are "poor . . . ill, unhappy . . . wicked . . . horrible", in Edith Nesbit's *The Story of the Amulet* (1906).

Hesba Stretton was the only writer who lent real dignity to the "silent majority" of the Victorian world. Her waif characters are "independent" in a real sense, for they must fend for themselves. She knew the difference between being inside the magic circle or outside. It was the difference between existing and not existing. "To be respectable, is to emerge from the anonymous, amorphous mass", she wrote.

Within the magic circle the characters we see developing in the most brilliant of children's fiction of the time are a more and more sophisticated blend of the Angel and the Scamp. As J. S. Bratton (*The Impact of Victorian Children's Fiction*) remarks, the "converted infant", has been transformed into the "child who can do no wrong." At one extreme are the "wonderfully uninhibited" Bastable children, as Mary Croxson describes them (*Signal* Magazine, May, 1974) – children of the new and fashionable Froebel mode of upbringing. As Mary Croxson points out, Edith Nesbit's is a secular concept of behaviour, derived in part from her membership of the Fabian Society, and in part from her passionate belief that the child should be free to develop its own sense of responsibility. It is an extension of John Ruskin's vision of the child who would do right without being told. As Froebel put it: "To young plants and animals we give space and time." It is not quite Jean Jacques Rousseau's child of nature, because Froebel's subject is carefully cultivated. In his equation of plant and child we see the dual meaning of the word "nursery".

At the other extreme, the child is like *Little Lord Fauntleroy* (1886), "loveable because simple and loving" as his creator Frances Hodgson Burnett sees him, or as Nesbit's Oswald Bastable saw him, "an insufferable prig".

The "frolicsome" child, whom Catherine Sinclair re-instated in *Holiday House* (1839) where little Laura was "quite as naughty as Harry", develops from the exception into the rule with the Nesbit family stories. Their security is never in doubt, even when playing at being "poor", always a favourite game of the well-to-do. If they get into a scrape they are to send a telegram. If their father is away, he is restoring the family fortunes. These assumptions, while they give the stories claims to be more "natural" than those which went before, keep them well outside the notion of the "average child" claimed for them by some critics. Always in the background, to be the butt of "ragging" or to clear up the mess when the pranks are over, is the anonymous figure of the servant. Servants are not "wonderfully uninhibited". The 13-year-old Bessie in Charlotte Yonge's story *Cheapjack* cannot understand the "fun and nonsense" of the children of the house. Their pranks just give her trouble. "Scullery maids", thinks Frances Hodgson Burnett's heroine in *A Little Princess* (1905) "were machines who carried coal scuttles and made fires." After the children in Nesbit's *The Phoenix and the Carpet* (1904) have wrecked the place, "no wonder" says Mary Croxson, "that the furniture as well as the servants . . . show signs of wear and tear".

In the 1890s and early 1900s, while the "free" child is wrecking the nursery and roaming the woods, half a million anonymous children went hungry to school. If they were lucky they got their soup ration at the police station or were given breakfast at the "Cinderella Clubs" organised by Robert Blatchford's *Clarion* magazine. No wonder Alice did not want to wake up and find she was Mabel. No wonder the Psammead angrily told the Bastables, "there's no room for half your children and no one to want them." Or as Hesba Stretton wrote in 1882, it was "the well fed and well clad citizens of the richest Christian city in the world, who . . . did what they could to perpetuate the sin and shame of having almost naked children to sweep the crossings."

But the poor were not just a shadow on the conscience of the well-to-do, they could also eventually be the means of their entertainment and self-indulgence. Hesba Stretton's "pathetic simplicity" (Edith Nesbit's verdict) copied by a line of followers, Mrs Walton, Mrs Molesworth, L. T. Meade, Evelyn Everett Green, became in their hands sentimentality for its own sake. As Harvey Darton (*Children's Books in England*) tells us, *Chatterbox* and other respectable magazines were full of "an abnormal number of shivering crossing sweepers" who were sure to catch the eye of a "long lost uncle or a peppery philanthropist". The sentimental, sensational exploitation of poverty with artists hiring bundles of rags from their owners was the other side to the coin in this era of "escape" from Evangelical moralising.

An interesting contrast to these stories can be found in contemporary American novels, some of which became popular in the English nursery in Victorian times. The work of Harriet Beecher-Stowe, Louisa M. Alcott, and Susan Coolidge, with its real life backgrounds, its relative absence of class-bound self-consciousness, its more democratic flavour, and above all, its more down-to-earth heroines, is more refreshing than most English writing of the time, Nesbit excluded. If one were to choose an English-born writer who most nearly captures their naturalness, then the name of Frances Hodgson Burnett comes to mind. Then one remembers that she lived a large part of her creative life across the Atlantic.

Another, and more fascinating contrast to the respectable nursery literature is described in Mary Cadogan and Patricia Craig's *You're a Brick, Angela*. In the down market area, the Amalgamated Press paper mill, with *Girls' Friend, Girls' Reader, Girls' Home*, offered "an amazing amalgam of mill girls, madcaps and Mothers Superior", a patchwork of remnants from popular tradition. To match the Black lad Pete of *Marvel* Comic, there is Coosha the Zulu girl defying superior people looking down on her as a "nigger". Meanwhile back in the nursery, the cannibal caricatures of Ballantyne's islands were reinforced by the *Sambo* of Helen Bannerman (1899) or the Gollywog playthings of Florence and Bertha Upton (1898).

There was, however, in the fantasies of Edith Nesbit, George Macdonald and Frances Hodgson Burnett, also a deal of anxious concern about the treatment of the poor. And a real fear that behind the well-behaved decent workers stood others who might destroy everything. These writers tried hard to overcome feelings of guilt about worth and value. There were, said John Ruskin, hard workers and idle among both rich and poor. George Macdonald assured his readers, "Whoever does what she is bound to do, be she the dirtiest little girl in the street, is a princess . . ."

"To be simple and loving . . . is to be born a king", as Frances Hodgson Burnett put it. Indeed, most of them, secretly were just that. Curdie the miner's son, one of George Macdonald's heroes, like Edith Nesbit's waif, Dickie Harding, turns out in the end to be of royal or aristocratic descent. Curdie's father, Peter, in *The Princess and Curdie* (1883) is told by the spirit lady: "It is a great privilege to be poor. You must not mistake however and imagine it to be a virtue . . . had you been rich, my Peter, you would not have been so good as some rich men I know."

Even the passive virtue of poverty, the last remaining element of the folktale philosophy, is thus declared to be not enough. Curdie indeed does not have the "faith" which Princess Irene has in *The Princess and the Goblin* (1872). He sees only the garrett and the straw, not the lovely vision she sees. In that sense he is like Kingsley's Tom who is only fit to join Ellie when he is cleansed of dirt and sin. Amid the moral and material transformations of Burnett's *Little Princess* and *The Secret Garden*, Becky the maid and Dickon the garden boy are to remain as they were, trusted, loyal and self-effacing.

Within the invisible bounds of circumstance beyond which all other people shade away into anonymity, the novel of the "real" child took its shape in the decades between *Alice* and *The Wind in the Willows*. The frontiers between real and fantasy world are broken down and the moral purpose melts into the fabric of the story. It is not that Nesbit, Macdonald, Carroll, or Kipling with his *Puck of Pook's Hill* (1906) and *Rewards and Fairies* (1910), were abandoning moral purpose. On the contrary Carroll was striving for a precise realisation of his aims. This becomes more clear in his second, less spontaneous story, *Through the Looking Glass*.

His fantasy, like Nesbit's magic, as Marcus Crouch says (*Treasure Seekers and Borrowers*) is "governed by inexorable rule". For them a make-believe world is not a means of escaping from the nagging demands of consistency and logic to write just as they please. In 1908, George Macdonald wrote: "The fairy tale cannot help having some meaning . . . everyone however, who feels the story will read its meaning after his own nature and development. One man will read one meaning into it, another will read another." Or, as the Duchess slyly remarks to Alice, "there's a moral there, if only you know how to find it."

The message, thought Macdonald, should be conveyed through the logic of composition, the very plot, action and development of character. "While without doubt for instance that I was actively regarding a scene of activity, I might at the same moment in my consciousness be aware that I was pursuing a metaphysical argument." His aim was to make the reader "think things for himself." So, too, Lewis Carroll is not breaking new ground by producing a story without a moral or meaning, but a story which while it entertains provokes the mind to think its own thoughts, or to examine others afresh.

Alice in her way is closer to the spirit of real young women of the time than are the heroines of most fiction for the young. The novels of Charlotte Yonge, and the pages of *The Girl's Own Paper*, launched shortly after BOP, carry warnings that girls seeking freedom would only give men an excuse for not behaving themselves. Lewis Carroll (or Rev. L. Dodgson) was in favour of admitting women to university, though he wanted them segregated.

Alice is a strange, indirect tribute to the influence of the growing women's movement. Mary Cadogan and Patricia Craig point out that this was given powerful impetus among the middle class ladies as they saw themselves by-passed for the vote by the working class male in 1867. They see this obliquely reflected in the "tomboy" stories of the prolific E. E. Green and L. T. Meade, and the more forthright Bessie Marchant. The model set by the boys' schools and magazines was accepted for the girls', with athletic, healthy young women streaming out on to the sports fields, active rather than violent like their fictional brothers. And just as the down market magazines offered more to the working class reader, so they did to the active girl of any class, more at least than respectable magazines like *Girls' Realm* and *The Girl's Own Paper*. (Though neither sort offered anything like Joanna Polenipper, female rustler and footpad, prison breaker and murderer, celebrated in one of the penny dreadfuls.)

It would be a long time indeed before children's literature would begin to do justice to some of the heroic young middle class women who, together with their working class sisters in the Co-op Women's Guilds, were then fighting for their own rights and those of others.

This alliance between militant middle class women and poor working class people is symbolised in the friendship between Eleanor Marx and Will Thorne. Thorne was a real life waif, a foundry worker at eight years of age, rising to be leader of the gasworkers' union for whom Eleanor Marx acted as secretary, and finally as MP, introducing into the House of Commons in 1906 a bill for education to the age of 14 for every child. One of the marks of her friendship was helping Thorne to learn to read and write. Thorne had to wait till 1983 for his life to be celebrated in a book for young people – *Will of Iron* by Gerard Melia.

Against all obstacles, the right to a free, publicly run, secular, full-time education up to the age of 11 was finally won before the First World War – though half-timers were to remain at work in the mills until 1922. Some small advances were made in secondary education, mainly doled out in scholarships to fee-paying secondary and grammar schools. The chance of such a scholarship before the First World War, says Brian Simon, was about one in forty. (When I went to elementary school in the 1930s, it was still around one in thirty.)

Slow as the advance was, it did have indirect effects on fiction for the young as described by Alec Ellis, in *A History of Children's Reading and Literature* (1968). One third of the new Board Schools had libraries, though usually with poor selections. Of the 340 councils who had by then agreed to start public libraries, about a third made provision for children, though still mainly for boys. The "box" system began to spread library books through the rural areas. School Boards and HMIs began to criticise the standards of prize books and school readers. Teachers were invited to suggest new books for purchase and the Library

Association began to assemble lists of approved children's fiction. Public libraries were cutting into the ground occupied by the commercial lenders, Boots, Newnes, Dents. The Publishers' Circular was hostile, for a while. If free fiction for the "poor classes", then "why not free games, free plays . . . free cakes and nuts for the boys?" it demanded in 1878. But by the end of the century, public lending had reached the level of one book per head of the population per year (today the figure is 12 per head).

The critical judgements of librarians, teachers, inspectors, as well as the critical discussion of writers like Charlotte Yonge, Alexander Strahan and Edward Salmon, in both religious and commercial magazines, was helping to create an atmosphere in which a broader range of fiction could be produced. As Edward Salmon remarked in 1890, the purchaser now looked for a "healthier and more natural tone." It was no longer enough to know if the book were published by "this or that religious society". And indeed the religious societies were beginning to mask their operations, the Religious Tract Society publishing books "from the offices of *The Boy's Own Paper*".

Summing up this crucial period of development in the literature, Brian Alderson (in his additional notes to Darton's *Children's Books in England*) writes:

> . . . the growth of critical awareness, like the growth of publishing activity itself, fostered an atmosphere which was conducive to free expression.

However, developments proved to be neither as straight-forward nor as inevitable as that. After the Golden Age there followed an Age of Brass.

12

The Age of Brass:
Children's Fiction Between the Wars

If the forty years before *The Wind in The Willows* (1908) were seen as a rich period in children's fiction, then the forty years that followed are judged by many to be poverty stricken.

The contemporary opinion of the Library Association Review in 1932 – "a few admirable books, submerged in an ocean of terrible trash . . . unreal school stories, impossible adventure, half-witted fairy tales . . . in every respect disgraceful" – is echoed by later commentators. John Rowe Townsend calls it "a great expansion of quantity, but a sad lack of quality"; Marcus Crouch, "a vast output of characterless, conventional writing, of some experiment and some achievement" (*Treasure Seekers and Borrowers*, 1962); Eric Quayle says "Few children's stories of the 1920s seem genuinely alive" (*Early Children's Books*, 1983).

Brian Alderson, having judged the First Golden Age to be the product of free interplay between ivory tower and market place, concluded that in 1932, "not even today's minimal progress had been made in literary circles, towards seeing children's books as having any cultural significance beyond quaintness." Eleanor Graham, active in the inter-war publishing world, says in *The Signal Approach to Children's Literature* (1980) that many people assumed all children's books were on the Angela Brazil level.

What had happened? The critical activity of the 1890s and 1900s was followed by a slump. The publishers' motto seems to have been, "never mind the quality feel the width." By 1937, nearly 1,600 "juvenile" titles were being published annually. But this was a trade mainly in "rewards" or prizes, written, according to Marcus Crouch, "to one of several approved formulae" and printed (according to Alec Ellis) on "featherweight paper, 70 per cent air." They were "swollen, puffboard monstrosities" in Margaret Meek's opinion.

Despite the fact that "juveniles" provided their bread and butter, says writer Wallace Hildick (*Children and Fiction*, 1974) most publishers treated their children's department as a Cinderella. If neither critics nor publishers were pulling their weight, what about the writers? Here we come across a paradox in the conventional view of what makes an age golden. If it is the presence of a number of outstanding writers, then surely the period which saw A. A. Milne, Hugh Lofting, Arthur Ransome, Alison Uttley, T. H. White, Mary Norton, P. L. Travers and John Masefield at work might qualify as golden or at least as silver. Perhaps it is after all the quality of the mediocre which determines the nature of the age.

But could the writers be blamed? Geoffrey Trease, in an article in Edward Blishen's collection *The Thorny Paradise* (1975), is emphatic that the conditions under which writers worked made good writing difficult. Many of them were "teachers in comic boarding schools". Certainly when invited to part with their copyright for a single down payment of £50 no writer could be expected to put heart and soul into it. The temptation to mine the surface of talent, working to formulae, preserving deeper emotions and ideas for better days, is clearly a factor.

One is drawn to the conclusion that what was lacking in the age was something that no single element or part of it could supply or restore. The spirit had gone. What to some people appeared a welcome development, the freeing of children's stories from moral constraint, may now be seen to have been the "demoralising" of children's books. Those twin pillars of belief, in Empire and Christianity, were crumbling. A vacuum was left, which the newly developing secular morality of the twentieth century was slow to fill. The "mood was, in one way or another, escapist", says Marcus Crouch, and the best books were fantasies. But then, so they were in the Golden Age. This, though, was fantasy with a slacker moral fibre. Katharine Briggs, comparing Kipling's Puck with the fairies which now lurked at the bottom of the garden, wrote: "an extreme tenderness and sensibility about children almost overwhelmed the folk fairies and turned them into tenuous pretty creatures without meat or muscles, made up of froth and whimsy." Rose Fyleman in particular, she adds, "got my goat" (*Signal*, September 1979). Rose Fyleman, however, was fashionable and in 1922 she inspired a young fairy-poetry writing teacher by the name of Enid Blyton.

Not only fairies lost muscle and backbone. The escapist or "protective" mood invaded all genres. "Adventures at home, school and abroad, were equally remote from everyday life", commented Marcus Crouch (*Treasure Seekers and Borrowers*). The Victorian family story, the "wild wood" story, the "waif" story, processed by the energetic, competent pens of L. T. Meade and Mary Wynn, blended to become the home-holiday-school interchangeable adventure of Elinor Brent Dyer and Enid Blyton. The formula, as Eleanor Graham noted caustically, was to get rid of the parents and plunge the children into "unlikely adventures".

The family model, in the hands of the competent prolific or the exceptional-inspired writer, was that of the well-to-do middle class like Masefield's Kay Harker leading his "wretched life" looked after by a governess, a cook and a maid. Bob Dixon in his study *Catching them Young* (1977) uses an ironic scale for measuring these families, as "one-servant, two-servant or three-servant poor". Even that welcome and vigorous version of the "Scamp" who arrived via *Home Magazine* in 1922, *William*, the brain-child of Richmal Crompton, lived in a family which managed on a diminishing number of domestic helpers as the 1920s gave way to the 1930s and the 1940s.

In the 1930s, according to a recent letter in the Radio Times, the "average family" had two or three servants. Thus the literary version of life replaces reality, and the majority below the Plimsoll line is culturally invisible. That in 1937, Eve Garnett's *Family From One End Street* should have been hailed, honoured with the newly established Carnegie Award and seen as a true picture of working life (it still is in some quarters) is an indication of the level of unreality that pervaded the family story.

And if there were illusions in children's literature about the way of life of the majority, at the level of the Establishment there was also hostility and contempt. The Newbolt Report on the Teaching of English in 1921 directed teachers' attention to their duty to teach pupils "who either speak a definite dialect or whose speech is disfigured by vulgarisms, to speak standard English and speak it clearly." They must combat the "powerful influence of evil habits of speech contracted in home and street".

This approach was carried on even more intensively in the 1920s and 1930s among the small minority of working class children who were granted scholarships to fee-paying secondary and grammar schools. Here the attempts to "cure" pupils of local accent and expression, thus detaching them from their families, caused a three-way split among them (as I recollect): an often sullen resistance, a painful conformity, or the survivor's response, a different way of speaking in classroom, street and home. The misdirected ingenuity and energy expended on all sides would have educated three generations.

Other battles were being fought or re-fought. The victory over the "penny dreadful" won by the irresistible combination of GOP, BOP and Amalgamated Press had it seemed to be won again, by yet other magazines. Conscientious parents were urged to buy Arthur Mee's *Children's Newspaper*, Blackwell's *Merry Go Round*, or *Joy Street*. "Comic" was still a dirty word, though most comics were now produced by solid and successful big business concerns. Amalgamated Press comics for both boys and girls now lost ground to the new D. C. Thomson comics which achieved competitiveness by barring trade unions from print shop and editorial office. With *Girl's Weekly*, *Rover*, *Wizard* and *Hotspur*, Thomson's forged ahead. In 1940, when A. T. Jenkinson published his important study of what boys and girls were reading, the Thomson comics had almost swept the board. E. S. Turner, historian of the comic movement, reckons that whereas Amalgamated Press kept a toehold on reality, Thompson publications abandoned it altogether.

Geoffrey Trease sums up the situation of the adventure story in the 1920s and 1930s – it "tended to be a fossil in which one could trace the essential characteristics of one written in 1880 or 1890." Whether at the level sanctioned by parents, or by the custom of the street, the age of brass lived off the age of gold. According to my own recollection, of the twenty most popular historical novels available in the 1930s and 1940s, eighteen were over 20 years old, twelve over 50, eight over 75 and others over a century old.

The focus of new adventures might shift from Africa or India to the Middle East, with desert kingdoms saved from false prophets, or from army to airforce as W. E. Johns and Biggles took over from Henty's heroes. Old ideas might be recycled. The BOP's Major Lumsden and Dilawar Khan (1879) magically reappeared as The Wolf of Kabul and his "clicky-ba"-toting Afghan follower in a Thomson comic. But the "values" remained fairly constant. As W. E. Johns explained, they were "decent behaviour". And that meant "loyalty to Crown, to Empire and to rightful authority".

This meant racism at all levels, whether at that of the *Wizard* story I recall of a school boy tempting his yellow-skinned, ape-like father to come for an interview with a teacher by laying a trail of banana skins, or at the refined level of the patronising caricatures of, for example, *Dr Dolittle's Post Office* (1923). The conventions of the young fiction in its broad notions of good and evil fell conveniently into the patterns of official domestic and foreign policy.

Conventions died hard. Talbot Baines Reed's schoolboys, in the 1890s, were a match for a gang of "half-tipsy cads". In the 1940s, a librarian complained of comic stories in which "one resolute youth aided by a comic Indian" could defeat a Nazi division. Even in post-war literature, as Eileen Colwell has noted in a much-quoted review, a gang of desperate men stood little chance against young fictional heroes.

Yet, between the wars as Mary Cadogan and Patricia Craig (*You're a Brick, Angela*) point out, it is popular literature which is marginally closer to reality. Topical references to Communism and rebellion appear in the 1920s in *William* books or the Nelson Lee Library. While *The Girl's Own Paper* was admiring the Hitler Youth, the down market *Schoolgirl* comic used fascist dictators as a synonym for bullying teachers. Sexton Blake, with his references to suffragettes, to profiteering, bad housing and other social ills, is more relevant than most up-market literature. Even when evacuation in the Second World War brought real East End and other city kids for the first time into close contact with the Home Counties, "respectable" magazines could not resist references to fleas and dirt. Such insults are generally absent from the "comic".

To the extent that social realities appeared and evoked the kind of response which is regarded as normal today, they were a recognition of a wider audience beyond the nursery. But it must be said that any working class children, such as the occasional factory lad or scholarship girl, who appear in comics of the 1920s and 1930s, are there for purposes of identification or pathos, and rarely convey a message likely to disturb the status quo. Though, as Cadogan and Craig again point out, the spirit of rebellion was not entirely absent from the comic appealing to the lower middle class and working class girl who had known the indignities of life in a "posh" school.

This ambivalence of the stories in pre-war comics attracted the scathing attention of George Orwell. In *Horizon Magazine* in 1940, he used his satirical talent to demolish the imaginary world of St Jim's and Greyfriars, created by the indefatigable Charles Hamilton (Frank Richards). It was, said Orwell, a kind of writing "sodden" with the worst illusions of the imperial past and was selling an escapist fantasy to the "scores of thousands to whom every detail of life at a posh public school is wholly thrilling and romantic."

To Orwell's surprise, Frank Richards replied. Looking back on the exchange it is difficult to repress the thought that Richards scored points. He had the advantage over Orwell, of course, in having a sense of humour. And Richards believed in the illusions he peddled. Orwell's illusions in his own class had been shattered and he never learned to know the working class beyond its down and out fringe. Thus he lacked the resources from which to restore his faith and confidence in humanity.

We can laugh at Richards when he says: "Most noblemen generally are better fellows than commoners." We can even laugh when he asserts that of course foreigners are funny – look at the Germans supporting Mr Hitler, he said. Unfortunately for Richards, many of his admired "noblemen", not to speak of the editors of *Girl's Own Paper*, were incautious in their admiration of the works of Hitler in the 1930s. The views of Scout leader, Lord Baden Powell, on women's place in society were disturbingly close to those of the Nazis.

But Richards was on firmer ground when he wrote:

Mr Orwell would have told him [the reader] that he is a shabby little blighter, his father an ill-used serf, his world a dirty, muddled rotten sort of show. I don't think it would be fair play to take his twopence for telling him that.

Richards, whatever his illusions about society, respected the reader in his way. Orwell could only, in a way not unknown among radicals, see the working class audience as manipulated by those in power. Not long after his debate with Richards, a *Tribune* magazine reader argued that there was merit in comics. They often showed poor people as better than rich. Orwell replied (July 1944):

> Film magnates, press lords and the like amass quite a lot of their wealth by pointing out that wealth is wicked . . . This business about the moral superiority of the poor is one of the deadliest forms of escapism the ruling class have evolved.

There Orwell betrays his ignorance of the roots of popular literature. The "moral superiority" of the poor is not an invention of the ruling class. It is one of two basic strands, along with the equalising function of the rebel rogue, in the ancient fabric of the tale. Both strands reflect the popular nature of audience and story-teller. Social and economic mastery of print, and the new fiction-technology, put control of the written story in the hands of the upper echelons of society. The popular story-teller, part of the working population, became the writer employed by the press owner – poised between the tastes and outlooks of employer on the one hand and customer on the other. This isolation engendered cynicism (Edgar Wallace expressed contempt for the "working man") or the amiable illusions of a Richards. The processing of popular tradition for this manufactured literature means that the "equalising" element is discarded or perverted, and the "compensatory" element of moral superiority among the poor acquires greater importance. But constant repetition, often without genuine conviction, reduces it to sentimentality, a calculated tugging on the emotions. Thus the whole development is one of the corrupting of popular tradition, not the cunning inventions of a conspiratorial and omnipotent establishment. The fruits of popular creativity had been appropriated. The popular tale was hi-jacked. J. S. Bratton, I think, uses the term "kidnapped". Orwell by his assumptions, implies nothing can be done to reverse or change the situation. If that really were so, then Richards was right. Better give a boy or girl a fair dose of illusions for their twopence.

But could nothing be done to rescue fiction, of the downmarket or up-market kind, from the slough into which it had slid? Some professional writers tried, in their own way, to bring a breath of real life to the literature. Arthur Ransome, with 12 children's books over two decades, brought a conscientious realism to "holiday adventure", while staying mostly within the magic middle class circle. Noel Streatfeild likewise stays within the circle yet, with *Ballet Shoes* (1936) and later novels, brings the world of work back to children's fiction. The much wider world of work and the working class generally, however, remains outside, though the novels of merchant seaman Richard Armstrong, from *The Mystery of Obadiah* (1934) onwards, pointed to the future.

Geoffrey Trease, with *Bows Against the Barons* and *Comrades For The Charter* (1934) brought the people back into the historical novel. Though as he later remarked, his "propagandist urge" lasted but a few years, it had remarkable impact. Both he and Jack Lindsay, who had a novel turned down by OUP because it showed a British officer "in bad light", were published by Left Wing publisher Martin Lawrence. Lawrence was unorthodox enough actually to offer Trease royalties for a children's book. Basil Blackwell's *Tales of Action* series drawing in writers like Rex Warner, and Eleanor Graham's launching of Puffins in the early 1940s in the face of much prejudice from the trade, were also early swallows.

But a general change in the commercial scene was not on the cards. The number of titles published annually was dropping, reaching 1400 a year just before the war. Dent, OUP and Heinemann had appointed children's editors, but these were still exceptional.

Change was at work in the institutional market. The launching in 1936 of the magazine *Junior Bookshelf*, by a leading library supplier, matched the founding by librarians of *School Library Review*, as well as the Carnegie Award, in 1936. While it is true that by World War II only 40 per cent of libraries had as yet any provision for the young, and school libraries were mainly in the grammar and private schools, still librarians were beginning to establish their own point of view and influence publishing developments. It was not a case of revolutionary librarians stirring up reactionary publishers, though when Eileen Colwell and her colleagues began setting up the Association of Children's Librarians (1937) the Library Association leadership looked on it as a sort of Communist plot. Nevertheless the small but growing band of children's librarians, those "sympathetic and good-tempered" ladies the professional journals advertised for, were pioneers of change. They were learning, teaching each other and restoring to the children's book world some of the moral fibre it had lost.

Beneath all this ran the groundswell of educational changes. There was no steady advance, but pendulum swings, as the demand from the Labour movement, with support from liberals, enlightened church people and many teachers, for universal secondary education met what economist Keynes called "hysterical" opposition from the industrialists. To say nothing of comic indifference from leading politicians. Prime Minister Baldwin looked round vaguely for "someone in the party interested in education". Changes in schooling were needed, he said, because "democracy has come upon us at a gallop" (this in 1928 when, after decades of struggle, all women over 21 at last had the vote.) Savage cuts in budgets set back advances as fast as they were made. In 1936 education spending was lower in percentage terms than in the 1913 budget. By 1939, says Brian Simon in his historical study of education, only 40 per cent of children over 11 went to secondary school. Free secondary education for all up to the age of 15, demanded by the Trades Union Congress during the Boer War (1900), was only achieved after the defeat of Hitler in 1945.

Hitler's bombs and submarines had meanwhile made their impact on fiction for the young. Denied supplies of newsprint from occupied Norway, the twopenny comics dwindled in size and vanished, some for ever. The Second World War (no "house match" like the First World War) changed the attitudes of GOP and BOP and caused some of the old snobberies to be discarded. W. E. Johns was induced to create a female Worrals to match

118

flying Biggles, for the benefit of the girl reader and the war effort. The Blitz, what is more, destroyed warehouses containing 20 million books. Rewards, classics, all went up in smoke. When peace came, the way was clear for a new start. The school population was to grow from 5 to 7 million in the next two decades. There was money in children's books in this new market. But it was a slow business. Reading surveys showed a lack of interest in reading among a substantial minority of boys and girls. Publishers, says Marcus Crouch, were slow to take up the challenge of the 1944 Education Act. Children's titles, down to 715 in 1945, began to increase again only slowly.

One writer, however, to the chagrin of her rivals, was going from strength to strength. Her work, for many different publishers, had secured her multiple paper allocations during the lean war years. Between 1942 and 1945, Enid Blyton produced 67 books. By 1950 she had written another 183, and by 1951 was producing nearly 70 a year.

She was one of the elements in the "gradual but considerable change in the balance of publishing" (Marcus Crouch) that post-war years were to bring.

13

Another Age of Gold?
1950–1970

"After the bleak 1940s, the new writers of the 1950s emerged into an atmosphere of unprecedented freedom", recalls John Rowe Townsend (*Fiction Magazine*, spring 1983). And it was Townsend who decided in mid-1960s that a Second Golden Age had arrived to match that of Carroll, Nesbit and Grahame. A decade later, in 1974, he was to modify this confident description. But he was not alone in his first assessment. Fred Inglis (*The Promise of Happiness*, 1981) thought a new golden age began in 1958 with Philippa Pearce's *Tom's Midnight Garden*. In her valuable introduction to *Twentieth Century Children's Writers* (D. L. Kirkpatrick, 1978) Naomi Lewis thought the 1950s and 1960s brought a second "flowering". Marghanita Laski in a 1965 review declared that "the last five years have seen an efflorescence of good writing for children of books that are plainly worth keeping on the shelf with the classics of the past."

Where had these flowers sprung from? Naomi Lewis, noting the greater post-war attention to children's literature, argues, "where a prestigious medium exists, the gifted come." Geoffrey Trease says, "more of the great general publishers were finding it worthwhile to build up a children's list". And unlike pre-war publishers they were offering proper contracts and royalties for children's books – there was a clear commitment to the future.

Also, adult fiction seemed to be running into the sands. As Edward Blishen remarks (*The Thorny Paradise*, 1975), "Writing for children grows stronger and bolder, as writing for adults grows more inward, more marked by self doubting intricacy." Among the post-war Carnegie winners were the names of established adult novelists like Elizabeth Goudge and Rumer Godden. Later, Joan Aiken, Nina Bawden, Peter Dickinson and

Penelope Lively, were to combine writing in both fields. Leon Garfield arrived in the 1960s, having found the adult fiction world less than hospitable. Today, about a third of the better known living children's authors are also adult authors. The expertise was there, the market was there. And conventional prestige came with *The Times Literary Supplement* (1949) producing its first children's books supplements, and papers like the *Guardian* supplementing the small band of mainly library review journals. Geoffrey Trease had his study of children's books *Tales Out of School* published (1949). Perhaps nothing shows the previous neglect more than Trease's amazement at being offered seven minutes' BBC time to talk about children's books.

Publishers began to abandon their "policy" of feeding off the past. At OUP, Frank Eyre, in Marcus Crouch's words, "threw off the reward trade". Together with the growing Puffin house, an association was formed which dominated children's publishing for another 20 years. By 1953 the pre-war annual total of titles had been surpassed. By the 1970s it was to double and pass the 3,000 mark. Sales rose year by year. Some publishers began eventually to count their turnover in millions, even without the captive school market. Staff who edited the new titles ("juveniles" no more) came out of the small back room to seats on the board.

My own recollections of this period is of colour and variety. I returned to the field in the 1950s as our family began to grow. My outlook was conditioned by pre-war experience of Sunday School prizes and the sombre bindings of library volumes. The post-war product – the vivid picture books, the jackets of the older readers' novels – promised well for the future. It seemed the book hunger many of my generation suffered from was to be a thing of the past.

This impression was to be qualified over the next 25 years when as parent, reviewer, literary editor and award panel member, I worked my way through some four or five thousand of the tens of thousands of books published. The question which arose time and again was: Are these books really, essentially different from the ones I had known as a child, or did they just look and sound different? It seemed that the literature, excellent as it might be, was in essence a re-making of the old to suit the modern tastes of the conventional audience.

The two pillars of the new "golden age" were the historical novel and fantasy and sometimes, as in the work of Joan Aiken, a blend of the two. Realism was very much a poor third. And beneath the peaks of excellence, Henry Treece, Geoffrey Trease, Rosemary Sutcliff, Hester Burton and Cynthia Harnett, the old historical novel was little changed. In the mid-1970s, out of 25 available novels about the Civil War, 14 were pro-Royalist, half a dozen "plague on both houses", and only one or two did justice to the Parliamentary side. Strangely enough, for all her fresh approach, Rosemary Sutcliff still took ancient British history very much from the Roman/Christian standpoint. Joan Aiken's comic-historical-fantasies were essentially nostalgic. Hester Burton said frankly that she was drawn to historical writing because of a sense of "how little I understand the present age", but "if I look back at a past age, however, the fog clears."

The excellence going into fantasy and history had little effect on writing about the present, if one excepts the golden Pearce and Bawden. Despite updating, the family novel remained until the 1970s, as Townsend observed (*Written for Children*), "the harmless, hygienic story of comfortable bourgeois life, written it seemed by comfortable bourgeois adults for comfortable bourgeois children." Or, as Brian Alderson comments (*Looking At Picture Books*, 1973), "tending towards average gentility". Stories of authentic working class life were thin on the ground. In 1980, listing some hundred books with working class children as their central characters, I found that most of them had appeared after 1970. In the language of criticism, there was a reluctance to call a spade a spade. Instead, there were references to "poor homes", "limited opportunities", "difficult backgrounds," "humdrum districts", "the dimmer suburbs", recalling the Victorian "boys and girls of the street" label. Books which ventured into the "street", often seemed like a sociological exploration of the inadequate, whether poorly done like Elizabeth Stucley's *Magnolia Buildings* (1956) or well done like John Rowe Townsend's *Gumble's Yard* (1961) or Sylvia Sherry's *A Pair of Jesus Boots* (1969).

So permeated was the literature with these values that there seemed to be a collective unwillingness at the lit-crit end even to consider the matter. It was for some a red herring. Others assured me that working-class children, known as "they", did not want to read about their own lives. As one charitable person remarked, "We don't want to rub their noses in it."

Geoffrey Trease, with his five *Bannermere* books in the 1950s, began to transfer the school story to a day school. But when E. W. Hildick attempted a more fundamental shift to working-class secondary modern school, he met with stiff opposition. He aimed mildly with his *Jim Starling* stories (1958 onwards) to allow the kind of pupils he knew "at least occasionally to read about their own kind". He was told that "working class kids disliked reading about such circumstances and craved nothing less than total escape." He was even, quite falsely, accused of "wanting to provide working class children with nothing but stories about children like themselves." Leila Berg, making a modest beginning with *A Box For Benny* (1958) had to meet, and overcome, more opposition when she later launched "Nippers" as an alternative to series like Ladybirds.

Later, other observers, like Sheila Ray (*The Blyton Phenomenon* 1982) were to judge that "the writers of the Second Golden Age had failed to make an impact on many children". But in the early 1960s such voices were not widely heard. The general publishing-conventional-literary success encouraged a self-confident, tolerant deafness. With public money, mainly from libraries, underpinning the structure, children's books was a secure and seemingly self-satisfied world.

A small world it certainly was. The "golden age" involved around twenty publishers, and of these about half a dozen claimed most critical attention. Reviewing centred on the *Times* group, the *Guardian*, occasionally *The Observer* and the specialist journals, which had now been joined by Margery Fisher's one-woman *Growing Point* – an impressive addition. On the fringes were the *Daily Mirror* and my own paper the *Daily Worker/ Morning Star* – the only two papers, incidentally, to aim at reviewing children's books each week and directing reviews to children.

Reviewing was done by another fairly small circle, journalists, librarians and not a few writers. Thanks to the anonymity rule, maintained by the TLS into the mid-1970s, it was possible for writers to encourage friends, destroy enemies, and make territorial signals to warn intruders off their chosen fields, without their identity being known. This reinforced the sense of an inner circle. The presenting of the Children's Book Circle's Eleanor Farjeon Award almost exclusively to reviewers in its earlier days gave further reinforcement to this impression.

One can get the flavour of the situation by looking at the catalogue of the Jubilee Exhibition at the National Book League in 1977. Covering the period from 1952, it was a retrospective on the second "golden age", by its cataloguer, John Rowe Townsend. Of the 200-odd books chosen, one third of the hardbacks and one half of the paperbacks had been published by two houses, OUP and the Longman/Kestrel/Puffin Group. Seven publishers out of 25 were represented by 150 out of the 200 exhibits. Of the 130 authors represented, nearly a score reviewed books for the *Guardian*, whose children's editor had mounted the exhibition, and who was a leading writer himself, published by OUP and Kestrel. The exhibition represented a careful choice by a competent and conscientious critic. Over the same period, half the Carnegie winners came from this stable. But to an outside observer, the dangers of self-perpetuating isolation from the real world outside were clear. There was also at this critical level a strong inclination to exclude consideration of the consumer, "that vast but largely non-participating audience" (Brian Alderson, *Children's Book News*, January/February, 1969). Parents, teachers, (and more rarely librarians) were often referred to disparagingly as ignorant and philistine in general articles on children's books. Calls in trade seminars for publishers to pay more attention to teachers' views were sometimes seen as unwelcome intrusions.

Yet this second "golden age" was more than a chance coming together of the right authors, publishers and critics at the right time. It was very much a child of the public. Community funds fed the expansion of the market. Guaranteed library interest enabled publishers to encourage authors as never before. And the private market was fed by the post-war boom in the birth-rate, and a new generation of parents with greater expectations, and a wider field of vision.

The library service expanded, borrowings reached 370 million in 1953–54 (they were nearly to double in the following decade).

There was plenty of room for expansion. The LA's Youth Libraries Section (later Youth Libraries Group) noted in the early 1950s that in many areas there was just one book per child, and one or two had only one for every 50 children. The area in which I grew up got its own children's library for the first time in 1976. Three years later, cuts had forced Saturday afternoon closing.

Sheila Ray (*The Blyton Phenomenon*) and Alec Ellis (*A History of Children's Reading and Literature*, 1968) chart the changeover from pre-war and war-time to modern peace-time conditions. Sheila Ray shows how among many leading librarians, the drive to stock and re-stock was informed by a desire to "reject the second rate and encourage quality", to urge the educative rather than the "light entertainment" side of the library. Whether intentionally or not this drive reinforced the tendency in criticism to treat customer tastes as irrelevant. On the one hand there was a belief that "children have a latent good taste", which would respond to the "gradual elimination of the inferior quality". On the other there was the more positively directed policy of working on the assumption that children do not know what is good for them. In 1949, *Junior Bookshelf* was arguing that the fact that "Little Tommy or Little Elsie may want Biggles and Blyton" should not influence purchasing policy. And in 1981 academic Fred Inglis declared that "*Tom's Midnight Garden* or *Puck of Pook's Hill* are wonderful books . . . whether or not your child can make head nor tail of them."

The only thing to do, said Inglis, was to "fill the shelves with the best books and persuade children to read them." This certainly also reflected many librarians' attitudes. As to what was "best", there was an unspoken determination not to let children's reactions influence the choice.

Sheila Ray provides a fascinating account of how all this affected one writer – Enid Blyton. At the peak of her publishing power when the attack opened in the 1950s, she was certainly affected by the growing hostility, although tales of librarians "banning" Blyton are mostly the hokum of a largely ignorant press. But the lukewarm to hostile library attitude to Blyton did reflect a critical view then busy in sorting out literature with a capital L and distinguishing it from "sub-literature" and "reading matter". The problem was, could one fill the shelves with the pure gold of the age? No. It is in the nature of elites to be self-limiting. But the shelves were filled with a thousand "nice" books, imitative or derivative of the golden. Many of the books published during the 1950s and 1960s were of this kind – acceptable to the purchaser, but not always to the consumer, and thus remaining unread on the shelves.

While the attack on Blyton and similar authors was in full swing, popular literature was under pressure from other directions. By the 1950s the old story comic – staple reading of millions of children, bookish and un-bookish – was dying. It succumbed partly to the challenge of television, but also to the profit hunger of an increasingly monopolised magazine trade. Any journal which began to show signs of faltering in those days was axed ruthlessly, not when showing a loss, but when the profit level dipped. Survivors like *Dandy* and *Beano*, in which some of the anarchic spirit lingered, made do on lower circulations, while the amount of reading matter in proportion to illustration was reduced. New arrivals on the scene, like *Eagle, Girl, Swift* and *Robin* (brain children of yet another clergyman seeking to improve young reading) were successful, but again with much less reading matter.

The old story comic was dying in other ways. In many post-war publications, Mary Cadogan and Patricia Craig (*You're a Brick, Angela*) see the lively character of pre-war comics degenerating into pathos, masochism, and worse, "vapid romanticism", a view supported by Bob Dixon's observations (*Catching them Young*). In the new post-war breed of "war" comics, the old imperial fervour subsided into a dull "bash the Boche" formula, repeated without conviction. It seemed clear that any revival of the old spirit of popular literature was not going to come from commercial sources. Worse, in the largely American horror comics of the 1950s, commercial opportunism, alienation of story-teller from audience and the cynical exploitation of readers' amazement and dread, went to the limit and beyond. The campaign to ban these comics, in which teachers played a leading part, re-stated what had been assumed too easily, that fiction for the young is a literature with responsibilities, that content and meaning are crucial and that values could not be left to fend for themselves in the market place.

But it was a more straightforward business to draw the line, to say what "popular" fiction should not be, than to produce a viable alternative. The old story comics had given their readers the equivalent of several books a year. The new comics provided a yearly equivalent of less than a single book. The young appetite for a story was fed more and more by television. Characters from TV as well as radio began to move in on the comic world. But these new magazines carried little enough reading matter. At this crucial point, where the coming of television coincided with the decline of the story comic, and helped it on its way, a post-war generation of children was being deprived of the very basic sort of pleasure reading. And those active in the making and diffusion of mainstream literature had their minds on other things.

It is interesting that critical attention could spare no time in this "vacuum" period to examine the much-despised Blyton's appeal. It is even more interesting that it was a teacher (and writer), Wallace Hildick, and a school librarian-lecturer, Sheila Ray, who were to examine Blyton's appeal in a serious non-hostile way.

It was in the child-centred schools, rather than in the book-centred literary world, that this problem was first faced. As Geoff Fox says in *Reluctant to Read?* (1977), it was "those who would hardly avoid children since they saw them all day in the class room" who were bound to raise the question: Good books – for whom? A. T. Jenkinson in his 1940 survey of what boys and girls were reading had asked for school libraries to include books "relating more closely to the books which the children themselves would select for leisure reading". The Newsom Report (1963) urged that reading should be more than just a skill to "turn symbols into sounds". It found that 60 per cent of schools were in some way lacking in library provision. Only one in four had a library exclusively used as such. This, despite the Ministry of Education's urging as early as 1952 that "individual rather than class reader" type books should be bought for the school library, and the School Library Association's calling repeatedly for libraries in every school, supplemented by class libraries and book corners.

What kind of "individual" books, though? In commercial bookshops Blytons were being bought by the tens of thousands. In this interim period (the children's paperback boom came a decade after the demise of the story comic) there were few authors capable of equalling the Blyton appeal. Blyton, W. E. Johns and Richmal Crompton all died between 1967 and 1968. At a time when careful study might have been made of the true nature of this appeal, critical opinion was instead using Blyton as a general yardstick for what was to be avoided. The impression was given that her popularity was her worse sin. And Dorothy Edwards, one of the few authors with really popular appeal at the time, was mortified to be told by one critic: "Dorothy, the children love your books, but they're not really literature."

New thinking then came from outside the literary world, and it came mainly from the schools. And when it came, it was not always agreeable. Elaine Moss noted (in Nancy Chambers' *Signal Approach to Children's Books*, 1980) that teachers saw their own experience in "large mixed ability classes with little time", as being far from that of the writer, especially the one who "claimed to be writing for himself."

The view from the inner-city classroom was already far from that of the ivory tower. And, by the late 1950s, the classroom, particularly in those cities, began to give yet another dimension to the word "child", a dimension not just of class, but of race. Black and brown faces began to mingle with the white. Problems of identification between child and book, never easy or straight-forward, became yet more complex and demanding.

The "golden age" was giving way to something quite different.

14

The Age of Strife
1970–

The 1970s and early 1980s were a time of change and upheaval, in which the earlier buoyant market, the cries of "too many books, surely", gave way to retrenchment, cut back and talk of the future of the book. New pressure groups, organisations and movements appeared with every year, genteel discussion and analysis gave way to bitter controversy. From a superficial look the 1970s seemed to be a battlefield between book people and child people, with the book people taking a terrible beating. From his confident "writers and publishers are resistant to being leaned on" (1977), John Rowe Townsend had passed in some seven years to "The Pressure groups have us at bay." The air was thick with the smoke of battle and the ground littered with the cartridge cases of abandoned arguments as defenders of the status quo retreated from one untenable position to another.

If positions appeared to be lost, it was because the children's book world was changing its composition and relationships. What had appeared in the 1950s and 1960s, to some, to be a set-up of beautiful simplicity with writers, publishers and critics in the centre and the various sorts of consumers arranged around them like minor planets around the sun, was replaced by "unparalleled confusion". Interest groups, with insistent, imperious demands, sailed in eccentric orbit through a cosmos where there was no respect for the old laws of precedence and the hierarchies of merit and excellence. In place of the old private market where producer and consumer were a mirror image of one another, was a vast public forum in which most of the people were strangers.

Commentators with a sense of history surveying the debates and demands of the 1970s thought they recognised the new voices, as the debate about the needs of the child reader shifted from analysis of the reluctance of the child, to a consideration of the inadequacy of the literature.

One had to go back many years to recall a time when outsiders had so determinedly tried to tell the writer and publisher what they ought to do, back not years, not decades, but more than a century.

A literature " . . . freed once for all from the rationalising of Maria Edgeworth or the sermonising of Mrs Sherwood", was now seeing "strenuous attempts at moral teaching of one sort or another which is increasingly apparent in contemporary children's literature" – Brian Alderson, (*Looking at Picture Books*, 1973).

Taking the cue, other critics began more freely to recall the strictures of Mrs Sarah Trimmer (relating her with more ease than accuracy to Mary Whitehouse) and talking of a "new Puritanism". But having discovered a historical parallel, none cared to pursue the logic of their discovery. If the ghosts of Edgeworth, Sherwood and Trimmer were walking the corridors of children's literature, what had raised them? What was it about the 1970s that so resembled the 1790s? Surely this re-staging of old debates had some deeper meaning? Why should writers in school, library and alternative magazines perversely wish to go back to square one, when decades of effort had been put into setting the literature free once and for all from its moral-didactic beginnings?

Surely, after the highly successful efforts to refine the literature, to turn a sow's ear into a silk purse, one should not have to return to the roughness and crudities of former times? Surely to force writers to un-learn all the aesthetic lessons of a century and a half was a form of oppression?

It was this sense of the disagreeable, the untoward, the bewildering, the unnecessary, that caused a good deal of the acrimony in the debates of the 1970s and early 1980s, when all parties could well have devoted more energy instead to analysing what was happening to fiction for the young, to the children's book world and the wider world beyond.

Printed fiction specifically for children was born in the eighteenth century, at a time of major social change, of technological and social revolution. It was one of the signs of the arrival of a new social group, whose economic activity, ideology and culture were to shape our modern society and world. In its arrival, in creating this literature as part of its visible presence, this class had raised in new forms ancient aspirations for more abundant life, for democracy, education, knowledge and enjoyment.

But because this group was a minority, those aspirations remained unfulfilled for the majority. The full use and control of reading and writing remained more a privilege than a right. But now, two centuries later, industrial militants, feminists, black power groups posed the question – why not the rights of *all* groups so far left out of consideration? And as in life, so the demand made itself felt in literature, not least in fiction for the young.

Here were questions still unanswered, an account still unsettled. Ghosts only walk when something from the past remains unremedied. In another age of change, today, other social groups have taken up the demands first made by the middling sort, and have moved into cultural visibility. The demands for recognition, whether in terms of purchasing power, or participation in society, can no longer be treated as irrelevant. Neither can the demands for a place, an existence in the literature. Today "people" must mean all people; "children" must mean all children, not one section deemed to represent the rest.

In 1970, Brian Jackson wrote that, though "ours is the golden age of children's literature", the so-called classics seemed to "have lost ground with kids." And the reason was that there had been a change in children, the creation of a "universal child public."

He went on, significantly: " . . . the overwhelming majority are different from the readers (or the read to) of the past, in that they are the children of the common man, and not of the middle class nursery."

It ought to be possible, argued Elaine Moss, four years later, to "use our experience to provide more approachable looking books and better written *stories* (her italics) for the broader mass of young readers." (*Signal*, May 1974).

This "broader mass" became visible during the 1970s, mainly because a new stage in the movement towards universal education was reached. Not an uninterrupted movement, because delaying tactics, opposition and misrepresentation dogged the advance as they had done at every stage during the past two centuries. With the raising of the school leaving age to 16, then the drive towards a more completely comprehensive school system in the 1970s, the "broader mass" could no more be ignored in literature than they could be in life.

When one looks back at the "golden age" of the 1950s and 1960s, one is struck by the complacency which watched the children's book business expand as school and library budgets expanded, without apparently asking whether or not this implied changes in the nature as well as the volume of the literature. The slogan "better books for more kids" was of great value during those years. It brought together disparate people in an important effort, which touched millions of children in one way or another.

"Better" books could not simply mean bringing up to date and making more attractive what was there already, nor simply producing more of the same. It also had to mean a different sort of book – for that different readership, the child of the "common man". And it was no use arguing, as did one commentator, that raising the question of the social image and nature of children's books "side tracked" efforts being made to increase the number of books available. The two could not be separated, as was to become apparent.

Provision of more books, meanwhile, became the aim of an alliance between educational publishers, the National Book League, and other interested parties, which kept on the heels of local authorities to ensure that the proportion of their rising expenditure which went on books for the pupil should be maintained or increased.

It may indeed have seemed like Christmas every day for some publishers and writers as, during the 1960s and early 1970s, the ratepayers dug each year deeper into their pockets, and as more and more libraries could be counted upon to buy one copy at least of each new children's novel. The number of titles published doubled between 1953 (when the pre-war total was once more passed) and 1979 when it soared over the 3,000 mark. Some thought this unhealthy, perhaps out of an elitist faith that "fewer means better" (a faith to which the 1980s cutbacks brought its own agnosticism). But there was an assumption that the job of the public and the public institution was to provide the funds, and let the producers get on with producing whatever they were inspired to do. Quality and content were still to be decided between ivory tower and market place.

This assumption was the grand illusion of the 1960s and it was to be shattered, not without alarm and discomfort, in the 1970s.

The citizens were advancing on the citadel of literature, their banners proclaiming "no taxation without representation". And the first to observe this advance were the teachers. They were to lead the way in calling for change and bringing it about.

E. W. Hildick, remembering "awkward moments in the classroom when trying to present children with books with middle class settings and values often quite foreign to my pupils", went on to write some of the first popular post-war school and family stories involving working class boys.

Aidan Chambers, recalling classroom moments using books which he "loathed almost as much as the children they were inflicted upon loathed them", went on to edit one of the most successful series (Topliners) for the "reluctant" reader, introducing new and controversial writers to the children's book scene.

Peter Kennerly noted that despite the "exciting, stimulating and sensitive" range of books, so many secondary school children were getting "no pleasure and satisfaction" from books. He noted, too, that if a child in Liverpool, where he taught, were given the price of a book, they might have to spend it getting to the nearest bookshop. And so he opened one of the first school bookshops.

Change came, but not without its confusions. At first the "reluctant" reader was barely distinguished from the child with reading difficulties, what Marcus Crouch called a post-war preoccupation with the "C-stream". Indeed the post-war school system had an enormous task in overcoming past neglect of child and book. Parents of most post-war pupils had left school themselves at 14 or even earlier. Many of these parents had never known secondary education of any kind. For many, books were alien to their whole way of life. But deprivation, generations of it, was only part of the picture. When one survey after another pointed to a proportion of between 35 and 40 per cent of children not enjoying reading, two conclusions were rapidly drawn, particularly at the level of general press comment.

One was that television, which had come within a decade to dominate home entertainment, had stopped children from reading. But the signals were confusing. Though the old style story comic vanished, book sales continued to climb, and sales of paperbacks, those books most likely to be bought by children themselves, increased even more. Some television programmes, it was noted, brought sudden demands for books which sometimes caught libraries and bookshops off guard.

Then the explanation was sought in the schools themselves and soon the view was abroad that children were not being taught to read, "as they used to be". If not television, then teachers, particularly "trendy teachers", were to blame. It took several years, until 1974, in fact, for the experts, HMIs, etc, to establish that reading standards had not dropped in schools. So clearly the matter was more complicated.

In fact the "reluctant" reader who emerged in the 1970s had been there all the time, but was discovered only when more children became culturally visible. In the pre-war school the question was asked, "Can the child read?" In the 1970s, the question was asked, though not universally: "Does the child read? Does the child read willingly and for enjoyment?"

Out of the confused discussion, particularly about "standards" some good emerged in the shape of more public attention to children and books. Most notable was the 1975 Bullock report on the use of books and the teaching of English in schools, together with the Schools Council Research Project on children's reading – the Whitehead Report (1977). Both reports generated concern and optimism. Bullock asserted the importance of print and books in the lives of children, emphasised that reading was not something to be restricted to particular occasions and purposes but something which should prevade all activities. By declaring that schools were responsible for making it possible for children and their parents to see, choose, and take home, a range of books, Bullock gave a powerful impetus to the school bookshop movement. The year after Bullock, a combination of publishers, teachers, parents and other organisations launched the School

Bookshop Association and within five years, some 6,000 to 7,000 bookshops were operating in schools, with a turnover of some £3 million a year, mainly in paperbacks.

The Whitehead Report published in 1977 underlined the gap between the general run of accepted fiction and the general run of children's choice – only C. S. Lewis of the accepted writers came into the same division as Enid Blyton. And it gave strength to the conviction of many that the school library was the place above all places where a child was likely to come in contact with books.

Sir Arthur Clegg, the famous educationist, drawing attention to the close link between ownership and keenness on reading, thought that the "school bookshop movement may go far to reduce the reluctance to read which poor teaching and too much testing can bring about".

Outside school, there was change too, not least among the new generation of post-war trained librarians, many of whom saw their task as not simply to meet the needs of the one in three who regularly used the public libraries. They also sought to "reach out" to those for whom libraries, like commercial bookshops, were often alien places. Janet Hill's *Children Are People* (1973), based on the experiences of Lambeth librarians seeking to take the book to the child, appeared in the same year as McLellan's study, *The Reader, The Library and the Book*. This gave a salutary reminder that although library use was "proportionately higher among the better educated", yet the numbers of people from the rest of the population using the libraries were "as great if not greater."

Along with "outreach" in the libraries and concern with the reluctant reader in the school, came a mounting public debate about the social content of books for children. Can they, asked Leila Berg, who pioneered "Nippers", "look at a book or hear a story and feel *that's me*?"

The organisation Librarians for Social Change was formed to combat the "more despicable manifestations of injustices such as racism, sexism and ageism" in children's books, and came in for violent counter-attack from Bernard Levin in *The Times*. Levin was one of a number of media personalities who were to make blundering excursions into the little-studied field of children's literature in the belief that they had discovered an issue of beautiful simplicity – the social engineer and censor versus the free writer. Similar hostility, incomprehension and alarm greeted the arrival of feminist groups campaigning against sex-stereotyping in children's literature, and the founding, in 1975, of the Other Award, by the Children's Rights' Workshop, aiming to encourage new writing free from sex, race or class bias.

The appearance of the new radical journals of children's literature, *Children's Book Bulletin* and *Dragon's Teeth*, alongside more conventional magazines like *Signal* and *Children's Literature in Education* in the seventies, broadened the debate and spread it through the field until it seemed that no writer, critic, teacher, librarian, publisher nor concerned parent could escape being involved.

Symptomatic of the debate was the running battle between a minority of writers in the Society of Authors and the editors of *Children's Books Bulletin* over "bias and censorship" in British children's books, which culminated explosively in press and television during the winter of 1980–81. Suffice it to say that after the sound and fury, there was a nil response to the appeal of the Children's Writers Group of the Society of Authors to its members for evidence of outside bodies exercising "undue influence" on the publishing of children's books. Indeed the following year, members of the Children's Writers Group, together with opposite numbers in the Writers' Guild, were contributing, along with publishers, teachers and others, to a study of Sex Stereotyping in School and Children's Books.

The problem of the book and the child had come to stay. Painfully or with pleasure, those responsible for the production and distribution of children's books began to respond.

Despite an unwillingness to admit that "the hustling of polemicists" (Elaine Moss's phrase) had helped to bring it about, change had come to the literature in the 1970s – and a change which affected all genres. In the prestigious field of the historical novel, new writers like Peter Carter and Susan Price opened up the neglected field of the industrial revolution, while Frederick Grice and Winifred Cawley introduced the General Strike (the Waterloo of working class history). Already established writers were venturing into new fields. Rosemary Sutcliff's *Song for a Dark Queen* (1978) not only saw Roman Britain from the British point of view, it gave a woman figure pride of place in the person of Boudicca.

In the field of the school novel and the family story, writers like Gene Kemp, Bernard Ashley, Gwen Grant, Robert Westall, Jan Needle and Dick Cate gave for the first time on any scale authentic pictures of working class children. When, in 1978, Gene Kemp's *Turbulent Term of Tyke Tyler* won both the Carnegie and the Other Award, it was recognised that a kind of turning point had been reached. The literature was changing under pressure from within and without.

Particularly in the field of the teenage novel and the novel about contemporary life, the wind from across the Atlantic, as a century ago, was a refreshing one. A range of authors such as Cormier, Zindel, Hinton and Blume, across the literary spectrum, presented a challenge in readable realism to British authors, and because of inadequacies in the literature over here, took a disproportionate share of the growing paperback market. They had the direct appeal to which the young reader responded.

There was a message here for writers and publishers which was not readily grasped. There was still a tendency to see the young person who did not read willingly as a special educational problem needing a special kind of book. As Margaret Meek points out in *Learning to Read*, the approaches to the "reluctant" reader which took "the reading scheme as their model" were based on a lack of understanding. Margaret Meek observes that "only real books make real readers". In many cases, publishers were producing second class books for second class citizens and ignoring the basic fact that a book which is not good enough to appeal to a keen reader is not good enough to offer to the reluctant.

Altogether some 100 series for the reluctant were produced. Some, like Topliner and Knockout, contained many books which would meet the above test. Many others did not. This may well be because in recruiting writers for this market, some publishers reverted to their bad pre-war practice of poor terms or outright purchase; or because publishers sometimes required a modern background to be accompanied by stories of the most banal and traditional conventionality. "Coming to terms with life" in this sort of book, usually meant some luckless hero or heroine accepting that they were in the wrong.

Critically it was supposed that the "reluctant" market could be supplied at one level while the search for the modern Arthur Ransome or Edith Nesbit might go on undisturbed at a higher level, and all at the ratepayers' expense. Writers and publishers working in the "reluctant reader" field found a great reluctance among the critics to evaluate their efforts. Critics were often reserved or suspicious or dismissive of attempts to reach out to a new readership. While children were deciding, in greater and greater numbers each year, that real books meant paperbacks, the critical coverage given to these very often implied that the opposite was the case.

There was on this level an unwillingness to face the possibility that the problem lay with the literature rather than with the child, that even in this very special and sheltered trade the customer could not always be wrong.

The inadequacies of the literature were however to become most painfully visible, when from the late 1960s it could be seen that the "broader mass" of children included not simply working class boys and girls, but black and brown as well as white. In their case it was less easy to pretend that exclusion, condescension and even hostility in the literature was a figment of the chip-on-shoulder imagination. But bringing change to the literature was not easy, and early attempts were subject to accusations of "social engineering". In publishing Errol Lloyd and Petronella Breinberg, the Bodley Head was a pioneer in this area, but black writers found their place only slowly as did their counterparts, the black teachers and librarians.

There were some signs of change. A rare exception to critical insensitivity was the *TLS* in the mid-1970s inviting Linton Kwesi Johnson to review for it, before his name became well known. And Farrukh Dhondy was brought into view by a combination of the publication in a non-nett series, Topliners, of his *East End at Your Feet*, winning the Collins Multi-Ethnic Award and the alternative Other Award, as well as a hostile press and racist campaign against his work. All of which might by some people be described as "social engineering".

Furthermore, the introduction of school bookshops and new

approaches in library purchasing were extending the market potential. By the 1970s Puffin paperbacks were joined by Armada and Lions, Carousel, Piccolo, Knight Books, Granada children's paperbacks and other imprints.

Social engineering was having other effects. The movement for the rights of women and ethnic minorities, and the legislation on race and sex discrimination which came in response to it, put further pressure upon publishers and writers. As said, it gave the literary debates in the world of children's books of the late 1970s a distinctly political tone. It was all too often seen in publishing circles as an attempt to make publishers do things against their will.

"If you do not like what we do, then the only solution is for you to go and publish your own books", a too persistent questioner was told from the platform of a publishing-bookselling seminar. And that, of course, was what happened in the 1970s, when community publishers and bookshops, linked to projects for helping people to learn to read and write, began to make their mark. The controversy over *Stepney Words* (1972), a volume of pupils' poetry gathered and published by teacher Chris Searle, in the teeth of official disapproval, was a signal of a new approach. Centerprise in Hackney, combining the functions of bookseller, publisher, community centre and creative writing college, produced work by working class people, black and white, young and adult. By the end of the decade a network of worker writers' groups and community publishers was established in the main cities.

The alternative publishing net, the small publishing movement which had grown out of the political and social turmoil of the 1960s when youth politics re-created something of the cultural excitement of the 1840s, had already achieved something remarkable. It had rescued poetry from obscurity, associating the printed word with the spoken again on a large scale for the first time in over a century.

As the latest wave of print technology made the small unit production of books viable again, it helped to make the publishing of fiction, and fiction for the young, possible outside the area of conventional commercial operations. Non-sexist children's books, teenage stories and memoirs, some of them written by formerly "reluctant" readers or even people once judged illiterate, began to appear. Some of the work was good, some was not so good, but it was new and it would not stop coming. It reached parts of the reading and non-reading population which mainstream children's literature had not succeeded in doing. One milestone was the winning of the Other Award by Roger Mills for his *A Comprehensive Education* (1979), probably the first time in history that the school story had been taken over by the school pupil.

Throughout the decade and across the spectrum, what had been a minority interest had become something of a mass movement, from the Federation of Children's Book Groups to the Federation of Worker Writers and Community Publishers. Fiction for the young, born out of a social movement, secluded into the area between ivory tower and market place, was renewing itself in the midst of a new social movement of incalculable extent and potential effect. In any case, after 30 years' expansion, there was trouble in the market place. International recession, in the early 1970s, coupled with big business concentration of power presented publishers with enormous problems which undermined their reprinting and backlist policies built up over decades. "Liquidity" problems began to bite into reprints during 1973–74. Lack of ready cash, coupled with the costs of maintaining huge warehouses full of books sold nation-wide from one or two centres of production, had an alarming effect. High interest rates took their toll. Even large companies such as Collins, one of the biggest children's publishers, and Penguin found themselves in temporary crisis.

The trade recovered, but the reprint situation did not. The trend inexorably was to shorter print runs. The National Book League, which since the mid-sixties had run its popular Children's Books of the Year Exhibition, began to discover that titles chosen might be out of print before the exhibition was mounted. There was talk of books with a life of no more than three months – this in a field of fiction where titles had been traditionally expected to last for years.

From 1975 the 5–14 population which had peaked at 9.1 million, began to drop, and fell to between 7 and 8 million by the early 1980s. The trouble was that the curve of children's book sales was dropping at a faster rate than the demographic one. If the child population was 8 per cent lower, children's book sales in cash terms were 38 per cent down on 1971 by the 1980s.

They did not fall however, so much as they were pushed. Cuts in public expenditure from the mid-1970s – based on the absurd notion that this would somehow revive the economy – took an enormous toll of school and library. Between 1976 and 1982 1,268 librarians' posts were lost, some 470 branch libraries and 593 mobile units were closed. Coupled with cuts in school expenditure, the knock-on effect on book sales by the early 1980s was staggering. Between 1979 and 1980 nearly five million fewer children's books were sold, including one million fewer hardbacks, which by one calculation was over 20 per cent of total output.

During the 1970s, some eighty per cent of sales of hardback children's books were "institutional". Publishers had complacently drawn on what *The Times* (March 14, 1983) called "this easily run and highly profitable market". The attack on public expenditure put a stop to complacency and led to a search for new private markets as well as public campaigns to restore the cuts.

Public expenditure can of course be defended, and eventually restored by social action. An education system which offers a chance, however qualified, to every child from whatever home, achieved after two centuries' agitation, is not to be lightly let go.

And a new literature, arising out of that new situation, is not going to die just after it has begun to be born.

But the future, whether better or worse than the present, or more possibly a mix of the two, cannot ever be the same as the past. The new literature, the new fiction for the young, will not go in cyclical fashion through the same historic process as did the old.

What may the future be, for readers, writers, critics, teachers, librarians, publishers, parents? That is a matter for much speculation and much discussion. The following chapters offer some of my ideas.

15

Critics' Choice:
Child or Book?

What future for the critic? Which critic, child- or book-centred? Eng-lit. critic or social critic? The critic who goes for rigour and respectability or the one who goes for relevance and response? More importantly, the professional or the amateur?

I see little future for the academic critic making an exhaustive study of *angst* in the writings of William Mayne, while I see an ever expanding future for the librarian, the teacher, the parent, above all, the child as critic. These I expect to become more active, informed, confident and demanding, as the former sort wilts on the vine. I hope DIY criticism will become the universal practice. Not before time, for I think a good deal of critical activity over the past 30 years has been misguided and has even done harm to the cause of literature which it champions. Criticism, taking its cue from the adult literary establishment, has failed to grapple with several basic contradictions in the historical development of fiction for the young.

First, the "childhood" which emerged with the literature was based on the assumption that "children" meant only a minority, and thus on a literary assumption that the minority represented everyone, and that the rest did not exist, were culturally invisible.

Secondly, even those deemed to be children were still regarded as inferior beings, the condition of their childhood was segregation, dependence, protection. And how can it be worthwhile or valuable for mature adults to concern themselves with a literature devoted to the inferior and immature?

Or, as Mrs Pinchard wrote in 1791, "To write with constant attention to the limited understanding or information of children, to restrain a lively imagination and employ a mind capable of the most brilliant pursuits on subjects of a puerile kind . . ." (quoted in Gillian Avery's *Nineteenth Century Children*).

Or as Lucy Boston wrote nearly two centuries later: "So I became a children's writer. I did not realise at the time what a step down this was." (Quoted in *The Cool Web*).

The third contradiction arises from what I have called the "demoralising" of children's books in the First Golden Age. Apparent creative and aesthetic advances were achieved by absorbing the moral into the fabric of the story, the assumption in place of the assertion. Overt moralising was deemed to have been banished. The result of the lifting of this moral burden was that in the first half of the twentieth century no one took children's books seriously at all.

In this period, fantasy became not only the premier type of fiction for the young; it became the only area where true excellence was discovered. All genres of fiction became a species of fantasy.

Fourthly, attempts in the 1950s and 1960s to get children's literature taken seriously at an academic level, what one might call making fiction for the young safe for adults, eventually declared the child irrelevant to critical judgement. Thus the literature which originally defined childhood and owed its existence to it, seemed finally to be expelling the child so as to maintain standards. The bath water was to be kept clean by throwing out the baby. And it was all done with the best of intentions.

In 1969, Sheila Egoff and her colleagues published *Only Connect*, a collection of essays, to show fiction for the young, as "an essential part of the whole realm of literary activity to be discussed in the same terms and judged by the same standards that would apply to any other branch of activity." This book became something of a bible for book-centred people. It was not seriously challenged at an academic level until 1977, when Margaret Meek and her colleagues published *The Cool Web*, evaluating literature in terms of the child's response. *Only Connect* saw not only the problem of getting children's literature reviewed more deeply. There was the problem of getting it taken seriously at all. C. S. Lewis was bothered by the "silly convention" in literary circles which caused people like him to "speak in playfully apologetic tone about one's enjoyment of children's books."

Defiantly, Penelope Mortimer wrote: "*Black Beauty* and *The Secret Garden* are more intelligent, even sophisticated than the average woman's magazine story. *Tom Sawyer* and *Huckleberry Finn* can be enjoyed by any fairly bright executive wanting a bit of escapism between ulcers." This recalls the banner headline in the *Boy's Herald* comic in the early 1900s, "you need not be ashamed to be seen reading this."

But it became more common for critics to use adult literature as a bench mark for excellence. Margery Fisher, speaking of "a crop of junior novels . . . some of which for style and content can and should stand alongside adult fiction", was certainly not alone in this. A great deal depended on – which adult literature? Some, like Edward Blishen, had noted the "self-doubting intricacy" of much written for adults. But in fact, it seemed that what we were approaching was not just adult literature as a model, but adult tastes as a yardstick.

C. S. Lewis wrote: "I am almost inclined to set up as a canon that a children's story which is enjoyed only by children, is a bad children's story." This sentence is often misquoted, but in any case, Lewis had already in 1947 nailed his colours even more firmly to the mast:

> No book is really worth reading at the age of ten which is not equally (and often far more) worth reading at the age of fifty – except of course, books of information. The only imaginative works we ought to grow out of are those which it would have been better not to have read at all.

To get the full, dogmatic flavour of this passage, one should apply it to C. S. Lewis's *Chronicles of Narnia*. Lewis's point of view marks a trend in criticism moving on from establishing "adult" standards, to the elimination of the child from the evaluation of the literature. An aesthetic tradition drawing on a distinguished line, from Samuel Johnson ("general and transcendent truths that will always be the same") to T. S. Eliot with his "existing monuments" which "form an ideal order among themselves", was thus adopted for special use. Nor was it simply adult tastes that were in question but the tastes of certain adults only. In his essay "On Stories" (quoted in *The Cool Web*), C. S. Lewis guessed that "something which the educated receive from poetry, can reach the masses through stories of adventure". He guessed, because he assumed the mass reader, child or adult, would be unable to explain what they got from "literature" anyway. Not just the child, but the child's family was to be put to one side. What began as an aesthetic judgement ended as an act of social discrimination.

Brian Alderson, who campaigned for "objectivity" in children's literature criticism, as an alternative to "a morass of contradictions and subjective responses", provocatively upheld "The Irrelevance of Children to the Children's Book Reviewer" (Quoted in *Signal*, May 1974). Some seven years, and many debates later, he was to amend this, writing of children and their parents as "short stay customers", compared with the "literati".

Peter Hunt with complete consistency laid out the argument in all its implications in an article in *Signal* (September 1974):

> Whatever critical theory we produce for children's literature, it will have little or nothing to do with children. Thus we must say Book X is literature (as opposed to reading matter) or Book Y is good literature (as opposed to not-so-good) regardless of whether children actually read it, or like it, or buy it.
>
> . . . I would as soon consider including her (Enid Blyton) in a study of children's literature as I would consider including say Mickey Spillane in a literature degree course.

Literary standards, then, were to be cloistered virtues, shielded by segregation, not tested in combat.

On the one hand there were the child-centred considerations argued by Townsend (*Signal*, May, 1974), "suitability, popularity, relevance" and on the other, the book-centred, "the merit of the book".

In practical criticism this meant, for example, Gillian Avery noting that in Kipling's *Rewards and Fairies*, the "finest story is incomprehensible to children." Now, Kipling himself said of *Rewards and Fairies*, "They had to be read by children, before people realised that they were meant for grown ups."

And indeed, what was encouraged during the Golden Age of the post-war years was very much the publication as children's books of works which were really meant for adult readers. And this migration into the field of children's literature, of adult novels about childhood, was accompanied by the cult among some critics, and some librarians and teachers, of the writer who writes for himself alone. This was seen as the guarantee of the purest inspiration. By contrast, Penelope Mortimer (in *Only Connect*) made clear her conviction that any book written specifically for a group of readers, by age, class or colour, would be "dishonest" and "spurious".

This complex of arguments led, naturally, to the separation of popularity from literary merit. Brian Doyle (*The Who's Who of Children's Literature*, 1968) pointed out that "several otherwise notable histories of children's literature, do not even mention many of its most popular and famous contributors." One critic, for example, went so far as to praise Helen Cresswell, for "not pandering to her readers". (Dictionary definition of *pander*: "One who procures for another the means of gratifying his base passions, procurer, one who ministers to evil designs.") To go out deliberately and specifically to the consumer, then, is not merely lacking in merit, dishonest or even spurious, but in the end evil. Who would not in such circumstances "write for himself alone"?

This high critical judgement had certain practical effects which were deplorable, not least in concentrating attention particularly on books for the upper age range. One could only with difficulty satisfy the adult criteria when writing for the under tens, for example. This had an unbalancing effect on awards like the Carnegie, and during the 1970s, a new generation of librarians began to speak more openly of the prize-winning novels which sat on the shelves unopened by most children, particularly the younger ones.

The so-called "reluctant" reader was in fact the great unrecognised critic of the 1960s and 1970s. These young people by their stout resistance, by their upholding of standards of readability, impelled in teachers and librarians, at least, a wish to rethink.

Do suitability, popularity, relevance, exist in a compartment sealed off from "literary merit"? Are children doomed to be exposed unwillingly to the kind of "literature" described in Dr Frederic Wertham's study of comics, *Seduction of the Innocent* (1954)?

"A good novel . . . may describe how a young boy and girl sit together and watch the rain falling. They talk about themselves and the pages of the book describe what their innermost thoughts are . . . this is what is called literature."

To which Sybil Burr's story, *Life with Lisa* (new edition, 1980) has the reply: "Literature . . . is books in libraries that are still like new because people do not take them out often."

A criticism which sets the child aside, which sees the reluctant reader simply as a problem to be dealt with in a literary ghetto, is wrong in principle and dangerous in practice.

The "reluctant" reader stands on the shrinking frontier of the whole literature. Survival of the literature depends upon expansion, upon winning new readers. "Filling the shelves with the best" may simply be placing books in a time capsule for future archaeologists. A book without readers, remarked Elaine Moss (in *The Cool Web*), is a film shown in an empty cinema. A literature which exists in despite of its readers, which cannot attempt to reconcile quality with popularity, is asking to be discarded. The parent, who as tax- and rate-payer contributed far more to the second "Golden Age" than any critic, may be prepared to pay to help the reluctant reader, but not to perpetuate a reluctant literature.

Is reconciling quality with popularity an impossibility, or simply a complex possibility which needs to be explored? Popularity can be measured; quality is subjective, and when "merit" is seen as a thing in itself, then it becomes more subjective still. The first step for the critic must be to consider the child. It is not desperately difficult. "Children," writes Marcus Crouch, "do not confine their reading to the best any more than do their elders . . . all is grist to their intellectual mill." Naomi Lewis adds "The youthful mind is immensely adaptable . . . taking the lowest when it is there, but capable of any feat required."

Eleanor Graham (in *The Signal Approach*) justified the exclusion of Blytons from her original Puffin books in the 1940s and 1950s, on the grounds that "they were not intended for that kind of public". Is there a "Blyton public"? I don't think so. How many adults will now admit that they may have, in their time, read Jane Austen when they felt like it and Blyton when they didn't?

What is it that makes certain writers appeal to those who read a little *and* to those who read a lot? To say, for example, that W. E.

Johns' stories are "swift and mindless" is to evade the question. Johns, like many of his kind, was not mindless. He knew what he was writing for. He had a scale of values he shared with more respectable writers of his day. Call him wrong-headed, call him single-minded, simplistic, perhaps – but mindless, no. What he had, and what superior writers often seem to lack, is the will to communicate with young readers. He liked sharing a story with them. So did Blyton. The will to tell a story that will rivet the audience, rather than the award panel, is the first gleam the critic needs to look for in a book. "It is astonishing," mused C. S. Lewis, "how little attention critics have paid to story in itself." Attention to plot, to story, is something which "lit-crit." left behind during the two centuries of sophisticated development after the oral tradition had been superseded. Style, like merit, is not a thing in itself. It is simply the way the author has chosen to say what the author wants to say.

A style that is "popular", argues Nicholas Tucker (*The Child and the Book*), "favours the description of plot rather than character since it does not lend itself easily to psychological analysis". Or, as I heard a teacher put it in a seminar, "They (the pupils) are not interested in character, all they want is action."

I'd suggest that "they" are very interested in character, though not in psycho-analysis. The most popular stories in folk tradition, comic, or television series, are those which base themselves on one or more clearly delineated characters. In these the great creative effort has gone into shaping the character before the action starts. But it is in action, rather than static introspective examination, that this sort of character shows itself. The basic story is based on the test and the quest which faces every human being. Identification lies at the heart of the popular story. It tends to be regarded as a mark of lack of sophistication by "lit-crit." exponents. But if sophisticated critics were to examine themselves they might discover that in making literary judgments, intended to stand for all time, they may simply be rationalising their likes and dislikes of the characters involved and their failure to identify with them.

Surely in the long history of the school story, *only* total identification on the part of the critics with the people and milieu involved could have prevented them from seeing anything wrong in the fact that this genre specifically excluded 95 per cent of all schoolchildren. If the literature, serious, comic, farcical, had not been so bound up with how they themselves saw the world, then surely their literary judgement would not have failed them in this. Likewise the failure to see, or be concerned at the way working class, female and black characters were treated in much fiction for the young before the 1970s – the whole range from omission or condescension, through ridicule to hostility. Might not this failure arise, not from a "pure aesthetic" approach, but from a total and complacent identification with the conventional characters and values of this often well-written but humanly inadequate literature?

The "popular" book may indeed have characters simplified to the point of caricature, a mechanical plot and absurdly simple language. But nothing should be assumed from its general reputation.

When new editions of the *Bunter* books were prepared in 1982, the adapter discovered how elaborate and rotund was the language of Frank Richards. No one-syllable man, he.

Aidan Warlow (in *The Cool Web*) says: "children will overcome all sorts of linguistic obstacles (usually by ignoring them) if the alternative world of the story is one that is desirable and comprehensible." I would say "skipping" rather than "ignoring", since children pick up many things subliminally as they cruise over the page. Only later do they realise that they learned something at this or that moment in reading a given book.

A story for children is (usually) a book with an adult at one end and a child at the other. "Will the children like it?" is not the only question for the critic. But it is the question no critic can avoid asking. "Accessibility" is one indispensable criterion. The reader must be in the mind of the critic as in the mind of the writer.

Professional critics work too much on their own, or with their own kind. What they hear is often the echo of their own voice. Too often they seem to be handing down opinions for lesser mortals to accept, rather than joining with others to sharpen their own wits. Criticism ought to be a DIY business. Much of it is practised alone by parent in bookshop or child in library. It is better practised in company, in selection meetings, in get-togethers of teachers, librarians, writers, anyone. One thing which distinguishes the Other Award from its more conventional rivals is that the award ceremony is a public occasion where choices can be debated and criteria considered openly by the audience. (See Appendix, p. 194.)

The critic is in an artificial position, thrust between writer and reader. If critics want to earn their bread in future – or simply to justify their existence – they need to work more closely with others in the field. I have got a great deal of benefit from the experience of attending library selection meetings, parents' group or school staffroom discussions and sharing in the exchange of views. If critics are to contribute to the renewal and thus the survival of the literature, then they must quit the ivory tower and go out among the many whose interest in this renewal/survival is as keen as their own.

16

The Shopping List:
Why "Social" Criticism?

Is "social criticism", with its basic consideration of the factors of class, race and sex, for example, simply a shopping list for the DIY critic, as someone suggested? A shopping list is a necessary thing, and every professional or amateur critic has one, though often when shopping they pretend to have left the list at home. But if it were not more than a shopping list, then the great debate which burst upon children's literature during the 1970s would hardly have taken place at all.

Social criticism is a shorthand term for a process which is a good deal broader than a method for choosing and rejecting books. It is part of the process of renewal of the literature itself. A good deal of the indignation in some quarters over the social critics seems to be based on the notion that children's literature is a "natural" product and social criticism an arbitrary and un-natural interference with it. But as I have tried to show, the literature itself is an artificial product, often as brilliant as the proverbial silk purse, but as artificial as the medium of print which gave it power to replace the sow's ear of narrative forms that went before. For all its brilliance, it lost some of the human breadth of the original story tradition. Its refinement, like all refining processes, discarded a great deal. As a representation of nature it left a lot of nature outside, and a great deal of human nature.

Seeking to renew the literature, social criticism attempts to restore the missing elements. This means, in one sense, going back to the beginning, setting the assertions of social criticism against the assumptions of conventional judgement. It often sounds crude. It often is crude, a kind of sow's ear of the aesthetic world. But it is crude because it is about life and it is alive. Nor is it anti-aesthetic. It cares a great deal about how the literature is written, not least because this is the key to regaining the universal story-audience which the book has lost. It is an attempt to renew and revive both literature and aesthetic. It is the kiss of life, however rough, and not the fate worse than death some affect to believe.

The basic problem for both literature and criticism is that in the refinement of the fiction, the all-inclusive real humanity of the oral tradition was exchanged for an artificial "universality" in which certain human types were deemed to represent all. It reflected a social scene and a world in which one group and one country dominated. In gaining acceptance for this un-natural artificial situation, came the attempt, reflected in the literature, to establish norms of right and wrong and notions of excellence which were denied to others, until the cultural existence of those others was cast in question. Finally, the assumption became so "natural" that it was accepted without any understanding of its abnormality. Thus the male, the middle class, the English, became a cultural norm.

> There's something unmanly about the best of girls . . .
> (E. Nesbit's *The Treasure Seekers*)

> Scullery maids . . . are not little girls.
> (Frances Hodgson Burnett's *A Little Princess*)

> Be yourselves . . . in the knowledge that a good-hearted English schoolboy is the summit of creation.   (R. M. Ballantyne)

> She had the vague idea that the army consisted mostly of public school boys.   (Angela Brazil, *A Patriotic Schoolgirl*)

> Julius Victor . . . the whitest Jew since the Apostle Paul.
> (John Buchan's Richard Hannay)

Once such norms become part of the flesh and bones of a literature, then they need not be crudely, snobbishly, jingoistically expressed. Becoming accepted, they undermine the critical sense of those who offend and the self-belief of those who are offended against, until the assumptions are accepted on both sides of the divide. When writers of the calibre of Farrukh Dhondy and Jan Needle can speak, in the late 1970s, of their original hesitation about writing for the young because of an inner conviction that children's literature was about "other people", one gets a sense of how the abnormal has been normalised. "Consider it exceptional, even if it is the rule", wrote Brecht and that might well be placed above the desk of every critic, social or un-social.

The problem has deep roots. It began when the spoken story was first recorded and interpreted. The sort of editing, refining process by which Perrault's eighteenth century *Cinderella* was accepted at the expense of some 300 other versions of this basic tale has had its effect on the representation of women in literature. In this process Burd Janet, Mollie Whuppie, Kate Crackernuts, the heroine who climbed the glass mountain in *The Black Bull of Norroway*, the bright girls in the stories of *The Gobborn Seer*, or *The Fish and the Ring*, the wise women of the *Fenland Strangers* tale, these and others were set on one side. Nursery literature was left with a type rather like the "angelic beauty who sighed for liberty and love in a cottage", ironically described by Maria Edgeworth in *Moral Tales* (1801). Only in chapbook and penny dreadful has there been a faint reflection of these women of the folk tale. And only after the efforts of twentieth century folklorists have we become fully aware how limited is the literary female.

Even modern collectors were not without their faults. The Chadwicks in *The Growth of Literature* describe how many valuable Slav stories were missed by "collecting" in the local tavern where no unaccompanied woman would go. Later collectors were able to fill the gap by visiting women in their homes. One reason why the basic East Prussian collection was so rich in stories told by women is that the pioneer collector Hertha Grudde was a woman herself. Stith Thompson *The Types of the Folk Tale*, 1961, who recounts this, himself betrays some of the assumptions when he says that in certain countries like Ireland, "men specialise in one kind of tale and *leave others to women*" (my italics). First choice for one portion of humanity is perhaps the deepest of these assumptions.

So deep are the assumptions of what we now usefully call "sexism" that, for example, even Iona and Peter Opie, renowned for their scholarship in collecting folk lore, allow themselves to deny the evidence they have in front of them. In *The Classic Fairy*

Tales, they argue that "the prevalence of step-mothers" in printed folk tale arises from the "shortness of life in past time." But did widows not re-marry? In a little-known version of *Cinderella*, the girl flees from home on her mother's death, because of her father's incestuous designs. "The mother", write the Opies, "is the indirect cause of the girl's distressed condition". The tale of Bluebeard, they say, is about the "fatal effects of curiosity, particularly female curiosity". But surely the bride's curiosity was a life-saver!

Class bias often lies alongside sexism. Discussing the British tale, *Three Heads in the Well*, the Opies describe the heroine's good fortune. By contrast, "her humpbacked sister who seeks to emulate her, obtains a disfigured face, foul breath and a poor cobbler for mate". Which misfortune is worst? In fact the story (in the Opies' version) says that the cobbler not only marries the sister but cures her of her afflictions.

This bias in the perception of stories so carefully collected and researched runs alongside a contradiction in the Opies' basic argument. At one point they say, "in the most popular tales . . . the proud and privileged are brought low and the meek and downtrodden raised above them." At another, though, they argue that "in the most loved fairy tales . . . the established order . . . is not stood on its head." However, people from on high may be brought low, to rise again when their human merit is shown.

The contradiction is interesting. Among the authors of Victorian nursery fairy tales from Thackeray to Nesbit, the theme of high-low-high is very popular. But the theme of the "meek and downtrodden" raised up and the privileged brought low was gradually squeezed out of nursery fiction. In popular fiction it survived but in a very weakened form. It is perhaps symbolic that when Robin Hood first reached television in the 1960s, the theme song told us he was "feared by the bad, loved by the good". The *rich* could sleep soundly.

Xenophobia, dislike of the stranger, shows itself in folk lore, though often in jokey form in tales about the dimwits of the next community. But the oral tradition had a certain rough fairness. The others could hit back. My own home village and its neighbour across the river both had ancient lore about the meanness of the other. Only when economic exploitation, the social divide, separates tale and teller from audience, does the process become one-sided and the mutual insult become unilateral condescension and contempt. And in the domination of one country by another, xenophobia turns into racism. With racism comes the conviction that one group is not merely different, but superior to the other, that one group is normal the other is not. *Funny Foreigners and Odd People* was the title of a geography book in early nineteenth century schools, as wars of conquest were leading to the building of Empire, and the Gulliver spirit of curiosity about the stranger gave way to the Crusoe spirit of domination. Charles Kingsley, compassionate author of *The Water Babies* and exponent of muscular Christianity, could be anti-Semitic, and describe the Irish as "white chimpanzees".

Charles Hamilton (Frank Richards) thought that by making foreigners the object of gentle mockery, he was educating the English out of prejudice. "It's part of British humour that we knock other nationalities", an IPC editorial director told an interviewer when discussing comics (*The Times*, February 24, 1974).

But these insults, bearable between friends, perhaps, were accompanied by injuries to those not strong enough to resist the English with their sense of humour. The tradition that foreigners did not appreciate the English type of humour became the conviction that foreigners basically had no sense of humour at all. But when matters went beyond a joke, with the plundering of natural resources, political and cultural subordination, then the inequality and injustice had to be seriously rationalised. Captain Marryat in his adventure stories brooded over the moral problem of an Englishman robbing an African. But, as Patrick Howarth (*Play Up and Play the Game*), shrewdly notes, "later writers organised their stories to avoid this question."

The process of rationalisation was remorseless. If subject races were servile, they were comic or contemptible. If they were rebellious, they were not only hateful to the British but essentially wicked. Even today the stereotype of the evil-intentioned nationalist, African, Latin American, Arab, haunts children's literature. Today the term "terrorist", borrowed from Imperial parlance in Ireland and Malaya, is a convenient catch-all. Official or government violence, no matter how terrifying, is never "terrorism".

The assumption influences even serious critical thinking. Margery Fisher speaks of "John Laputa's sinister ambitions", in discussing *Prester John (British Children's Books)*. Fred Inglis (*The Promise of Happiness*) refers to Rider Haggard's "picture of British imperial benignity . . . a decent ruler imposed with foreign help".

Along with hostility and condescension goes the denial of identity. Crusoe's first act was to rob Friday of his own name. Countless maids in real and fictional life became "Mary" and "Ellen" at the whim of their mistress. "All boys", said Tom Brown, "are sent to a public school in England". And in fiction for the young until recently all children have indeed been sent there, though in real life 95 per cent have gone to state schools. That real 95 per cent just disappeared.

Symptomatic of the problem is that in writing, post-war, about Eve Garnett's *Family From One End Street* (1937), Marcus Crouch should find it remarkable that the Ruggles family was made "funny with condescension" – the exception that proves the rule. Brian Alderson on the other hand, (*The Times*, March 13, 1974) thought in retrospect the Eve Garnett book looked like "a dim comedy at the expense of washerwomen and dustmen".

If critical judgements could ignore, and the concept of "literary merit" could conceal, the social inadequacy of the literature, the judgement of the modern classroom and city library was harsher. The new audience looked into the literature and often did not find what they were seeking.

"Most people can find no meaning, no order, cannot even recognise their existence until they have formed their perceptions into words or found them reflected in someone else's words", writes Aidan Chambers (*Introducing Books to Children*, 1973).

For black, working class and often female children, entry into the world of fantasy was achieved at the cost of a surrender of identity. Or the child retained its identity and rejected the literature, if it could not find anything to identify with.

Attacks on the assumptions of a literature are seen as attacks on literature itself. And since social criticism is harshest with the literature of the past it is here that the first "defence" is made. Earlier writers who were clearly guilty of racism, sexism or class bias, are defended on the grounds that they were "innocent of harm" (a reviewer's verdict on Helen Bannerman's *Little Black*

Sambo). Hugh Lofting, says John Rowe Townsend (*Written For Children*) was guilty only of the "insensitivity of many Englishmen of his time to whom all foreigners were funny and those of a different colour were doubly funny." A. A. Milne, says his son Christopher (*The Enchanted Places*, 1974) was guilty of "snobbishness and class consciousness", but it would be unfair to blame him for what were "current" attitudes. Nicholas Tucker (*The Child and the Book*) says W. E. Johns shared the "anti-black prejudices common to his time".

The notion that each "time" comes complete with its uniform package of attitudes is a commonplace in this debate. But is it valid? In a given age, certain attitudes may be dominant, or appear from the literature to be dominant. But that neither makes them universal, nor natural or acceptable, then or now. Elizabethan times saw a powerful debate on the worth and value of women. There were Christians who questioned slavery. The joke about the Scots minister who "loved all men – Jew, Hindoo – aye and the English, too", is as Elizabethan as is the bricklayers' guild declaration in the 1580s: "All men are equal, made by one Maker of the same mire".

If no one could stand up for fair play in the sixteenth, seventeenth, eighteenth or nineteenth centuries, by what miracle did our twentieth century selves come to possess what Nicholas Tucker calls "current liberal orthodoxies"? And, as we make our critical time journey, whose side are we on? Lofting in fact privately believed that all human beings given a chance had the same "batting average". But in his Dolittle stories he allowed conventional racial caricatures to shape his creative effort.

Guy Arnold in his frank, but not unsympathetic, biography of G. A. Henty (*Held Fast For England*) deals with the back-dated justification of such attitudes. "To suggest that Henty was expressing no more than what half his contemporaries felt is to denigrate his power and influence. He was a propagandist for Empire and British interests and a highly successful one, too, in his way". In his day, church people protested at the "inflammatory" nature of *The Boy's Own Paper* stories. The Socialist journal *Justice* exposed Board school text books with their "160 references to war and bloodshed and 60 to peaceful reform". During the 1920s and 1930s teachers criticised the glorifying of Empire in school text and ceremony. Such criticism caused the London County Council to give the lead in changing Empire Day to Commonwealth Day, a lead followed nationally after the war. In 1928, while Lofting was happy with his "cannibals", F. Tennyson Jesse wrote *Moonraker* (1928), an adventure story celebrating black and female liberation. Naomi Mitchison began her series of historical adventures which featured real heroines.

At no time, then, have "current attitudes" remained unchallenged. So, what motive can un-social critics have for entering this retrospective defence? If writers may be excused for conforming to racist and sexist attitudes of yesteryear, can they also be defended in the same breath for refusing to "conform" to today's reformed attitudes? By defending yesterday's conformist and today's non-conformist, the suspicion is left that what is being defended is not the writer but the attitudes, both in crude earlier form, and more modern, refined form.

But social attitudes *have* changed. No editor would dream of accepting characters like "Conkey Ikestein", the Jewish looter in the *Union Jack* comic before World War I, without comment. How have they changed? A critical judgement confining itself to "literary merit" could not possibly have changed them, any more than conventional criticism made any difference to the social content of the school story. Socially motivated writers from Trease to Hildick, Ashley and Kemp, busy changing the story, made the difference. Likewise for the historical novel, Trease's pre-war "propagandist urge" did what a thousand pure aesthetic urges could not do, change the course of a genre.

Form which reaches its peak through the inherited efforts of generations of writers, which has produced its classics, its "monuments", tends to the conservative. Critics concerned with pure "excellence" without asking, *for what? for whom?* look to the past for their yardstick. In such a critical environment, the new expresses itself first not in terms of form, but of content, the message, the meaning, the assertion. Sometimes the new wine breaks the old bottles, bringing cries of distress from the connoisseurs. But it is with the crude new, rather than the accomplished old, that the future lies.

Hence the crucial role of the social critics, social engineers, polemicists, propagandists, Black Power agitators, feminists, radicals of all description, in the often disturbing, yet fruitful debates of the 1970s. They brought back seriousness to children's books, not solemnity, but seriousness of purpose, lack of which had brought the literature to its low point in the 1920s and 1930s, when the pure aesthetic was powerless to help. Secondly, through their influence in schools and libraries and in publishing houses, too, they helped create a new market, enabling publishers to generate a new sense of purpose themselves and to encourage new talent, from the regions, from ethnic communities.

New writers have come. Established writers have changed. None has been unaffected. Anyone doubting this might like to consider three new books (1983–1984) – *Dan Alone* by John Rowe Townsend, *Dragonfly Years* by Mollie Hunter, and *Handles* by Jan Mark, and ask whether what these books say about class, race, and sex prejudice owes nothing to the new climate.

One critic has offered the hope that the "pressure groups will fade, perhaps leaving behind them a useful legacy of the issues they raised." Fade they will, when the literature and aesthetic are renewed and refreshed by this new set of values. Thus when people speak of children they will mean just that, and no less.

17

What the Writer can do

What future for the writer? As story-teller, the writer has an unlimited future. If one medium goes out of fashion, the writer can hopefully switch to another. But that does not solve the problem of the writer's isolation from the rest of the world. So complex has the situation become, with a succession of intermediaries between writer and audience, that many have preferred to let the matter be resolved "between ivory tower and market place" – consciously or unconsciously allowing the publisher to represent the outside world to them, and them to the outside world. Geoffrey Trease, in a significant reference to his pioneering days of the 1930s, writes:

> By 1938, however, I had got the propagandist urge out of my system and I was finding it possible to say what I wanted to say without instantly antagonising an ordinary general publisher. (*The Thorny Paradise*).

Yet the publisher is not always an adequate go-between, as Writers' Guild and Society of Authors members know all too well. One of the early members of the Society of Authors, in the nineteenth century, Harriet Martineau, however, looked on this situation as temporary,

> ... a transition stage between old patronage and that free communication between speaker and hearers, writers and readers which must be arrived at sooner or later. (quoted in *Writers by Profession*, Bonham Carter, 1978).

In this transition stage there are often tales of exploitation, cavalier treatment, undue pressure from publishers. But on the other hand, when the general public is in a demanding mood – and in children's literature it has recently become very demanding – writers are not above sheltering behind their publishers. When the missiles start to fly, when angry readers demand the burning of a book because of a rude word on Page 94, then it's tempting to curl up in the ivory tower and let the publisher deal with the common foe.

But the notion, albeit unspoken, of the public foe, is at the root of the writer's problems. The nature of print, turning the story from a service into a commodity gives the writer a freedom and independence which are also isolation and alienation. Beatrix Potter told her publisher: "You are a great deal too much afraid of the public for whom I have never cared a twopenny button." This much admired remark, with its implication that integrity equals contempt for the reader, is not untypical. It fits in with the notion of the writer who writes for himself. As Arthur Ransome observed, "You write not for children but yourself and if by good fortune children enjoy what you enjoy, then you are a writer of children's books."

A writer's subjective attitude is the writer's own affair. But when it is objectified as a critical statement we are in a different game: Marcus Crouch writes of T. H. White's *Sword in the Stone*: "so spontaneous an outpouring of fun and beauty and wisdom could only have been written to please the author."

So developed is this convention, that an author may well be told, not asked, at meetings: "Of course, you don't really write for children, do you? You just write for yourself and hope they like it."

Yet is the public, the consumer, obliged to accept such a take-it-or-leave-it attitude, being grateful if the artistic arrows shot in the air find their target? What happened in the old story-telling days? If the audience did not appreciate the genius of the story-teller, did that individual stalk off, supperless, into the night? Actual experience of story-telling suggests something different. You match story to audience, as far as you can. You may even adapt or "edit" the story as you go, concentrating on the fine tuning of audience attention. And there is an art in so doing, the enjoyment of which must be experienced to be appreciated.

Parents and teachers often do it, editing certain overblown passages of classics when reading to a modern audience. There is an interchange between story-teller and listener, something alive and creative, an interchange which has become confused, problematic, sometimes oppressive with the printed word. Not that print in itself is alone responsible. There is that in a socially divided society which gives rise to alienation of artist from audience. In his book *From Script to Print* (1945), H. J. Chaytor quotes a fascinating exchange between two French minstrels in the twelfth century. Linhaire, one of the jongleurs, having said that he believes that it is up to everyone how and for what audience they compose, asks why it should be wrong, "If I work late and turn my rest to weariness for that reason (to make my songs simple) . . . Why compose if you do not want all to understand? Song brings no other advantage".

The other minstrel, Girault, replies: "I produce what is best at all times. I care not if it be not so widespread. Commonplaces are no good for the appreciative. Gold is more valued than salt." One can find echoes of this dialogue in many modern debates. "Gold is worth more than salt", is a social rather than a literary assumption. It avoids the question, for whom and in what circumstances? Midas and his touch is an enduring figure of legend. Yet the core of the argument is there. Is a popular audience, particularly a younger, less experienced audience, not a threat to the development of the artist?

You can overcome what Edward Blishen calls the "thoughtless notion of the inferiority of writing for children", but are you working for flesh and blood children, or the shadowy "child you once were?" Or is the writer to concentrate on winning the approval of the intermediary – adult, parent, teacher, librarian? "Buy only those books you like yourselves", I heard a writer urge a librarians' conference.

I would argue that such distancing from the audience is wrong, unwise and unnecessary. It is especially wrong in the case of the young audience for whom writers share with the rest of the community a deep and vital responsibility. It is unwise since today's young audience, unlike yesterday's, has its say in the purchase of books, through the school bookshop. It also has its say through the increased attention that parents, teachers, librarians pay to winning the young for reading rather than imposing it on them. Children are conscript readers no more; they have alternative ways of getting a story.

It is unnecessary, because as any one of the 150 authors who each year meet children in school or library can tell you, the contact is invigorating, a help to the inner self and no threat to "the child you once were." Geoffrey Trease recalls how his Bannermere series was begun after two girls approached him at an early "Writers in Schools" meeting to ask for day school stories.

Trease as a trouper thought a lot about the salt-gold argument. Unlike some writer-critics he did not accept the false notion that quality should equal unpopularity, but pleaded for popular books which set higher standards in form and content than books of the Biggles school. Sheila Ray (*The Blyton Phenomenon*) shows how the approach that "the good will drive out the bad", did not dispose of Blyton. The anti-Blyton campaign left her the best known author of the second golden age.

Absolute notions of "good" and "bad" are unworkable. They are never based on realistic comparison. They are unworkable because of the broad spectrum of tastes among young readers which accommodate a remarkable mixture of subject matter and quality. They are unworkable because often what is deemed good is chosen for qualities that do not render it popular even with the omnivorous "keen" reader. Thus one had in the past "children's children's authors" and "librarians' children's authors".

A more recent approach has been the search for writers with popular appeal, but creative and content merit, not with the aim of wiping out Blyton, but with providing a broad and viable alternative, writers who stand comparison with Blyton in the child's eyes, rather than the adults'. "What we want", a publisher remarked to me a few years ago, "is a working-class Enid Blyton", a writer with that ability to captivate children, but minus the snobbery, suburban prejudice, acquisitiveness, golliwog-racism, which she shared with more respectable writers but spread a good deal more effectively than they did.

Some ask if the two elements can be separated: some have asked, "Does not simplicity in the writing go naturally with simplistic and reactionary notions about the world?" Or, "Aren't the masses basically reactionary anyway?"

But writers do not have to be simplistic to win readers from beyond the magic circle. Theodorakis, a modern minstrel, who would relish the salt-gold debate, says wisely: "If you want a dialogue with people, you can't use avant-garde forms, but with simple forms you can say complicated things."

One has to consider carefully what is being aimed at. Enid Blyton belonged to a line of writers now departed, like L. T. Meade and Evelyn Everett Green, who spanned the nineteenth and twentieth centuries, who learned the art of popularising in the old religious school and worked with equal ease for magazine or book publication. That was a popular extension of their role as writers which is only enjoyed by modern writers if they write for television. They were happy hacks and so was she. She only resented it if someone suggested she did not write every word herself.

Blyton was a communicator. She wrote direct to the kids. She answered their letters by the thousand. She used, without much scruple, the ideas she gained from them, and offered small presents, for example, for the idea which set off the Secret Seven adventures. She did not sigh for feedback but organised it. She ran blanket and silver paper|collections long before *Blue Peter* was heard of. She encouraged children to write to each other, town to country and so on. She never stopped writing. She could not. She was inspired. Her own personal creative image of a film screened in the cinema of her mind is a sign of inspiration. In the end, it seems, she was worn out. Her last illness shows all the signs of long-term exhaustion. Anyone who thinks "easy" writing is easy writing, that it means less effort, should study her life and find some of the reasons why there are not many like her.

Television and radio have in any case altered the rules of the game. A writer, televised, may for a short time outsell Blyton and the other old popular writers. Meade and Green with their 300 titles and Blyton with her 600 will not come again. Nor need they. In Blyton's day the number of children's writers was small compared with today. The burden of replacing her, or matching that appeal, does not rest on any single pair of shoulders. Already, to judge from the "Children's Choice" publishers' promotion campaign of summer 1984, children do not automatically choose Blyton as favourite.

But it is worth a look at the elements in Blyton's success, her compound of virtue and vice. She absorbed the world of children and gave it back to them. Her first writings were directly for the children she taught. As someone said of her, "she knew just how children like a story to be." That was the ace in her pack. She started them young: no complaints about the customer from her. She fed the children, from four to fourteen, on themselves. She satisfied them and left them hungry for more of the same. She gave children what they liked, though never what they wanted. She did not allow her readers to advance a fraction beyond where she held them. There is part of every child that does not want to grow up, and she catered for this part. Keen reading children will return to Blyton, when they are tired or ill.

Aidan Chambers (*Introducing Books to Children*) and Nicholas Tucker (*The Child and The Book*) sum up how this affects the content of her work – "Collusion in a game of those adults versus us kids . . . openly and unembarrassedly . . . let's have fun at the expense of the grown ups." (She) "quite deliberately places her second self at the side of the children in her stories and the readers she deliberately looks for . . . an anti-adult fantasy world."

All this is true, and it is close to the world of the comic, what Tucker calls the "saturnalia" element, where "authority is flouted and made ridiculous by characters who are themselves absurd and unreal." Comics, like Blyton, take what is left of the old "equalising" element of the folk tale, what John Buchan called "the survival of the unfittest", the weak against the strong, and make use of it, draining it of all social meaning. Blyton mixed this "us and them" element, with what Tucker calls the "darker" side of children, their apparent willingness to pick on others, ganging up against the outside world, but also ganging up against weaker "outsiders" of their own kind.

Blyton unconsciously but unscrupulously perverts the "us and them" theme away from its anti-authority context. The targets for her mockery are not powerful people at all. They are working class parents like the Sticks, whom her characters insult with impunity. Plod the policeman may represent authority, but at such a low level as to be almost a servant. I say "unconsciously", because, surely, no one could deliberately set out in creative terms so to pervert the child's anti-authority impulses to the ends of snobbery and suburban prejudice. And there's the rub. Any writer who seeks to develop this "saturnalia" element in their writing, in combination with a genuinely and uncompromisingly anti-Establishment attitude, may run into trouble with the critics.

"To make fun at the expense of authority . . . is to reduce story-telling to the lowest level of entertainment", writes Eileen Colwell in her *Storytelling* (1981). Yet fun at the expense of authority has an honourable folk tradition behind it. And there is enough force in the image of the under-dog for it to be summoned in the most unlikely causes. Two leading children's writers, Lynne Reid Banks and Philippa Pearce, in articles in *The Times* and *The Guardian* written within ten days of each other during December 1976, showed just how the matter can be confused, by comparing criticism of the middle and upper class with National Front type attacks on Jews and Asians. Thus an attack on privilege becomes an attack on a "minority".

Even a critic of the experience of Brian Alderson can complain of writers who make modern developers the villains of their stories as though this were somehow impermissible. With the question of power relations in society thus thrown into confusion, by ostensibly non-political commentators, the task of a writer seeking to restore genuinely popular elements to the children's story is rendered more difficult.

The process of getting rid of the age-old image of the rich and powerful villain from fiction for the young, inevitably drives the story towards villains of the "lower class" criminal type, the "half-tipsy cads" of Talbot Baines Reed, or the vulgar outsiders of Blyton and Malcolm Saville stories. When in his comic *Uncle* books, J. P. Martin (one of the last of the clergymen in children's writing) made a huge joke out of a millionaire landlord defeating a tenant's revolt by violence, the inversion of the old folk *motif* had reached its limit. It has led inevitably to the corruption of the popular element in the story and is the truth behind the apparent "reactionary" nature of much writing of this kind.

A genuinely popular children's writing needs to resolve this problem of attitudes to power in society and restore to the book the essential equalising element of the original story. If writers are to side with children, then the real enemies with the real power must be identified, not a set of scapegoats, and the game must be played out with total commitment. This may involve the kind of "propagandist urge", which Trease says he got "out of his system". But I would argue that a literature which gets such urges totally out of its system is one which is in danger of losing its reason for existence.

Such urges are not programmatic. Programmes are for parties not for writers, just as novels are about people with problems not about problems with people assigned to them. Above all novels are about moral choices. The fabulist, as Kipling and William Golding have reminded us, is a moralist. The fabulist, says Golding, "tells the ruler what he does not want to hear". Where does the moral lie then? It depends on your judgement of human nature. Of *Lord of the Flies*, Golding tells us (in *The Cool Web*) with all the authority of a private schoolteacher, "I have lived for many years with small boys and I know them with awful precision." Golding knew one sort of small boy, but it is the habit of the middling sort to imagine they are representative humanity. For Golding goes on: "Man is a fallen being. He is gripped by original sin. His nature is sinful and his state perilous."

If that is Golding's fable-moral, then most rulers would be delighted to hear it. Original sin, the innate wickedness of human beings, totally believed in, can justify institutional wickedness, exploitation and oppressive government.

I prefer the judgement of two other writers. One from some 80 years ago, G. K. Chesterton, writing about the "penny dreadful", says, "The vast mass of humanity, with their vast mass of idle books and idle words, have never doubted and never will doubt that courage is splendid, that fidelity is noble . . ." Modern author S. E. Hinton (*The Outsiders*), writes of her young readers, that they

> . . . know a lot today. Not just things out of a textbook but about living. They know their parents aren't superhuman, they know that justice doesn't always win out and that sometimes the bad guys win . . . give them something to hang onto. Show that some people don't sell out and that everyone can't be bought. Do it realistically. Earn respect by giving it.

My own conviction about humanity and its virtue is not a simple act of faith. I suppose I am as likely to be mistaken as is the believer in original sin. But there is more pleasure each time my convictions are confirmed.

Morality in a story does not speak simply from the mouths of characters, nor in introspective examination of their souls. It is in the spirit of the book itself and shows in the shape of the story, its choices, its changes and its conclusion. If half the battle is in the content, then half the battle is in the form, in the telling, and I believe that the key to the acceptance of writing by young people lies in what I call the narrative thread. It is something about the story which can be grasped from the beginning and followed through the twists and turns of plot. It may well be couched in simple language, but that is not essential. The thread may take the form of a known and popular character. A conference lecturer, analysing *Grange Hill Rules OK?* declared that the story with its multiple main players was too complex. He could not follow it. But the children could. They could follow switches of presence and point of view, even within the same page, with ease.

So also with moral and meaning. If the readers can make their way safely through the story, as one follows a path through an unfamiliar wood, the journey is everything. Things observed will make their impact on the mind later. But to observe one must get into, and through, the wood.

Narrative thread is something the writer shares with the story-teller within every child. Writers often recall how, as children, they made up stories for themselves before they went to sleep. My own discussions with children of different ages show how widely this bedtime story making is practised. Dreams of day or night are the basic human facility for narrative at work. Our minds are always busy composing stories, for whatever motive.

The belief that this capacity is limited to certain individuals is part of the alienation of writer from reader in our society. It reduces the child without genuinely elevating the writer. It merely sets them apart one from another. Fred Inglis is honest enough to say, in *Promise of Happiness*, what some believe but will not express openly: "It is self-evident that some individuals with every opportunity in the world just are without any imagination at all." Which individuals, what sort? Anyone except ourselves, perhaps.

Yet all humans, young or old, dream. And for each one their dreams have a special vividness. I have spent many hours with boys and girls in discussion of their dreams. Listening to them and to their stories, I feel I begin to know what it is they want of a writer, not just what they like in a writer.

This of course is the special aspect of writing for the young which gives such writers a fortune not shared by others. The audience is real, it is there. It can be found, every day of the week, five days a week, 38 weeks of the year, in the same place. Those who pioneered the "Writers in Schools" scheme years ago conferred a blessing on their craft. It has provided a means of bridging that gap between storyteller and audience which has burdened us for so long: that "lamentable gap" which Joseph Jacobs wrote of in the 1890s (*English Fairy Tales*), "between the governing and recording classes and the dumb working classes of this country, dumb to others but eloquent among themselves."

The notion that in the interests of social control, one could foster reading, a love of literature and knowledge, while discouraging the majority from writing, from self-expression, was one of the illusions of the Victorian age. It cannot be maintained today. There should not be players and spectators in literature, any more than there was a passive audience for the told story. Working in writing workshops with young people, reading my stories to them before and after publication and listening to theirs in hundreds of schools, has shaped my style of writing more than I can easily describe. What they have taught me is not to waste words, to make every word pay.

It has helped me in my search for a balance of interests between what I want to say and what they want to hear. To seek a popular style is not to surrender integrity. The opportunist bid for cheap laughs or thrills is as alien to genuinely popular writing as is the elitist bid for critical approval. It is a dialogue calling for honesty on both sides. I am very much concerned with comic writing and aware of how the comic sense grows in a human being. I have made a simple rule for my writing. If when reading a story, the children laugh but the teacher doesn't, five marks out of ten. If both laugh, ten out of ten. If the teacher laughs and the children don't, nought out of ten.

This *is* a special literature. Its writers have special status in home and school, free to influence without direct responsibility for upbringing and care. This should not engender irresponsibility – on the contrary. It is very much a matter of respect, on the one hand for the fears and concerns of those who bring up and educate children, and on the other for the creative freedom of those whose lives are spent writing for them. I have generally found, in discussion with parents or teachers, including those critical of or hostile to my work, that these respects are mutual.

18

The Age of Change:
Publishers, Librarians, Teachers

We have not decided if because life is so complicated nowadays, everyone has to be better at reading and writing than ever before, or whether we want to give everyone the powerful privileges of the literary elite, the professional readers and writers who shape and mould public opinion.

Margaret Meek – *Learning to Read*

Fiction for the young is going through a period of crisis while it works out who it is for. Are these "powerful privileges" to become human rights – shared by everyone? The future of the literature is linked very much with the expansion of democracy in all aspects of life. Reading, writing and the vote have been linked from the beginning. The future of literature for the young, with fiction at its heart, forms an important part of our striving for a better life for all. So the literature which came into existence to give children a more abundant life cannot now declare that it has no more lessons to teach and that when it says children it doesn't mean children.

Each of the separate parts of what is known as the children's book world, parents, teachers, librarians, publishers, writers and booksellers, has a very real interest in the future success of the literature. History shows that success depends upon the working together of those parts. The potential for this symbiotic relationship is enormous. Crisis, doubts, hesitations have arisen just when the means of making enormous advances had come to hand.

During the 1960s and 1970s, there were complaints of "too many books". There never were, though it seemed sometimes "too many" titles were being published. But if publishers, even when they agreed there were "too many", never seemed to heed the mournful cries, it was not due to ill-will or stupidity. Economic developments external to publishing caused them to depend upon borrowed money to service the storage and turnover of their incredibly varied produce (does any other trade have 250,000 stock items?). Thus publishers were driven more and more to boost turnover, not simply to raise profits, but to pay the bank. This led to shorter print runs on the one hand and a feverish interest in best-seller flagships for their sales campaign. Those same economic trends fed the belief in business circles that somehow private commerce might flourish if public expenditure could be reduced. For publishers, and for children's publishers especially, this was like cutting the veins to increase the blood circulation. Some publishing directors may privately treasure the high-income bracket tax cuts which have been the "reward" for all the book budget cuts, the closed branch libraries and sacked librarians. But public sector misfortunes have been visited rapidly upon the private sector. Big cuts in library expenditure have been followed by massive drops in hardback book production.

This has not led, as might be presumed, to a rise in quality. Loss of confidence, sometimes disorientation as publishers look round for alternative markets, do not create an atmosphere in which new talents may be sought and encouraged. Courting the "conscience"market, or cajoling parents into buying books for their offspring by advertising in child-ware shops, may help. Wild experiments with puzzle books, competition books, computer books, may generate some cash, but will leave the essential future market, an expanding young reading and buying public, insufficiently involved and affected.

One problem is that children's publishers do not sufficiently study nor easily understand this market, going generally by what has sold rather than what might sell, or even less, by what is wanted. If publishers' editors would sit, for example, in library selection meetings and see the books proferred by the trade, not neatly arranged in exhibition stands, but in piles where the repetitiveness of theme and treatment invites the careful-spending librarian's rejection, they might have second thoughts about their own policies. Consultation between publishers, librarians and teachers is at a fairly low level. Opportunities to meet are lost.

The habit, for example, of publishers sending not editors but promotion people to library and education conferences indicates a one-way approach.

Editors by upbringing and education are not automatically in touch with the way of life and thinking of the majority of consumers. This may change over the years, as the proportion of ex-comprehensive pupils recruited rises and that of ex-private school pupils correspondingly drops. But the will to share experience is the main thing and any editor who is prepared to spend several weeks in the year, in classroom or library, sitting in on bookshop sessions at lunch time, observing discreetly what kids pick up and put down, what they say, would gain immense and valuable experience.

There has to be the will to develop lists as part of a literature which aims to appeal to young people right across the spectrum of ability and interest, instead of, as too often, the two-tier approach which puts prime editorial effort into producing potential prize winners and hives off the rest to specialist attention, producing books for the "reluctant reader"and so on.

The trouble is not all on one side. Librarians and teachers will, or should, admit that they understand little of the problem of finding new writers, for example. Yet it is in this library-school network and through its lines of communication to the community, children and parents, that some of these problems may be most fruitfully discussed and perhaps tackled.

Getting to know the reader sounds a fairly trite aim, but I would hazard a guess that lack of such knowledge is one of the greatest obstacles to giving children's literature a broader appeal. Yet the readers, nearly 8 million of them, from 5 to 18, are there to be met. It is from the school library that two thirds of the children may get hold of a book. A properly run school library should have most children visit it, one way or another.

The school librarian is the most active of all intermediaries, can do the most good or the most harm, in bridging the gap between reading under compulsion and reading for pleasure. Where the school library is connected with, provides room for, or runs the school bookshop the influence on taste and choice as well as the knowledge of these is considerable in the best cases. It is an area of knowledge little tapped by those who make books. For the visiting writer, the school librarian is a key figure, particularly if seen as ally and not outcast by the English Department. The modern well-run school library is the ideal place for the writer to meet the reader, and that goes for other book-makers. The school bookshop is the perfect example of a successful public/private operation. It retains the merit of the market, in that the girl or boy can choose, buy and own the book they wish. But one has to face the fact that it would not exist without public backing. This it gets in the form of funds from school or parents, and a great deal of unpaid work by teachers, school librarians, often pupils and parents.

I made a rough calculation that this unpaid work amounts in any year to something like half a million pounds. And that does not figure in the accounts of the School Bookshop Association. The SBA and its magazine *Books for Keeps*, founded by a coming together of publishers, teachers, parents, librarians and other groups, is one of the success stories of recent years. Publishers' backing is still needed for its survival, though independent status is within reach. One would hope though that this will not be independence from the rank and file teachers who run the shops. They need to be associated in a much broader way with the running of the movement. The opening of 6–7,000 school bookshops in a period when some commercial bookshops have closed, and others were kept going only by the dedication of their owners, is a remarkable thing. Even more remarkable is the fact that if one were to ask the MD of the average publishing house, Did you know that nearly 7,000 new retail outlets had opened since the 1960s? – the response would be a baffled stare. School bookshops account for some £3 million worth of sales each year, by one estimate. For many young people – and in some cases their parents – they bring a bookshop within reach for the first time. A school bookshop can also be a community bookshop.

In her study of ten school bookshops in *British Book News* (spring 1980), Yvonne White gives a fascinating picture of the choices made by pupils. Humour, the supernatural, fantasy, science fiction and school stories come first and poetry, historical and classics come at the bottom of the list, a complete reversal of the conventional orientation of the literature. Ms White points out that in children's choices, factors of price, the influence of teacher and friends, availability, and the opportunity to meet live authors, play an important role. And she indicates the role of the school bookshop in reaching beyond the circle of "good" readers to a new market.

The number of school bookshops could double before saturation point is reached, since "shop" in this context can mean anything from a special room with display stands, to a box of books on a table in the hall of a village school on a Friday afternoon. What limits the potential for development is the failure to take school bookshops seriously – both on the part of many publishers (at top level rather than the children's department) and on the part of many schools. The existence of the bookshop along with the library is a guide to how seriously the school takes reading. My own observations show, unfortunately, that a number of schools regard books, other than specific texts, as either irrelevant or a positive distraction from the serious business of getting students through the exam funnel. But the same observations (in nearly 500 schools) show that in a sympathetic school the efforts of one or two teachers keen on reading for pleasure can transform the situation. One can assert that until such opportunities to borrow, buy and keep are freely available to all children, no final judgement can be made upon whether books appeal to them or not.

Another casualty of the piecemeal and unequal development of education and children's literature is the class reader, which accounts for an enormous part of publishers' production. In many cases it is the only book a boy or girl has regularly in their hands, and this is often a misfortune because the class reader, despite some attempts to improve the situation, is still the Cinderella of children's literature. Writing of Falkner's *Moonfleet*, Brian Alderson (*Children's Books in England*) puts a not untypical point of view: "By a quirk of misfortune this masterly historical novel was published by a company with an educational list and for many years it had to struggle to make its way to readers in the guise of a text book reserved for such occasions as reading round the class".

Yet why should reading in class be a disaster for a book? Writers do sometimes feel there is a stigma attached to being used as a class reader, arguing that readers should be "free" to choose.

In fact, quiet consumer resistance does play an increasing role in changing the choice of class reader. If the class reader has a bad reputation from the past, though, the solution is not to try and save "good" books from the fate, but to improve the quality and appeal of the class reader. If the pupils find the book provided is enjoyable, then they are more likely willingly to buy or borrow others. There is no reason why the same popular book should not be class reader, borrowed from the library and bought in the bookshop. The discovery that my own book *It's My Life* was being used as class reader and stolen to keep at home by pupils, was a compliment worth a row of reviews.

Yet no school on its own can offer the range of books which a properly stocked area library provides, nor the opportunity of linking reading with spare time activity which the club atmosphere of such a library, run by welcoming staff, can give. It is in the area library that the community can best give to all children an equal opportunity to enjoy the widest variety of books, often in association with audio visual material, games and vital information. Librarians who see it as their duty to safeguard books from children are a vanishing species. The librarians who are trying to make the library a place where young people spend their spare time comfortably and enjoyably, increase in number. Here again the cuts have come at a moment of real breakthrough in attracting youngsters beyond the one third who regularly use libraries.

A key question, is, who is the typical library user? Peter H. Mann in his pamphlet *Book Publishing, Book Selling and Book Reading* (1979) has something to say on the subject which reinforces McLellan's evidence about the "social profile" of the library customer.

> As middle class people read more than working class people so there is a danger of thinking of reading being a predominantly middle class activity. This is a dangerously wrong viewpoint. The working classes are roughly twice the size of the middle classes, so if one looks at a profile by class of those people now reading books, more than half of them will be working class.

Assumptions about book reading and borrowing, and this is confirmed by Jennie Ingham's studies of children during the

Bradford Book Flood experiment, have to be revised in favour of a broader view of the reader and potential reader.

The area library is very much involved in the business of winning readers, and a key problem is not simply whether the library is gloomy and forbidding or modern, light, well-stocked and entertaining, but what choice of books it offers. An inspired librarian can win children into the library and make them happy with Yellow Pages. But mostly even inspired librarians need books that will do some of the work. Books generally fall into three categories.

Category A books draw the kids in to look for more of the same and, hopefully, others. These books may be forgettable. Nevertheless they are indispensable. Kids like them. But often they are memorable and they are the ground bait of the profession. Category B books, once the kids are inside the library, will grab them, perhaps after some nudging from the librarian. They will satisfy and stimulate them, though they may be more discreet than Category A. Some of these are forgettable, but many more are memorable. Category C books are those to which the kids who have liked A and B can be led to. If they are completely hooked then Category C books are a whole area of discovery. That is, the best of them. But are they less accessible because they are deep and many layered or because they are pretentious, remote, obscure and boring?

The best "C" books are memorable. The worst are worse than forgettable. They may turn the kids off and out through the door again.

What counts is where the centre of gravity of the library and, eventually, the literature is seen to lie, where the creative productive and distributive effort is going, whether the literature is for young people or whether the children's library is a haven for non-viable literature which is judged worthy of preservation – the "time capsule" approach.

At this point in the argument, murmurings are sometimes heard from those who feel writers are going to be put to the rack to make them produce books for the "down market" child whether they like it or not. No unwilling horse should be led to water. One of the most significant developments of the 1970s was the arrival of new authors from social and geographical areas outside the old

177

magic circle. A renewed literature means a fresh stock of authors supplementing the existing. There is room for both.

This is why creative writing in schools is of importance far beyond the English Department. I have tried to show historically how writing (the means to command) has been given much less importance in education than reading (the means to obey), particularly where the schooling of working-class children is concerned. *They*, after all, are the descendants of that story making population whose oral tales, often in local dialect, were relegated to second class status and obscurity by print and the social attitudes of those who controlled it. As the Opies' *Lore and Language of School Children* (1959) has shown, much of the oral tradition has survived in the school yard. Bringing that creativity of the spoken word into the school classroom, and taking it out into the wider community through the medium of writing, is an important part of the renewal of a literature which will make sense to the young. Its social potential is enormous. It has been recognised in a totally negative way by John Rae, head of Westminster School, writing in *The Observer* in February 1982:

> The overthrow of grammar coincided with the acceptance of 'creative writing' in social behaviour. As nice points in grammar were mockingly dismissed as pedantic and irrelevant so was punctiliousness in such matters as honesty, responsibility, propriety, gratitude, apology and so on.

Giving what Margaret Meek calls the "privilege of the literary elite" to the "ordinary" child, then, involves a challenge to the existing order. It is an order which is in difficulties now, because all too often its "punctiliousness" was artificial and its qualities were reserved for social equals and not extended to lesser breeds at home and abroad.

Creative writing, in its broadest sense of allowing children to bring into existence from their own minds and selves what was not there before, however modest that may seem to an outside observer, is more than a question of restoring a cultural heritage to its rightful owners. It is a vital necessity for development of language and literature. For it is the invisible majority which constantly renews the spoken language, to the fury of pedants, inventing new words and recalling old ones from the past, changing their meaning by using them "wrongly" just as it is the "guardians" of the obsessively correct use of written language who are slowly squeezing it to death. Speech among the majority of children varies widely still from area to area and constantly from month to month and year to year. Any writer attempting to quote verbatim the latest street talk in dialogue may find when the book is published nine months later that the terms are already out of date. Yet it is the speech rhythms, idioms, cadences, metaphors of this spoken language which is the resource from which the literature may be renewed.

A little late in the day, the strength, variety and value of "non-standard English" is gaining recognition. Why restrict oneself to the handful of synonyms in a thesaurus when each county dialect offers a complete stock of its own? The very richness of non-standard English is in itself a challenge to the whole system of education and literature, but a challenge that must be met. London schools at the moment are grappling (or not grappling) with new streams of language like Creole. In the Spring 1984 issue of *Dragon's Teeth* magazine, children's writer Petronella Breinberg discussed this problem, contrasting claims about "multi-cultural education" with "an objective attempt to eradicate the social speech and language of one cultural group, eg. the blacks of Caribbean background". Her conversations with Black pupils vividly recall the experience of working-class pupils in pre-war grammar schools where the local dialect was the object of "eradication" and the confused and contradictory response this evoked in the pupils who were being culturally "straightened out."

What is striking is that the dynamic writing from within the black community, for example from writers like Linton Kwesi Johnson, proved to appeal to young people both white and black, and the "non-standard" nature of the language proved no barrier, but part of its appeal.

Can mainstream publishers make sure of these new generations of young writers? Some, perhaps. One or two, like the Bodley Head, are making the effort. It is a matter of whether the publishing system is flexible enough. But there are alternatives to orthodox publishing: there are community publishers, neighbourhood councils, bookshops, literacy classes, worker writers' circles, WEA classes, teachers' centres, schools themselves, local libraries. Sometimes "local" publication is anything but restricted. Centerprise reached a sale of over 10,000 copies with the poems of Vivian Usherwood.

In these publications local dialect, local language colour is not a disadvantage as it might seem to publishers with their national base and heavy central capital involvement. Nor is it essential that the critical apparatus should be able to digest or even understand the alternative publication, provided it can meet the critical response of its readers. The verdict of Arts Council pundits that the works published by worker writers' circles lack literary merit is being reluctantly abandoned.

Mainstream publishers *can* work with the alternative publishing network; indeed they neglect it at their peril, because this is where new writers are most likely to appear. So far the alternative publishers have not made great inroads into the field of fiction for the young. There have been some feminist stories for small children, some teenage writings, original and re-told folk stories from ethnic minorities. These are modest beginnings. The important thing is that, unlike the alternative movement of Chartists days, they are not abandoning the "wide and fruitful plain" of young reading to others.

Our new Renaissance, like our New Reformation, undoubtedly means a great deal of change and upset for conventional attitudes in the children's book world. Both have all the problems of the new, and the promise. The book will survive the age of change if the new is recognised and welcomed by the established, if all the public and private elements work together for a new literature looking outwards for its new readers.

19

What Future for the Book?

Is there a future for the book, or rather is there a future for fiction for the young in book form? Few would say "Yes", without hesitation. Even if we are not pessimists, and I do not think pessimists stay around the children's book world for long, we think long and hard before answering. The present, as we have already seen, is unsettling. The recent school and library cuts, a blow at the unhampered development of literature from a direction not foreseen in the 1984 myth, has caused alarm and despondency, as well as searches for alternative markets, some of which in themselves raise questions about the future of the Book as we have known it.

Political attacks on the wider diffusion of literature are not new. If the history of libraries is studied, it will be seen partly as a battle between book lovers and philistines – those, for example, who could write to the press in the 1890s "I would rather a young man went into a public house than a public library", those who delayed the provision of libraries in some areas right into the mid-twentieth century. Such people may have fallen silent between 1945 and 1975, but once again the cry of "why should we pay for other people's reading matter?" is heard.

But there is more to it than the periodic rise and fall of the philistine. The world of children's books, a product of this social and economic system, is sharing in its general crisis. Everything associated with this culture and its categories seems to have gone into the melting pot in the 1980s. Did not some miners vote for Mrs Thatcher in 1983 and do not ladies and gents in Town Hall and Whitehall go on strike and march with banners? Is any strand in our social fabric now whole?

Fiction for the young, it has been said, came with the onset of "childhood", children dressed as children, taken into protective custody in the nursery, the approach of adult cares delayed. Today, mums, daughters, dads and sons all dress alike, picture books are published which only adults can appreciate, OAPs in flight from the modern novel take refuge in the children's section of the library. Has children's literature served its purpose, and become redundant?

The "domesticated family" now seems socially and morally in disarray. The family of literature is no longer typical of life. Even the family as the bastion of virtue seems in danger. In *The Times* on June 2 1983, a parent who shared "adult" videos with the children, was reported as saying: "If anyone is going to be corrupted, it will only be us."

Is the book, symbol of the "literate" and civilised society with all the values implied, to go down into the darkness?

The video, known widely and inaccurately as the vehicle of the disgusting, is only part of the new surge of technology connected with communication, information, entertainment and ideology. The rapidity and power of this surge seems a threat to the book. "Are Books becoming redundant?" asked Sir Robert Lusty in *The Bookseller* (June 21, 1980). Dr Christopher Evans in *The Mighty Micro* (1979) speaks of the "death of the printed word . . . the 1980s will see the book as we know it and as our ancestors created and cherished it begin a slow but steady slide into oblivion."

A vision of a bookless, computer-run video indoctrinated and soothed society is conjured up, a situation like that in *Fahrenheit 451*, the book and film whose vision of the future shows books and book lovers as the hunted and persecuted freedom- and culture-loving minority, sandwiched between a dominant technocracy and a torpid television-watching majority.

All these warnings come from the heart of the book-loving minority of the population. And it is a minority still, though experts disagree on its size. The most optimistic conclusion, by UNESCO, is that even in countries where universal education is the rule, some 50 per cent of people read relatively little. We would be wrong to disregard these warnings. But we would also be mistaken if we did not examine them for traces of elitism, self-satisfaction, cultural conceit and social guilt. We need to avoid the trap of seeing the book as synonymous with education and culture and as being the base line from which everything else should be assessed. Some of the alarm at the prospect of the book's decline stems from the sacred aura the book has acquired in our culture – as the embodiment of the truth. With the notion of truth goes that of power. The idea that "they would not have written it if it were not true", is potent and dangerous, especially today, when 90 per cent of our daily press is owned by fewer people than would fit into the average minibus. Some of these people own TV and book publishing, not to speak of computer companies. When the truth/ power aura of the book is transferred to television, where we have two transmitters and twenty million receivers, we have the same problem writ larger. In this age we need the spirit of the early pioneers of bible and free press and it is the democratic element in the history of the book which needs to be enlarged.

For all its "sacral" quality, the book is in danger because its truth and power were largely annexed by one section of the population. A literature which throughout its history seemed to exclude, now in the audio-visual age stands in peril of being excluded because of its very exclusiveness. Television has out-flanked the book, which is ironic when you consider that without the book TV could not have been invented.

TV's advantage over the book lies largely in the fact that, though it is not as democratic a medium as the book can be, it is a popular medium. To be viable it needs a mass audience. It must overcome the barriers which have surrounded the book. With the told story there are no reluctant listeners, with TV one does not hear of the reluctant viewer. Ironically, the audio-visual media appear to be threatening the book at a point in its history when mass education and advanced printing technology could set the book on course for a new great era of development.

If one looks at the past 100 years, the picture is one of complexity, of co-existence and mutual stimulation between media, of rises and falls in fortune. But TV and film have not been guilty of the open hostility shown by the book towards the oral tradition. There has been no campaign of destruction on grounds of morality or ideology. On the contrary.

When the film arrived, it did not immediately challenge the book. At first its dialogue had to be printed, making the film like a large illustrated book whose pages turned independently of the reader. When sound track was added, freeing the new medium, much of its raw material came from the old. Before the war most people would not accept that a film adaptation could be better than the book. "Nothing like the book", was the usual criticism. Only in the 1940s did we hear the catch phrase, "I'll wait until I see the film." As film and then TV rose in public esteem (TV appeared to be destroying the film, but ended by feeding on it), both fed from the book, and as the supply of famous books diminished unknown works were adapted and became famous in their turn. TV carried these aspects to a new level. For it did its work within each household, doing it every day and not on occasion, publicly, like theatre and film. You *saw* a film, you *watched* television.

Like a permanently stationed rather than itinerant story-teller the television brings back to us old films like half forgotten remnants of a folk tradition. The long-running TV series with its teams and successions of often anonymous writers, its running story line, with endless variation and renewal, resembles the epic of pre-writing days. Television is more "primitive" than the book. To enjoy it you need what nature gave you, eyes and ears. Books on the other hand, in reading and writing, need a skill, artificially and recently developed. It is easier to watch TV than read a book. If a hunter-gatherer from the old stone age came into our home and found one of us watching the television, another reading a book, he would feel at home more rapidly with TV. The latest rumour is of nomadic tribes in North Africa delaying their time-hallowed departure from the oasis, to watch the last episode of *Dallas*. TV, behind the back of the book, has picked up strands from our earliest lives: acting, talking, dancing and singing which all belong with the oral tradition.

TV reminds us that the oral tradition has survived. Playground lore now uses advertising jingles to supplement the old nursery rhymes and music hall songs. With the help of the electronic media, our spoken language is renewed at a faster rate (or corrupted, if you are a purist) by a constant stream of new words. It is too simple to say that succeeding media destroy earlier forms. Old ways are changed, live elements persist. We live in a multi-media society; hence our confusion, hence our opportunity.

When writing was first invented, its potential for setting the mind free, by lifting the burden of memory, was recognised. The new media increase the possibilities of storage and retrieval (by reading) and so we may now begin more easily to realise the full potential of our minds, not only for retaining the past but exploring the future, making sense of what the whole of humanity has learned to date.

The ability to discern a pattern in nature, the material world, or in knowledge, is the hallmark of intelligence and its development should be the aim of learning. And since intelligence and emotion are linked together in the mind, fiction provides the incentive of pleasure in perceiving the pattern, the "plot" of life. The ability not only to read stories but to write them, the essence of the discovery of life's patterns, an active rather than a passive involvement, should be encouraged in every child.

Television reminds us with force that the book is not the only vehicle of the story. Its monopoly is broken. There is no future for the book if it is seen as the only true and valid bearer and developer of the story. The book has never been alone. It has always been linked with other media. When the Italian Punch and Judy show came to London in the 1820s, an enterprising publisher took down the dialogue and wrote the first "tie-in" book. Dickens was plagiarised in theatre and magazine simultaneously. *Alice in Wonderland* and *Wind in the Willows* owe much of their popularity not only to stage and film, but to reading aloud in class. *Worzel Gummidge, Toytown, Jennings, Dick Barton, My Naughty Little Sister, Grange Hill*, came to books via radio and TV.

Television has affected children's reading, though not in a straightforward way. During the years of the rise of TV, the story comic declined and the children's paperback flourished. But TV has changed what is published for children, and is helping to shift the centre of gravity of the literature as well as shifting the power of choice somewhat from adult to child.

The hierarchy of books is challenged by a new notion of success. When an author is asked by a school pupil, "Have you been on telly?" and seen the look of relief when the answer is "Yes", then it is realised that you begin to "exist" when linked to the new dominant medium. This is a change of fortunes indeed for book people, whose favoured medium, in its time, has caused many other people to cease to "exist".

Thanks to the television, in fact, there is an enormous new readership to be reached. Known at one time as the reluctant, or even "backward" readers, these have come now to be recognised as the unsatisfied readers. Can the literature respond to them? Does it have to? Does it want to?

Writing in *Fiction Magazine* (Spring 1982) John Rowe Townsend puts openly what others sometimes feel privately:

> The view that all children should be reading books for pleasure and that if they are not doing so there must be something wrong with the books, is mistaken in my opinion and leads to the dangerous demand that writers should produce simply written, easy, superficial books geared to the tastes of the unbookish child . . . it is not an obligation on the writer to produce books for the unbookish any more than it is an obligation on a composer to write music for the unmusical . . .

These are colours nailed to the mast of a sinking ship. To survive, a literature needs books, of all kinds, and it needs readers of all kinds, and above all it needs more of every kind.

As the UNESCO Report on *The Future of the Book* says, the book's fate in the decades to come depends first of all on whether these "under-consumers" can be won over to regular and pleasurable reading. This "popular" readership of books not only guarantees the continued publication of the "easy" and the "superficial", but also guarantees the future of the Literature with a capital L. Indeed, it has already done so. Literature with a limited readership appeal often depends for its life on two subsidies, one from the public, whatever their taste in books, and one from more popular authors on the publisher's list. A long line of such writers from Blyton onwards has helped indirectly to maintain the "quality" literature even while its authors were privately and publicly disparaging the "popular" authors.

Books which draw in the wider readership are the life-blood of the literature. It is they which maintain standards by making variety possible. Without them, without the backing of the wider public, much that is highly regarded among critics may wilt and die.

So without the "unbookish", the book *will* die. Like it or not, the book must live with the other media, and compete with them because without them, it might be less healthy. Likewise the other media have already seen the value of the book. TV companies invest in publishing, and every successful series must be crowned with its book or books.

This poses a new challenge to writers, not only what happens to their books if they allow someone else to adapt them, but what happens when a television firm or series is turned into a book. Is it to be packaged scripts, with "he said", "she said", inserted at high speed, or is it to be the book expression of the essence of the television? TV tie-ins are often judged to be of poor quality. Some are, but then, the same might be said of many "real" books, some of them written with the highest literary pretensions. Good and bad must be judged objectively and not by category.

What cannot be disputed is that the rivalry and cooperation with television has affected the writing style of every author writing for young people, giving dialogue greater importance, trimming down "purple" descriptive passages. One may test the extent of this by taking books written twenty years ago and compare them for pace with books written today. This change affects writers whether or not they have had direct contact with television writing; and indeed, the writer who seeks to work in various media is more and more typical.

If television has stolen a march on the book by drawing on the appeal of the oral tradition (life is an audio-visual experience when all is said and done), then the book can do no less. Writers who work directly with children, not only reading their own stories aloud, but helping the young story-maker to master the craft, reach the audience beyond the book. This audience may be bookish or unbookish, but it loves a story, and will take it from wherever it comes most pleasurably. Why not from the book? To abandon the quest for true universality, which was once held to be the great merit of the book, just when the goal is in sight, is to abandon the future of the book.

When writers go round to schools they restore the old contact between story-teller and audience, and restore it at a new level. This is because, unlike the story-teller of old, they do not depend upon the unsupported memory of their own minds and those of the audience. In the book they have an unparalled treasure store of stories old and new, long and short, simple and complex, from every language under the sun.

No longer isolated ivory tower dwellers, they increase their own number, and in numbers lies safety. Children for whom writer and writing are demystified are people who at last see the point of the book. They are the future of the book, its readers and its writers.

Showing children the pleasure and value in creating stories from their own existence and imagination is one key to unlocking to them the pleasure store of reading. The book, portable, hideable, repeatable, inexhaustible, a story to have and hold miles from the nearest power point, is still the cheapest way of getting a story when and where you want it, and likely to remain so for some time to come.

We live in a multi-media world. This offers great opportunities. The book will have its place, not an exclusive, nor a dominant place, but an indispensible one, a constantly changing and challenging one.

Not long ago, I was in a library in the Midlands, talking with and reading stories to a crowd of 12- and 13-year olds. In the adjoining room other young people were studying the library's stock of tapes and videos, yet others were searching the bookshelves, a few more were gathered round a games table. From the corner of my eye, I noticed that some were pausing to listen, through the open doorway. Others carried on with what they were doing, but I had the feeling they, too, were listening.

Bibliography

ALDERSON Brian (editor) see Darton, Harvey
(Translator) *The Brothers Grimm, Popular Folk Tales* (Gollancz, 1978)
ALTICK R. D. *The English Common Reader* (Chicago, 1951)
ARNE Antti and THOMPSON Stith *The Types of the Folk Tale* (Helsinki, 1961)
ARIES Philip *Centuries of Childhood* (London, 1962)
ARNOLD Guy *Held Fast for England: G. A. Henty, Imperialist Boy's Writer* (Hamish Hamilton, 1980)
ASHTON John (editor) *Chapbooks of the 18th Century* (1882) with new foreword by Victor Neuberg (Seven Dials, 1969)
AVERY Gillian, and BULL Angela *Nineteenth Century Children* (Hodder & Stoughton, 1965)
BARTON Griselda (see MEEK Margaret)
BLISHEN Edward (editor) *The Thorny Paradise* (Kestrel, 1975)
BONHAM CARTER Victor *Authors by Profession, Vol I* (Society of Authors, 1978)
BOWRA C. M. *Landmarks in Greek Literature* (Weidenfeld and Nicolson, 1966)
BRATTON J. S. *The Impact of Victorian Children's Fiction* (Croom Helm, 1981)
BRIGGS Katherine *A Dictionary of Fairies* (Allen Lane, 1976)
BULL Angela (see Avery, Gillian)
BURNETT John *Destiny Obscure: Autobiographies of Childhood, Education and Family, from the 1820s to the 1920s* (Allen Lane, 1982)
CAMDEN Carroll *The Elizabethan Woman* (New York, 1952)
CADOGAN Mary and CRAIG Patricia *You're A Brick, Angela: A New Look at Girls' Fiction from 1839–1975* (Gollancz, 1976)
CHADWICK H. M. and N. K. *The Growth of Literature* (Cambridge, 1940)
CHAMBERS Aidan *Introducing Books to Children* (Heinemann, 1973)
The Reluctant Reader (Pergamon, 1969)
CHAMBERS Nancy (editor) *The Signal Approach to Children's Books* (Kestrel, 1980)
CHAYTOR H. J. *From Script to Print* (Cambridge, 1945)
CLANCY M. T. *From Memory to Written Record* (London, 1979)
COLLINS A. S. *Authorship in the Days of Johnson* (London, 1928)
COVENEY Peter *The Image of Childhood* (Peregrine, 1967)
COX Jack *Take a Cold Tub, Sir: The Story of the Boys' Own Paper* (Lutterworth, 1982)
CRAIG Patricia (see Cadogan, Mary)
CROUCH Marcus *Treasure Seekers and Borrowers* (Library Association, 1962)
CUTT Margaret Nancy *Ministering Angels: A Study of Nineteenth Century Evangelical Writing for Children* (Five Owls Press, 1979)

DARTON F. Harvey *Children's Books in England: Five Centuries of Social Life, Third Edition* revised by Brian Alderson (Cambridge, 1982)

DIXON Bob *Catching Them Young (1) Sex, Race and Class in Children's Fiction (2) Political Ideas in Children's Fiction* (Pluto, 1977)

DOYLE Brian *The Who's Who of Children's Literature* (Evelyn, 1968)

EGOFF Sheila and others *Only Connect: Readings on Children's Literature* (OUP Toronto, 1969)

ELLIS Alec *A History of Children's Reading and Literature* (Pergamon, 1968)

EYRE Frank *British Children's Books in the 20th Century* (Longman, 1971)

FISCHER Ernst *The Necessity of Art* (Pelican, 1963)

FISHER Margery *Intent Upon Reading* (Brockhampton, 1964)
Who's Who in Children's Books (Weidenfeld and Nicolson, 1975)

FORRESTER Wendy *Great Grandmama's Weekly: A Celebration of the Girls' Own Paper, 1880–1901* (Lutterworth Press, 1980)

FOSTER John L. (editor) *Reluctant to Read* (Ward Lock Educational, 1977)

HILDICK Wallace *Children and Fiction* (Evans, 1974)

HILL Janet *Children are People* (Hamish Hamilton, 1973)

HOWARTH Patrick *Play Up and Play the Game* (Eyre Methuen, 1973)

INGHAM Jennie *Books and Reading Development: The Bradford Book Flood Experiment* (Heinemann Educational, 1981)

INGLIS Fred *The Promise of Happiness: Value and Meaning in Children's Fiction* (Cambridge, 1981)

JACKSON Donald *The Story of Writing* (Studio Vista, 1981)

JACOBS Joseph (editor) *English Fairy Tales* (London, 1898)

JAMES Louis *Fiction for the Working Man* (London, 1974)

KENNERLEY Peter (editor) *Teenage Reading* (Ward Lock Educational, 1979)

KIRKPATRICK D. L. (editor) *Twentieth Century Children's Writers* (Macmillan, 1978)

LEAKEY Richard and LEWIN Roger *People of the Lake* (Collins, 1979)

LEESON R. A. *Travelling Brothers: The Six Centuries' Road from Craft Fellowship to Trade Unionism* (Allen & Unwin, 1979)

LINDSAY Jack *A Short History of Culture* (Muller, 1967)

MCLUHAN Marshall *The Gutenberg Galaxy* (Routledge & Kegan Paul, 1967)
The Medium is the Message (Penguin/Allen Lane, 1967)

MANN Peter H. *From Author to Reader: A Social Study of Books* (Routledge, 1982)

MEEK Margaret *Learning to Read* (Bodley Head, 1982)

MEEK Margaret, BARTON Griselda; WARLOW, Aidan *The Cool Web: The Pattern of Children's Reading* (Bodley Head, 1977)

MILNE Christopher *The Enchanted Places* (Eyre Methuen, 1974)

MORLEY Dave and WORPOLE, Ken *The Republic of Letters: Working Class Writing and Local Publishing* (Comedia, 1982)

MUIR Percy *English Children's Books, 1600–1900* (London, 1954)

MARSHALL Margaret *An Introduction to the World of Children's Books* (Gower, 1982)

NEUBERG Victor (see Ashton, John)

OPIE Iona and Peter *The Classic Fairy Tales* (Paladin, 1980)
The Oxford Dictionary of Nursery Rhymes (London, 1951)
The Lore and Languages of Schoolchildren (OUP, 1959)
ORWELL George *Collected Essays, Journalism and Letters, Vol 1: An Age Like This, 1920–1940* (Penguin, 1970)
PONS J. *L'Education en Angleterre entre 1750 & 1800* (Paris, 1919)
QUAYLE Eric *Early Children's Books* (David and Charles, 1983)
QUIGLY Isabel *The Heirs of Tom Brown* (Chatto and Windus, 1982)
RAY Sheila *The Blyton Phenomenon* (André Deutsch, 1982)
SIMON Brian *Studies in the History of Education, 1780–1870* (Lawrence & Wishart, 1960)
Education and the Labour Movement, 1870–1920 (Lawrence & Wishart, 1965)
The Politics of Educational Reform, 1920–1940 (Lawrence & Wishart, 1974)
STEINBERG S. H. *Five Hundred Years of Printing* (Penguin, 1955)
STINTON Judith (editor) *Racism and Sexism in Children's Books* (Writers & Readers, 1979)
THOMPSON George *Marxism and Poetry* (Bombay, 1953)
THOMPSON Stith *The Folk Tale* (New York, 1946)
Types of the Folk Tale (with Arne, Antti)
TONGUE Ruth L. *Forgotten Folk Tales of the English Counties* (Routledge & Kegan Paul, 1970)
TOWNSEND John Rowe *Written for Children* (Kestrel/Pelican, 1964, 1974, 1983)
TREASE Geoffrey *Tales Out of School* (Heinemann, 1949, 1964)
TUCKER Nicholas *The Child and The Book: A Psychological and Literary Exploration* (Cambridge, 1981)
TUER Andrew W. *Old Fashioned Childrens' Books* (London 1899/1969)
TURNER E. S. *Boys Will be Boys* (Penguin, 1975)
VICINUS Martha *The Industrial Muse* (Croom Helm, 1974)
WALVIN James *A Child's World: A Social History of English Childhood 1880–1914* (Pelican, 1982)
WARDROPER John *Jest Upon Jest* (Routledge & Kegan Paul, 1975)
WARLOW Aidan *See Meek, Margaret*
WORPOLE Ken *See Morley, Dave*
WILLIAMS Gladys *Children and Their Books* (Duckworth, 1970)

Shorter Works, Reports etc.

ANON *The Bookseller* (in the London Tradesman, 1747)
ALDERSON Brian *Hans Christian Andersen and His Eventyr in England* (Five Owls Press/IBBY, 1982)
Looking at Picture Books (National Book League, 1973)
BIRD Jean *Young Teenage Reading Habits: A Study of the Bookmaster Scheme* (British National Bibliography Research Report, No 9, 1982)
BULLOCK A. *A Language for Life: Report of the Committee of Inquiry* (London HMSO, 1975)

CAM Helen *Historical Novels* (Historical Association, 1961)

CHILDREN'S RIGHTS WORKSHOP *Sexism in Children's Books: Facts, Figures and Guidelines* (Writers and Readers, 1976)

CUNNINGHAM Catharine *The Children's Market: A Discussion Paper* (Book Marketing Council, 1982)

FISHER Margery *British Children's Books* (National Book League, 1972)

GAULT Michael *The Future of the Book, Part II: The Changing Face of Reading* (Unesco Studies on Books and Reading, Paris, 1982)

H. M. INSPECTORATE *(Aspects of) Secondary Education in England: A Survey by H. M. Inspectors of Schools* (HMSO, 1979)

H. M. INSPECTORATE *Primary Education in England: A Survey by H. M. Inspectors of Schools* (HMSO, 1978)

JENKINSON A. J. *What Do Boys and Girls Read? – 1940* (Methuen)

LEESON R. *Children's Books and Class Society, past and present* (Children's Rights Workshop/Writers and Readers, 1977)

MANN Peter H. *Book Publishing, Bookselling and Book Reading* (Book Marketing Council, 1979)

MOSS Elaine *Children's Books of the Year 1972–1978* (Hamish Hamilton/NBL)

MOSS Elaine and Barbara SHERRARD-SMITH *Children's Books of the Year 1979* (Julia MacRae NBL)

NATIONAL BOOK LEAGUE *Working Party Report: Books For Schools* (NBL, 1979)

NATIONAL BOOK LEAGUE *(Public) Library Spending in England and Wales* (NBL, 1982)

RAY Colin (editor) *Story in The Child's Changing World: Papers and Proceedings of the 18th Congress of IBBY* (Cambridge, 1982)

RATHBONE Nicky *Mirth Without Mischief: An Introduction to the Parker Collection of Early Children's Books and Games* (West Midlands Library Association Occasional Pamphlets, No 2, 1982)

SCHOOLS COUNCIL *English in the 1980s: A programme of support for teachers* (Eyre Methuen, 1979)

SHERRARD Smith Barbara *Children's Books of the Year, 1980–1982* (Julia MacRae/National Book League)

STONES Rosemary *Pour Out the Cocoa, Janet: Sexism in Children's Books* (Schools Council Programme 3/Longman, 1983)

TOWNSEND John Rowe *25 Years of British Books* (National Book League, 1977)

WHITEHEAD Frank and others *Children and their Books* (Schools Council Research Studies, Macmillan, 1977)

Articles in Journals etc.

ASHTON Paul and SIMONS Michael *A Look at Books for Slow Readers* (English Magazine 1, Spring, 1979)

BALLANTYNE R. M. *Personal Reminiscences (1893)* Signal Reprint (Signal, 15, September, 1974)

CROXSON Mary *The Emancipated Child in the Novels of E. Nesbit* (Signal 14, May, 1974)

GREGORY Gerry *Working Class Writing: Breaking the Long Silence* (English Magazine, 4, Summer, 1980)

HUNT Peter *Criticism and Children's Literature* (Signal, 15, September, 1974)

HILL L. E. *A Readability Study of a Junior School Library* (British Journal of Educational Psychology, February, 1981)

JONES Martin *Where Charity Begins . . .* (Guardian, August 8, 1982)

LEESON R. *The Spirit of What Age?: The Interpretation of History from a radical standpoint* (Children's Literature in Education 23 Winter, 1976)

MACDONALD George *The Fantastic Imagination* (1908) Signal Reprint (Signal 16, January 1975)

MANN Andrew and STONES Rosemary *Censorship or Selection?* (Children's Book Bulletin, 3, Spring, 1980)

STRAHAN Alexander *Bad Literature for the Young* (1875) Signal Reprint (Signal 20, May, 1976)

SALMON Edward *Should Children Have a Special Literature?* (1890) Signal Reprint (Signal 11, May, 1973)

TOWNSEND John Rowe *The Outlook for Children's Fiction* (The Fiction Magazine, Vol 1, No. 1, Spring, 1982)

TUCKER Nicholas *Trends in School Stories* (Children's literature in Education, No 45, Summer, 1982)

Appendix:
The *Other Award* Criteria

The Other Award, for non-biased books of literary merit in the field of children's literature, was founded in 1975. The criteria employed by the Award Panel are regularly discussed, amended and published afresh each year for public debate.

The Other Award Panel considers books that have been published in Britain during the last year, including reprints and paperback editions. The Panel looks for books (fiction or non-fiction, realistic or fantasy, prose or poetry) that:

will be accessible, in form and content, to children and young people and will give pleasure and enjoyment.

have, as appropriate, imaginative, dynamic, credible, interesting features, i.e. the story-line and situations, illustrations, characterisation, sequencing and development and use of language.

contain credible depictions of all people, whatever their background, culture or occupation. For example:

a) more varied depiction of sex roles:

b) an accurate picture of the realities of different cultural and ethnic groups in society both in industrialised countries and in those countries experiencing "Third World" development and under-development;

c) accurate representation of the lives and occupations of different groups and classes in society, especially those usually ignored, patronised or misrepresented.

are historically accurate, and in text and illustration, present a people's history of events, not just of rulers and elites.

do not condone or take for granted the explicit or implicit values of compretititive individualism, the accumulation of wealth, hierarchical social organisation, the inevitability of superior/inferior social categories.

Book Choice:

A bibliography of progressive books for young readers selected by Rosemary Stones

This 1985 bibliography is a selection of children's books–novels, picture books, biography, poetry–published in the main in the sixties, seventies and eighties in Britain (althouth a few are from an earlier date) which illustrate the creative responses that progressive writers for children have made to recent social conditions.

It is not a comprehensive bibliography: I have tried to include only books in print at the time of writing (with a few exceptions) so that the list may be of practical use to those working with children and their books. I have also tried to avoid repeating information that is easily available from other sources and on occasion I therefore refer users of this bibliography to other publications. Space prevents me from including all the books I would like to have included and I have sometimes been obliged to list only one or two books from particular authors when I could have included all their work. The publication date given for each book is the date of first publication, either in Britain or elsewhere. I have given ISBN numbers for ease of reference.

Some of the books listed here are designated as *Other Award* winners. This annual award for progressive children's books was established in 1975 to draw attention to books which accord their rightful place to groups of people usually ignored, patronised or misrepresented in children's literature.

Rosemary Stones, 1985

History and Politics in Children's Books

1934 saw the appearance of Geoffrey Trease's *Bows Against the Barons* (a socialist view of Robin Hood) and *Comrades for the Charter* (the story of the Chartists from their point of view). These pioneering titles were the creative outcome of Trease's attempt to revitalise the fossilised adventure story of the period which was still, as Orwell remarked, "sodden in the worst illusions of 1910". And while the Cavaliers-are-a-good-thing approach to historical novels can still be found today, the number of progressive writers for children – both of historical fiction and of novels and picture books that treat contemporary political issues – has steadily increased since the 1930s.

But while recent books have touched on Northern Ireland, South Africa and even the Falklands, what is remarkable is what is still not covered in contemporary writing for children. The Palestinian Question is just one of today's burning political and moral issues that simply does not exist for British children's books.

ALLAN Mabel Esther
The Mills Down Below (1980)
Abelard   0 200 72638 2
The daughter of a mill owner, fourteen-year-old Eleanor, learns from working class Tom about the exploitation of the mill workers. The arrival of her Suffragette cousin Amy completes her education and the novel ends with Eleanor demanding to go to a local school and choose her own friends and future. A romantic story that nevertheless emphasises opportunities for girls outside marriage and women's struggle for equal rights. 10 years and upwards.

ANDERSON Rachel
The Poacher's Son (1982)
Lions   0 00 672251
Rural England before the First World War is the setting for this strongly told story of poverty and oppression as the Betts family are turned out of their cottage when the father is sacked unfairly from his job as gamekeeper. 10 years and upwards.

BALLARD Martin
Dockie (1972)
Kestrel   0 7226 5498 7
Lions   0 00 672228 8
With a background of unemployment and poverty in the London docklands of the 1920s, fourteen-year-old Moggy decides to try to find a way out as a boxer. Meanwhile Union activity is increasing in the docks and violent conflict with the police occurs on the picket line. A strongly written story based on working class history, but the book has dated – particularly in its depiction of women. 10 years and upwards.

BRIGGS Raymond
When the Wind Blows (1982)
Hamish Hamilton   0 241 10721 0
Penguin   0 14 00.6606 3
A bitterly ironic tale, in cartoon strip, of a retired couple, Jim and Hilda, who trustingly follow County Council leaflets as they build their 'Inner Core or Refuge' as nuclear attack threatens. This searing anti-nuclear story makes devastating use of the cartoon strip format.
(*Other Award* winner 1982). 10 years and upwards.

CARTER Peter
The Black Lamp (1973)
Oxford University Press   o 19 271356 6
Archway Novels   o 19 271497 X
The livelihood of the Lancashire weavers is threatened by the supplanting
of handlooms by machines in the early 1800s. Daniel, a weaver's son, is
one of those who marches to a rally in Manchester to protest – an event
which becomes known as the Peterloo Massacre. An outstanding book for
its powerful indictment of child labour in the mills and the effects on the
weavers of mechanisation. 10 years and upwards.

CARTER Peter
Under Goliath (1977)
Oxford University Press   o 19 271405 8
Puffin   o 14 03.11132 7
Alan, a young working class boy in the Belfast of 1969, is a 'Protestant of
sorts' and a lambeg player in an Orange Order band. Fergus is a Catholic
who pipes in a Catholic band. Their friendship falls victim to the divisions
of bigotry, unemployment and social injustice out of which the Civil Rights
movement is beginning to emerge. 10 years and upwards.

COOKSON Catherine
The Nipper (1970)
Puffin   o 14 03.05807
Sixteen-year-old Sandy's love for the pony he has reared but is forced to
sell, when he and his mother lose their farm jobs, leads him to take a job
in the mine where 'The Nipper' is now a pit pony. Terrible working
conditions, low pay and employment of young children from the workhouse drive the miners to fight for improvements. The novel ends
romantically (and unhistorically) but it is nevertheless firmly rooted in the
North-East mining experience of the early 1800s. 8–12 years.

COPPARD Audrey
Nancy of Nottingham (1973)
Heinemann   o 434 93302 3
Poverty following the introduction of the enclosure system forces Nancy
and her brother to Nottingham to live with their uncle, a hosier. When
Luddites begin to smash the new stocking frames, Nancy helps to unmask
a spy and she meets 'Captain Ludd'. An excellent portrait of working life
in the Nottingham of the period and one of the few novels about industrial
life to feature a girl as the central character. 10 years and upwards.

DARKE Marjorie
A Question of Courage (1975)
Kestrel   o 7226 5903 2
Lions   o 00 671212 6

A Long Way to Go (1978)
Kestrel 0 7226 5485 5
Each novel stands on its own but the two are connected by the women's
rights issue. In *A Question of Courage* working class Emily, a Birmingham
seamstress, joins forces with upper-class Louise in the fight for votes for
women. Darke spares the reader nothing of the realities of force feeding
and police violence as Emily moves to London and becomes one of Mrs
Pankhurst's bodyguards. London during the First World War is the
setting of *A Long Way to Go*, a richly devised novel which underlines the
links between the Suffragette movement and the continuing struggle, in
the munitions factories and elsewhere, for equal rights. Against this
background, mixed-race twins Bella and Luke face up to the implications
of Luke's decision to refuse his call-up papers, helped by Bella's new
friend Emily, once a Suffragette. 10 years and upwards.

EDWARDS Dorothy
A Strong and Willing Girl (1980)
Methuen 0 416 88630 2
Magnet 0 416 24590 0
Set in Victorian times, these vigorously told stories about a ten-year-old
working class girl, Nan, tell how she goes into service to support her
family. Based on her own family history, Dorothy Edwards presents a
lively and detailed account of the life of a young servant at the turn of the
century. (*Other Award* winner 1981). 8–12 years.

FOREMAN Michael
Dinosaurs and All That Rubbish (1972)
Hamish Hamilton 0 241 92234 7
Puffin 0 14 050.098 7
Moose (1972)
Puffin 0 14 050 073 1
War and Peas (1974)
Hamish Hamilton 0 241 89013 6
Michael Foreman's allegorical picture books blend his distinctive
illustrations, notable for their luminous tonality and sometimes menacing
imagery, with seemingly simple story lines that, together, express complex
ideas about society in ways that can be understood by the very young.
Thus in *Dinosaurs* his theme is pollution and the distribution of wealth; in
Moose it is the fate of the poor nation caught up unwittingly in the wars of
the super-powers; in *War and Peas* it is the relationship between the
industrialised nations and the Third World. Under 6 years.

GRAY Nigel
The Deserter (1977)
Lions 0 00 672029 3
Four children find a soldier who has deserted from Northern Ireland and

is on the run. As they hide him they learn about the war in Northern Ireland and the hard choices that faced the soldier when he served there. 10 years and upwards.

GRICE Frederick
The Bonny Pit Laddie (1960)
Oxford University Press 0 271498 8
Puffin 0 14 03.1190 4
The son of a miner, Frederick Grice's best work is those novels that embody the history and spirit of the Durham mining community he grew up in. Set at the turn of the century, *The Bonny Pit Laddie* tells how twelve-year-old Kit is obliged to leave school and go down the pit to support his family as his father, a strike organiser, has been refused work. *The Oak and the Ash*, Grice's other outstanding novel, has long been out of print. (A 1977 *Other Award* winner for his contribution to children's literature.) 10 years and upwards.

HUNTER Mollie
The Ghosts of Glencoe (1966)
Hamish Hamilton 0 241 89478 6
Robert Stewart, an Ensign in the King's army, is moved by the dignity and culture of even the poorest of the Glencoe Highlanders amongst whom he is billeted. When he is given his orders to take part in their massacre he refuses and risks his life and his future career. A carefully researched and compelling story based on the events and people of the Massacre of Glencoe. 10 years and upwards.

HUNTER Mollie
A Pistol in Greenyards (1965)
Hamish Hamilton 0 241 89152 3
The 'Clearance' of Greenyards in 1854 when Highland tenant farmers were brutally evicted from their homes to make way for sheep farming is the historical background to this powerfully written story in which young Connal Ross attempts to defend his home with a pistol and must then flee for his life. 10 years and upwards.

IRWIN Hadley
We are Mesquakie We are One (1980)
Sheba 0 907179 25 8
As Native American peoples are forced on to the reservations their culture and very survival are threatened. Hidden Doe, a Mesquakie woman, is determined that the Mesquakie way of life shall survive. 10 years and upwards.

JONES Toeckey
Go Well, Stay Well (1979)
Bodley Head   o 370 30176 5
Lions   o 00 672030 7
South Africa, 1976, and a friendship develops between Candy, from the
prosperous white suburbs, and Black Soweto dweller Becky, both sixteen-
year-olds. This unusual friendship becomes the vehicle for drawing
attention to the injustices of apartheid with its pass laws, Bantu 'education'
etc. This part of the book will help young readers to understand
something of the reality of South Africa but the fundamental racist notion
that white people would inevitably lose their freedom under democratic
Black majority rule (a view expressed by Candy) is not countered or
discussed. This book is included here as one example of how crucial
present day political issues are being treated in children's literature.
10 years and upwards.

KHERDIAN David
The Road from Home, The Story of an Armenian girl (1979)
Julia MacRae   o 86203 050 1
In 1915 the Turks began a systematic persecution of the Armenian
community and thousands of Armenians were massacred. David Kherdian
recreates in this moving novel the story of his Armenian mother's
miraculous survival and her emigration at the age of sixteen to the U.S. as
a 'mail-order bride'. 10 years and upwards.

KOEHN Ilse
Mischling Second Degree (1977)
Puffin   o 1403 1356 7
Germany 1937 and eight-year-old Ilse's parents inexplicably divorce. War
breaks out and Ilse is sent to evacuation camps and she joins the Hitler
Youth Movement. It is only at the end of the war that she learns that she is
a 'mischling' (half-Jew) and her parents' separation was for her protection.
A memorable autobiography. 10 years and upwards.

LEESON Robert
'Maroon Boy (1974)
Lions   o 00 672097 8
Bess (1975)
Lions   o 00 672218 0
The White Horse (1977)
Collins   o 00 184136 x
Lions   00 672252 0
Spanning the reign of Elizabeth I to the Civil War, this picaresque
adventure trilogy breaks new ground by its inclusion of aspects of our
history not previously treated in children's historical fiction. Thus in
'Maroon Boy, a merchant apprentice, Mathew, goes to sea but he is to free

his ship's cargo of slaves and join forces with the Cimaroons. In *Bess*,
Mathew's sister Bess refuses to accept conventional notions of a woman's
place, and dresses as a man as she seeks her brother in far-off lands, while
in *The White Horse* Bess' son Matt rides at Cromwell's side in the Civil
War. 10 years and upwards.

LEWIN Hugh
Jafta – My Father (1981)
   0 237 45545 5
Jafta – My Mother (1981)
   0 237 45544 7
Jafta – The Journey (1983)
   0 237 45676 1
Jafta – The Town (1983)
   0 237 45677 x
Evans; illus. by Lisa Kopper.
A white South African who spent seven years in prison for opposing
apartheid, Hugh Lewin wrote the *Jafta* stories for his own children to
explain to them something of the life of a Black child in a South African
'homeland'. Jafta's father must live away from his family in the city to
make money and *My Father* describes Jafta's grief at his absence and
memories of the happy times they had together. *My Mother* is a companion
portrait of a woman alone, caring for her children and labouring
ceaselessly, yet finding time to hug and talk to her children. In *The
Journey*, Jafta and his mother make the difficult journey to town to see his
father, while in *The Town*, Jafta describes the fun they had together before
the next painful separation. The young reader is presented with a family
whose hard life and separation are the result of an inhuman régime. These
books are written in strong, poetical cadences and the illustrations, in a
sepia brown, are well researched and full of feeling. Under 6.

MARUKI Toshi
The Hiroshima Story (1983)
A & C Black   0 7136 2357 8
A true account of what happened to two victims of the Hiroshima atom
bomb, seven-year-old Mii-chan and her mother, told and illustrated by an
artist who went into the burnt-out city to try to help survivors. 10 years
and upwards.

MELIA Gerard
Will of Iron (1983)
Longman Knockouts   0 582 20036 9
The early life of Will Thorne, the founder of the General and Municipal
Workers' Union, inspired this sensitively written play which traces the
struggle of Thorne and his fellow workers to overcome the hardship and
poverty of their condition and take steps to organise themselves into a

Union for the unskilled. (*Other Award* winner 1983). 10 years and upwards.

NAIDOO Beverley
Journey to Jo'burg: A South African Story (1985)
Longman Knockouts   0 582 25208 3/0 582 24391 2
Thirteen-year-old Naledi and her younger brother Tiro are scared that
their baby sister will die. They decide to run away to Johannesburg (300
kilometres away) to fetch their mother who has had to go and work there,
separated from her children. On their way the children meet kind people
who feed and hide them and the reader builds up a picture of life for
Black people in the racist regime of South Africa. Written with great
clarity and simplicity, this moving story will shock and anger young
readers. 8 years and upwards.

PRICE Susan
Twopence a Tub (1975)
Faber   0 571 11660 4
Based on local records and family memories of the Dudley miners' strike
of 1851 for twopence per tub of coal filled, this outstanding novel
powerfully and realistically depicts the exploitation and suffering of the
mining community. And there is no happy ending – the miners are forced
back to work with a cut in their wages to three farthings a tub. (*Other
Award* winner 1975). 10 years and upwards.

REES David
The Green Bough of Liberty (1979)
Dobson   0 234 72187 1
A significant chapter in the long and bloody history of the Irish struggle
against the British was the rebellion of 1798 in which more than 30,000
died. Movingly written, this sensitive novel recreates the incidents and the
people of the time. (*Other Award* winner 1980). 10 years and upwards.

REISS Johanna
The Upstairs Room (1972)
Puffin   0 1403 1139 4
The Jewish de Leeuw family in German-occupied Holland are forced to
separate and go into hiding. Ten-year-old Annie and her elder sister Sini
spend over two years in the upstairs room of a kindly farming family until
liberation comes. A tragic and moving story based on Johanna Reiss' own
experience of hiding from the Germans. 10 years and upwards.

SEARLE Chris (Ed.)
Wheel Around the World (1983)
illus. by Katinka Kew
Macdonald   0 356 09213 5
An outstanding collection of poems from around the world which
celebrate the diversity and the unity of all peoples, recognising their

struggles against oppression now and in the past. Poets range from Langston Hughes, Paul Robeson and Bertold Brecht to children. (*Other Award* winner 1984). 8–12 years.

DR SEUSS
The Butter Battle Book (1984)
Collins 0 00 195005 3 (Hardback)
0 00 195006 1 (Paperback)
A rhyming story from the exuberant nonsense poet Dr Seuss which puts its finger on the absurdity of the arms race and the threat of nuclear weapons. A wall divides the Yooks and the Zooks and war escalates between them to the point where each side threatens total destruction. A brilliant anti-nuclear fable that will help young readers to understand the moral issues that face the world. 6 years upwards.

SUTCLIFF Rosemary
Song for a Dark Queen (1978)
Pelham 0 7207 1060 X
Knight 0 340 24864 5
The story of Boudicca (Boadicea) has always represented in the public imagination resistance against foreign occupation. This powerful novel recreates the woman and the tribe who were to sack three Roman cities and to bring about – almost – the end of Roman imperialism in Britain. (*Other Award* winner 1978). 10 years and upwards.

TREASE Geoffrey
Bows Against the Barons (1934)
Hodder & Stoughton 0 340 04043 2
First published in 1934, this adventure story version of the Robin Hood legend emphasises the oppression of the peasantry within the feudal system and the economic reasons for the Crusades. The book has dated (characters say 'Good Lord!' and 'Grab him!') but it is vigorously written and its socialist perspective is as refreshing today as it was in the 30s. 8–12 years.

WATSON James
Talking in Whispers (1983)
Gollancz 0 575 03272 3
Lions 00 672378 0
This tensely written novel draws on the tragic events of the last decade in Chile depicting and discussing the political realities of this military dictatorship and paying homage to the courage of those who continue to confront and struggle against the repressive régime. 10 years and upwards. (*Other Award* winner 1983).

The Freedom Tree (1976)
Gollancz 0 575 02094 6

Based on the recollections of veterans of the International Brigade, this is a novel that uses the conventions of the adventure story to portray international solidarity and the struggle against fascism in the Spanish Civil War. Will from Jarrow joins the POUM, experiences fighting at the Front and is in Guernica when it is obliterated by Nazi air power. 10 years and upwards.

WILLARD Barbara
The Iron Lily (1973)
Kestrel 0 7226 6040 5
Puffin 0 1403 0741 9
One of the 'Mantlemass' novels, set in Ashdown forest in Sussex, which trace the history of two families from the battle of Bosworth Field to the Civil War and which include a number of interesting female characters, none more so than in this novel in which Lilias Rowan becomes an iron master with her forge. 10 years and upwards.

Changing Community: Stories of Home and School

As Bob Leeson wrote in *Children's Books and Class Society* (Writers & Readers 1976), "the modern school story must essentially come to grips with the life of working class children and their home background." Leila Berg in *Look at Kids* (Penguin Education 1972) wrote of the "laughter of acceptance, of recognition" with which working class seven-year-olds greeted her stories about the children recognise the presence of disabled people in the community, the multi-racial . . . had seen themselves portrayed in preserves that hitherto were middle class and alien. They didn't have to pretend to be someone else anymore. They were released."

Today, books which portray our changing community are also books which recognise the presence of disabled people in the community, the multi-racial nature of British society today and the real and changing place of women. Some of these concerns are developed in other sections of this bibliography.

ABUK Chris
Maxine's Piano (1983)
Longman 'You and Me' books 0 582 39250 0
A young Black girl, Maxine, loves making up songs on her piano – but when her family move into a flat the piano is too big to fit into the lift or go up stairs. Then Maxine remembers her friend Junior, the crane driver . . . A warmly told, brightly illustrated small format paperback. Under 6.

ASHLEY Bernard
High Pavement Blues (1983)
Julia MacRae 0 86203 105 2
Saturday market stall holder Kevin meets hostility from the traders at the next pitch when he sets up his mother's stall but he cannot count on

anyone to help him out. A toughly written novel of family break-up and
London street life. 12 years and upwards.

ASHLEY Bernard
Linda's Lie (1982)
Julia MacRae   0 86203 099 4
Linda's Dad is unemployed and there is no spare money for school
outings, and no question of 'favours' from the school being accepted.
Linda loves the ballet and tries to cover up the truth when a trip to the
ballet is being organised – but events get out of hand . . . A sensitively told
story with a Black central character. 6–8 years.

AVERY Valerie
London Morning (1969)
Pergamon English Library   0 08 006432 9
Born off the Old Kent Road in 1940, Valerie Avery completed the first
draft of this lively autobiography when she was sixteen and a pupil at
Walworth School, one of the first comprehensives. This funny, touching
book records family and school life in her working class neighbourhood –
the trauma of failing the 11+, getting her high heels stuck in a grating on
a first date, etc. 12 years and upwards.

BERG Leila
A Box for Benny (1958)
illus. by Jillian Willett
Magnet   416 45350 3
A collection of stories about a small Jewish boy, Benny, who plays a game
of exchange hoping to come by the shoebox he needs for a children's
street game. Based on Leila Berg's own Salford Jewish childhood, this
acutely observed and warmly told book builds up a convincing portrait of a
street community and of a child's imaginative world. 6–8 years.

BROWNE Anthony
A Walk in the Park (1977)
Hamish Hamilton   0 241 89397 6
Working class Mr Smith, daughter Smudge and dog Albert meet middle
class Mrs Smythe, son Charles and dog Victoria in the park. Class barriers
break down between the children and the dogs who enjoy playing
together, but the adults remain aloof. A brightly illustrated picture book,
full of surreal detail, that comments cleverly on the divisions between
people in class society. Under 6.

BURR Sybil
Life with Lisa (1958)
Puffin   0 1403.1172 6
'I thought they [posterity] might want to hear about another Ordinary

Person (me) because my life is very interesting in parts', writes twelve-year-old Lisa, a student at Secondary Modern School in the fifties, to explain her decision to write this extremely witty and acute diary which looks sharply at the class divisions and pretensions of the community she lives in. 12 years and upwards.

CATE Dick
Old Dog, New Tricks (1978)
Hamish Hamilton   0 241 89949 4
Puffin   0 14 03.1270 6
Set in a mining village near Durham, *Old Dog, New Tricks* is one of four short novels about Billy and his family (the other titles are *Flying Free, A Nice Day Out?* and *A Funny Sort of Christmas*). It charts with subtlety and humour the upheavals that suddenly affect each generation of Billy's family – his Dad loses his job in the pit, his sister and her miner husband must move away to find work and his Gran buys an impossibly volatile dog in Durham market. Written in robust local language, this beautifully constructed short novel is a warm family portrait within which each member emerges in her or his own right, regardless of age or sex, to tackle the problems that confront them. 8–10 years. (*Old Dog, New Tricks* was an *Other Award* winner in 1979)

CAWLEY Winifred
Gran at Coalgate (1974)
Oxford University Press   0 19 271366 3
Silver Everything and *Many Mansions* (1976) (in one vol.)
Oxford University Press   0 19 271389 2
Based on Winifred Cawley's own Tyneside childhood in the 1920s, these two lively, humorous books tell how, when Jinnie is eight and her father has not found work for a year, the family put all they have left into a shop in a different part of town (*Silver Everything*). In *Gran at Coalgate*, Jinnie, now eleven, spends a holiday away from her strict Chapel parents with Gran who lives in a Northumberland mining community. It is here that Jinnie learns about strikes – and about dances, short skirts and bobbed hair. 10 years and upwards.

DE LARRABEITI Michael
The Borribles (1976)
Bodley Head   0 370 10898 1
Piccolo   0 330 26857
The Borribles go for Broke (1981)
Bodley Head   0 370 30413 6/0
Piccolo   0 330 281 763
Two extraordinary fantasy sagas in which the working class Borribles (scruffy, tough Londoners with pointed ears) first defend Battersea Park from the posh Rumbles who are trying to colonise it and then, joined by

some Bangladeshi Borribles from Spitalfields, fight to the last to free their captured friends. 10 years and upwards.

DICKINSON Mary
Alex and Roy (1981)
illus. by Charlotte Firmin
Deutsch　o 233 17347 8
Scholastic　o 590 70161 4
Alex, a small white boy who lives with his single parent Mum, is in a bad mood when his Black friend Roy comes to play – but then he doesn't want Roy to go home. A warmly told picture book that captures the reality of pre-school friendships. Under 6.

DOHERTY Berlie
How Green You Are! (1982)
Methuen　o 416 20940 8
Lions　o oo 672210 5
Narrated in the first person by eleven-year-old Bee, this lively collection of short stories tells of the exploits of a group of children who live in the same street in a working class neighbourhood near Liverpool. Bee's mother works at a laundry and 'Toad', one of the best of the stories, tells how she organises her fellow workers (all women) to go on strike over working conditions – much to the amazement of Bee's Dad. 8–12 years.

GARNER Alan
The Stone Book Quartet
Collins (1976–78)　o 00184282 x/00184289 7
The history of a Cheshire village family of craftspeople from the 1860s to World War II is traced in this quartet of books, based on Garner's family history, each one recalling a childhood in a particular generation and yet interweaving with the other stories to recreate a universe of shared skills and knowledge. 12 years and upwards.

GIFFORD Griselda
Jenny and the Sheep Thieves (1975)
Gollancz　o 575 02019 9
Nine-year-old Jenny convalesces at her grandparents' farm and makes friends with children from a new town nearby, catching some sheep thieves on the way. Jenny turns out to be as good at fighting (and better at tree climbing) as the boys and the book also has the grandparents sharing the work of house and farm. 8–12 years.

GRANT Gwen
The Lily Pickle Band Book (1982)
Heinemann　o 434 94137 9
Lions　o oo 672081 1

Lily Pickle lives in a mining town on the 'far tip of Nottinghamshire' and this bouncily written first person account of how a children's band was formed, and the people in it, is pacily and amusingly told. 8–10 years.

GRANT Gwen
Private – Keep Out (1978)
Lions 0 00 671652 0
Knock and Wait (1979)
Lions 0 00 671762 4
One Way Only (1983)
Heinemann 0 434 94136 0
Lions 0 00 672290 3
The youngest of a large Nottinghamshire family (Dad is a miner, Mum works in the fields and does cleaning), Gwen Grant's stubborn, high-spirited heroine is eleven in *Private – Keep Out*, the first volume of her 'diary', which begins in 1948. Each of these three books chronicles her experiences humorously and with gusto: in *Knock and Wait* she describes the painful year she spends at an Open-air school to cure her anaemia, far from her family, while in *One Way Only* she is confidently back on home ground and we have reached 1950. 10 years and upwards.

HAIGH Sheila
Watch for Smoke (1978)
0 416 86380 9
Watch for the Champion (1980)
0 416 87390 1
Methuen Pied Pipers
Two books from a number of lively adventure stories featuring a group of school friends from different social and family groupings (Smoke lives with her foster mother; Dan's Dad is made redundant and his family are in debt). The books also stand out for their non-stereotypical treatment of sex roles – in *Watch for Smoke*, Smoke helps Dan overcome his fear of swimming while in *Watch for the Champion* Angus and Dan encourage and support Smoke while she trains for a gymnastics competition. 8–10 years.

HUTCHINSON Lindsay
The Victorious School Strike (1979)
illus. by Squim
from Bookbane, 7 Mary Road, Handsworth, Birmingham
A racist teacher insults a Black school student and the students eventually go out on strike, growing in confidence as they manage their campaign. Hutchinson's style is rather awkward but she conveys the feel of racial tension and her use of different characters to symbolise aspects of the struggle comes off well. 12 years and upwards.

HEASLIP Peter
The Terraced House Books: Sets A–F (1980–1983)

photos by Anne Griffiths and John Bennett
Methuen Educational
Each set of four simply written beginner readers in this outstanding series
focusses on everyday happenings for the urban child at home, at school
and in the community and reflects unselfconsciously, via compelling
photographs, the multi-racial composition of British inner cities and the
extended family, as well as presenting women and men in non-
stereotypical roles. (*Other Award* winner 1981). 6–8 years.

HUNTER Mollie
A Sound of Chariots (1972)
Hamish Hamilton   0 241 02368 8
Lions   0 00 67 2092 7
Bridie McShane is the fourth daughter of a poor working class Scottish
family in the twenties, and she writes poetry. The burdens of poverty and
of a rigidly class divided society are added to by the traumatic death of her
father, and Bridie withdraws into herself. A sensitive, partly
autobiographical story of a working class girl who is determined to write.
10 years and upwards.

KEEPING Charles
Shaun and the Cart-Horse (1966)
    0 19 279624 0/0 19 272110 0
Joseph's Yard (1969)
    0 19 279651 8
Through the Window (1970)
    0 19 279655 0
Oxford University Press
Born and brought up in Kennington, Charles Keeping produces
atmospheric picture books (worked in black or coloured inks) that portray
the streets, yards, docks and markets of working class South London with
detail, sympathy and often with emotional intensity (Joseph watching a
flower grow). Under 6.

KNUTTSON Rolf
Torkel (1970)
Burke 'Read for Fun' books   0 222 99338 3
One of the first picture books available in Britain about a single parent
family, *Torkel* (from Sweden) is about a five-year-old boy who lives with
his Dad and visits his Mum who lives nearby. One day he and Dad are
followed home by a stray cat – will Dad let Torkel keep it? Under 6.

LEESON Robert
Harold and Bella, Jammy and Me (1980)
Hamish Hamilton   0 241 10722 9
Lions   0 00 671606 7
A finely told series of semi-autobiographical stories narrated in the first

person about a Northern small town childhood which ends with a scholarship to the grammar school and the outbreak of World War II. 10 years and upwards.

The Demon Bike Rider (1976)
Lions   0 0067 1320 3
Challenge in the Dark (1978)
Lions   0 00 671648 2
The Adventures of Baxter and Co. (both titles in one vol.)
Collins   0 00 184124 6
In their last year at Primary school, Mike Baxter and his friends think the story of a ghost on Barker's Bonk is a joke – until they see the 'demon bike rider'; while in *Challenge in the Dark*, Mike's first week at the comprehensive means coping with a bully. Narrated in the first person by Mike, these two brisk, lively stories are strongly rooted in their Northern working class community setting. 8–10 years.

Candy for King
Collins (1983)   0 00 184136 X
A sparkling, tongue-in-cheek account of the rites of passage of the proverbial innocent abroad, Kitchener Candeford, expelled from school in the Northern town of Barnswick in the fifties. After many adventures, encounters and travels (Candy joins the army) he learns his true parentage and, on the way, much about British society. 12 years and upwards.

The Third Class Genie (1975)
Hamish Hamilton   0 241 10623 0
Lions   0 00 671633 4
Genie on the Loose (1984)
Hamish Hamilton   0 241 11177 3
Lions   0 00 672294 6
Two fast-moving, funny novels about Northern teenager, Alec Bowden, and his friends which incorporate fantasy into a working class community and school setting. In *The Third Class Genie* a Black genie materialises only to be classified as an illegal immigrant while in *Genie on the Loose* a young, inexperienced Black genie creates havoc but also manages to help defeat the school's racist bullies. 10 years and upwards.

LINGARD Joan
The Clearance (1974)
    0 241 89021 7/0 600 20299 2
The Resettling (1975)
    0 241 89258 9/0 600 20300x
The Pilgrimage (1976)
    0 241 89399 2/0 600 20301 8
The Reunion (1977)
    0 241 89753 x/0 600 20302 6
Hamish Hamilton/Beaver
Four lively, warmly written stories about working class Glaswegian

Maggie, a bright spark always full of ideas who encourages her family to move and start their own plumbing business when her mother cannot cope with living in a tower block. Maggie also plans to read anthropology at university and her ideas about female behaviour are not the norm for her peer group. Lingard is one of the most accessible writers for younger teenagers today. 10 and upwards.

MACGIBBON Jean
Hal (1974)
Heinemann   0 434 94986 8
Wheaton   0 08 025619 8
Puffin   0 1403.0968 3
Hal, or Gloria, as the West Indian heroine of *Hal* is really called, coaxes invalid Barry back to health as she persuades him to leave his lonely flat. Her dynamic personality pervades this story of London children from different cultural backgrounds who are trying to build an adventure playground on a derelict site. (*Other Award* winner 1975). 10 years and upwards.

MARK Jan
Hairs in the Palm of the Hand (1981)
Kestrel   0 7226 5728 5
Puffin   0 1403 1441 5
Two witty short stories about school life: in *Time and the Hour* a class in a boys' school work out how much time is wasted each school day, while in *Chutzpah* Eileen spends her first day at a comprehensive inciting different classes to act on issues of democracy and women's rights – only to exit mysteriously at the end of the day. 10 years and upwards.

MOORE Inga
Aktil's Rescue (1983)
Oxford University Press   0 19 279772 7
When reggae fan Aktil sees that Izzy of the 'Rat Racers' needs help, he gets caught up in a dramatic kidnapping. An imaginative picture book adventure for older readers with witty touches of the contemporary reggae scene. 6–8 years.

NAUGHTON Bill
The Goalkeeper's Revenge (1961)
Puffin   0 14 03.0348 0
My Pal Spadger (1977)
Puffin   0 14 03.1379 6
Two funny, laconic yet moving books about the lives of working class communities in the industrial Lancashire of the twenties. *The Goalkeeper's Revenge* is a collection of thirteen short stories including the hilarious *Seventeen Oranges* about a thief who eats the evidence and *Maggie's First Reader* about a housewife who turns to writing. *My Pal Spadger* traces the

friendship of two young men in Bolton who leave school together to work in mill and mine. *The Goalkeeper's Revenge* won the 1978 *Other Award*. 10 years and upwards.

NEEDLE Jan
The Bee Rustlers (1980)
Magnet   0 416 29310 7
Losers Weepers (1981)
Magnet   0 416 30170 3
Two short novels set on a Yorkshire farm which reflect the lives of country children with great zest and reality. In *The Bee Rustlers*, Carol and Tony discover a gang of honey thieves about to raid their Mum's hives – but Tony is afraid of bees. And in *Losers Weepers* their discovery of an antique sword leads to unexpected complications. 8–10 years.

A Pitiful Place (1984)
Deutsch   0 233 97560 8
A collection of ironic, pessimistic, sometimes funny short stories about the lives of a handful of teenagers who have just left school – Christine has her baby taken into care; Wally is a soldier in Northern Ireland; Milly hangs around a far-right group; David becomes a casualty of the Falklands war. 12 years and upwards.

NOSTLINGER Christine
The Cucumber King (1972)
trans. by Anthea Bell
Andersen Press   0 86264 057 1
Beaver   09 933940 4
When a deposed monarch who looks like a cucumber seeks asylum in the Hogelmann household, trouble begins. Dad takes a liking to the sly, petulant autocrat but Wolfgang and Martina discover the king's sinister plans for his ex-subjects. A witty fantasy that comments unobtrusively on the way power is used within the family and in society. 8–10 years.

Conrad the Factory Made Boy (1976)
Andersen   0 905478 037
Beaver   0 600 32002 2
Mrs Bartolotti is always sending away for special offers, so when a large can arrives she is not surprised. When it turns out to be a mail-order son who says 'Hullo, Mummy!' on seeing her, she gets more than she bargained for especially as Conrad has been programmed to be very truthful and well behaved. If he's to survive at school drastic measures are needed . . . A comic tale that is very astute about the way people are taught to behave towards each other. 8–10 years.

PRICE Susan
From Where I Stand (1984)
Faber   0 571 13247 2

Kamla Momen is known as a quiet conscientious sixth former who does not react to racist comments. But when Kamla joins forces with Jonathan Ullman who is obsessed with the twentieth century's record of war, death camps and genocide, she decides it is time to speak out about racism at school via a public news-sheet. A tough school story that breaks new ground in its complex discussion of anti-racist struggle by young people. 12 years and upwards.

SHYER Marlene Fanta
Welcome Home, Jellybean (1978)
Granada   0 583 30485 0
A toughly realistic, sensitively told story about the pressures and frustrations that Neil's family faces when his active mentally handicapped older sister returns home for good. Love and understanding, but also misery and despair are recorded in this pioneering and unsentimental USA novel. (*Other Award* winner 1982). 8–12 years.

SMITH Vian
Come Down the Mountain (1967)
Kestrel   0 7226 5311 5
Working class Brenda, a grammar school fifth former, is a timid unassertive girl until her compassion for a neglected horse and the need to care for it force her out of her shell. A sensitive, strongly written story full of class conflict set in a rural Dartmoor community. 10 years and upwards.

WILSON Jacqueline
Nobody's Perfect (1982)
Oxford University Press   0 19 271463
Lions   0 00 672159 1
Fifteen-year-old *Spare Rib* reader and aspiring writer Sandra is fed up with her very ordinary (and overweight) family: mother, stepfather, stepsister. She decides to have a go at finding her father who might be an improvement. Her friend Michael (small and puny) is not perfect either . . . A comic, touching book about a girl finding her feet. 10 years and upwards.

YOUNG Helen
What Difference Does it Make, Danny? (1980)
Deutsch   0 233 97248 X
Lions   0 00 672219 9
Nine-year-old Danny has epilepsy but that does not stop him doing sport until a new games teacher arrives at his school. A lively school story that helps to dispel myths about epilepsy. 8–10 years.

The Impact of Black American Writers

The substantial Black British presence in the inner cities of the fifties and sixties created a more obvious discrepancy than before between the ideas, the values and the people portrayed in children's literature and the audience for that literature. Young Black Britons reacted by seeking out books by Black American writers. As Julius Lester put it (*The Black American in Books for Children*, The Scarecrow Press 1972), "Blacks know their condition on a gut level, but to have that articulated, to read about it in a book is to become conscious where before one was unconscious. It is the black writer's job to tell black people about themselves."

Black British teachers Keith Ajegbo and Roxy Harris in their useful selections from Black American writers (listed below) have responded to the need to make such writings more easily available. In the seventies some of the finest Black American children's writers began to be published in Britain and their books underlined the need for new directions in British publishing.

AJEGBO Keith
Black Lives White Worlds (1982)
Cambridge Educational   0 521 28463 5
A skilful selection of extracts from 20th century Black American writing, which all tackle the relationship of Black people to white society, while also providing a record of changing Black consciousness. A powerful introduction for teenagers to such important writers as Toni Morrison, James Baldwin, Ralph Ellison and Richard Wright. (*Other Award* Winner 1982). 12 years and upwards.

CAINES Jeanette
Daddy (1977)
illus. by Ronald Himler
Harper & Row   0 06 020923 2
A young Black girl longs for Saturdays when her father will come to collect her. A picture book that tells, with tenderness, of the relationship between a father and daughter who no longer share the same house. Under 6.

GUY Rosa
The Friends (1974)
Gollancz   0 575 01839 9
Puffin   0 14 03.0933 0
Edith Jackson (1979)
Gollancz   0 575 02607 3
The Disappearance (1980)
Gollancz   0 575 02804 1
Ruby (1981)
Gollancz   0 575 03052 6
New Guys Around the Block (1983)

Gollancz 0 575 03271 5
Born in Trinidad, Rosa Guy is a Black American writer who became
president of the Harlem Writers' Guild and whose dramatic,
compassionate, very contemporary novels treat the lives of Black Harlem
teenagers. *The Friends, Edith Jackson* and *Ruby* are novels that stand alone
but each is related to the others, developing characters and relationships
over a time span of a few years and probing in depth the options open to
young Black women – Phylissia, Edith, Ruby, Daphne.

The Disappearance and *New Guys Around the Block* have a teenage boy,
Imamu Jones, as the central protagonist and the setting is again Harlem –
but Guy now also includes Black middle class characters for whom
Imamu's street world is unknown territory.

The Friends is justly popular with British school students (and is now a
set book for one examination board) but until they are made available in
paperback Guy's other books will not reach the wide audience they
deserve. 10 years and upwards.

HAMILTON Virginia
M. C. Higgins the Great (1975)
Hamish Hamilton 0 241 89214 7
Justice and her Brothers (1979) OP
Hamish Hamilton 0 241 10152 2
Dustland (1980)
Julia MacRae 0 86203 080 3
The Gathering (1981)
Julia MacRae 0 86203 037 4
Virginia Hamilton is the grand-daughter of a slave who escaped from the
South to Ohio and *M. C. Higgins the Great* reflects the preoccupation of
her earlier books (not all published in the U.K.) with Black history and
cultural identity as Black teenager M.C. defends his mountain home, the
place where his slave grandmother came as she escaped with her child.

Justice and her Brothers, Dustland and *The Gathering* represent a move
away from the roots/identity theme; they are a cycle of fantasies, again
with Black protagonists, about the nature of future society and the genetic
information that we will bring to it. 12 years and upwards.

HARRIS Roxy
Being Black
Selections from *Soledad Brother* and *Soul on Ice* (1981)
New Beacon 0 901241 39 3
Short extracts from George Jackson and Eldridge Cleaver's famous books
with explanatory notes and questions to consider are presented here by
teacher Roxy Harris as a response to young Black school students' "strong
desire for reading material with which they could make some connection,
and which would enable them to explore their own experience." 12 years
and upwards.

LESTER Julius
Long Journey Home (1973)
Puffin   0 14 03.0903 9
Basketball Game (1974)
Puffin   0 14 047.106 5
A Taste of Freedom (1983)
Longman Knockouts   0 582 20128 4
Julius Lester's beliefs that "history is the lives of the people" and that the
role of the Black writer is to "tell Black people about themselves" find
powerful expression in his short stories about slavery times (*Long Journey
Home, A Taste of Freedom*) and in his memorable portrait of a Black middle
class family in the Nashville of the 1950s (*Basketball Game*) whose 14 year
old son breaks the unwritten rules by becoming friends with a white girl –
but it can't last. 10 years and upwards.

TAYLOR Mildred
Roll of Thunder, Hear My Cry (1977)
Gollancz   0 575 02384 8
Puffin   0 1403.1129 7
Let the Circle Be Unbroken (1982)
Gollancz   0 575 03084 4
Puffin   0 1403.1605 1
Drawing on her own family history, Mildred Taylor traces in these two
outstanding novels the story of a Black Mississippi farming family, the
Logans, during the Depression years. Narrated by Cassie Logan (nine in
Roll of Thunder, eleven in *Let The Circle Be Unbroken*), the books reveal
starkly the everyday injustices suffered by the Black community. The
Logans' belief that they have "some choice over what they make of their
lives" makes them an obvious target for the "nightriders". 10 years and
upwards.

Britain Through the Eyes of Black British Writers and Illustrators

I do not cover here books for the multi-racial society already covered in other
booklists such as Judith Elkin's *Multi-Racial Books for the Classroom* (Youth
Libraries Group 1980, from The Central Library, Paradise Street, Birmingham
B3 3HQ), Ruth Ballin, Jean Bleach and Josie Levine's *A Wider Heritage* (The
National Book League 1980; from Book House, 45 East Hill, London SW18
2QZ); and Anne Kesterton's *We All Live Here* (1983, also from The National
Book League). Children's books for the multi-racial society do now exist, if not
in profusion, then in sufficient numbers for an assessment of their value and
impact to be possible and necessary.

The disjuncture between the audience (Black and white) for such books and
the small number of writers and illustrators with sufficient knowledge, sen-
sitivity and skill to write and illustrate them is a continuing problem. It is a
problem most imaginatively tackled by the Black community itself with the

emergence in the sixties of Black bookshops like New Beacon (established 1966) and Bogle L'Ouverture (established 1969 and now renamed The Walter Rodney Bookshop) which also began to publish books – some children's books too. One of the first such books was Phyllis and Bernard Coard's *Getting to Know Ourselves* (Bogle L'Ouverture 1972), a colouring book for under sixes which explained, simply and clearly, the links between African and Caribbean peoples. It was intended, as Jessica Huntley of Bogle L'Ouverture wrote in a publisher's note, "to assist the young Black child in his search for his identity. [Books] should help to bridge the gap between our peoples in the Old and New Worlds."

In 1985 there are still too few Black British writers and illustrators for children:

AGARD John
I Din do Nuttin (1983)
illus. by Susanna Gretz
The Bodley Head   0 370 30459 4
Magnet   416 49760 8
Born in Guyana, John Agard has lived in Britain since 1977. He has broken new ground by writing one of the first poetry books for younger children in Creole to be published by a mainstream British publisher. Talking about his poetry Agard commented: "We function in a bilingual way, some of the poems grow out of me in straight English, some in Creole." *I Din do Nuttin* is a collection of funny, lively poems, some set in Guyana, some in Britain, some written in "straight English", some in Creole and featuring Black and white children. 6–8 years.

BELL Mal
Marcia's Birthday Wish (1984)
illus. by Gilroy Brown
Affor   0 907127 11 8
from Affor, Lozells Social Development Centre, 173 Lozells Road, Lozells, Birmingham B19 1RN.
Marcia's secret birthday wish every year is to go to school like her big brother Omari, but only when she reaches her fifth birthday does her wish come true. An amusing and warmly told story about a small Black girl from the white author of *The Black Rose* (now sadly OP) with pictures by a new Black illustrator Gilroy Brown. Under 6.

BREINBURG Petronella
My Brother Sean (1973)
Bodley Head   0 370 02025 1
Sean's Red Bike (1975)
Bodley Head   0 370 10781 0
illus. by Errol Lloyd
Puffin   0 14 05.0253 X
The first full colour picture book from a Black writer and a Black illustrator about a Black British family, *My Brother Sean* appeared in 1973.

It is the story of a small boy Sean who "always wanted to go to school" but who has ambivalent feelings about it on his first day there ("Sean cried"). Lloyd's strong, bright pictures convey Sean's mixed emotions dramatically. Despite its quality and its pioneering example as an authentic representation of the Black British experience, *My Brother Sean* did not appear in paperback until 1978 and this has now long been out of print. *Sean's Red Bike* has a slightly older Sean saving up for the red two-wheeler he longs for and doing odd jobs for neighbours and friends to earn money – looking after a baby cousin, cleaning a neighbour's car. Domestic and street scenes convey a strong sense of a multi-racial neighbourhood. Under 6.

Sally-Ann's Umbrella (1975)   0 370 10752 7
Sally-Ann in the Snow (1977)   0 370 01809 5
Sally-Ann's Skateboard (1979)   0 370 30166 8
illus. by Ossie Murray
Bodley Head
Written in response to a request from girls at a South London Infants' School for a "companion for *Sean*", *Sally-Ann's Umbrella* is a picture book about a small Black girl, Sally-Ann, who lives with her mother and her aunt. Sally-Ann takes her new umbrella to school to show her friends but it is blown away in a gust of wind and has to be rescued.

In *Sally-Ann in the Snow*, Sally-Ann overcomes her fear of tobogganing ("I'll never be scared of that old slope again") in a story that infectiously conveys the fun of snow fights and sleighs. In *Sally-Ann's Skateboard* there is a dramatic chase down the street when a boy goes off on Sally-Ann's brand new fibreglass skateboard. All three *Sally-Ann* books, with their bright chalk illustrations, reflect life in multi-racial South London in a positive and relaxed way. Under 6.

Brinsly's Dream (1976)
illus. by Margaret Theakston
Puffin   0 1403 11112 2
Brinsly (of West Indian origin) is obsessed with football to the point where he often forgets about anything else. His team has a good chance of winning the football trophy – until Brinsly is kidnapped. The family scenes in this story are traditionally sexist but the characterisation of Brinsly is lively and appealing. 6–8 years.

Us Boys of Westcroft (1975)
Macmillan Topliner   0 333 18815 2
A Black South Londoner, Walter has been taken into care and sent to a "posh" school where sharp lines are drawn between the local well-off "lads" and the boys from the Home. When a Black teacher, Miss da Sousa, arrives, conflicts come out into the open. Told in the first person by Walter, this is a sharply realistic story of life at a very tough school. 10 years and upwards.

THE CROSSFIELD FAMILY
Seven of Us (1978)
arranged by Alix Henley
photos by Jeremy Finlay
A & C Black 'Strands' series   o 7136 1830 2
The West Indian Crossfield family (Mum, Dad, Aunty and four children)
describe their lives in London and the adults also remember their
childhood in Jamaica.

This kind of photo-story, which is intended to provide information
about ethnic minority history and culture as well as providing a positive
portrayal of an ethnic minority family in Britain, is typical of many such
books published in the last few years by A & C Black ('Strands') and more
recently (and for a younger age range) by Hamish Hamilton (see for
example, *A Day with Ling* by Ming Tsow).

Such books have been criticised for giving a "worthy" and "community
relations" view of multi-ethnic Britain. Certainly the lives of ethnic
minority families in Britain are more problematic, dynamic and interesting
than these series have so far been able to convey, but given the paucity of
material which reflects the ethnic diversity of our society, these books
continue to have a valuable role – especially, as so many teachers have
attested, for children in Primary schools. *The Crossfield Family* was the first
of these books to be written by an ethnic minority family about themselves.
8–12 years.

DHONDY Farrukh
East End at Your Feet (1976)
Macmillan Topliner   o 333 19962 6
Come to Mecca (1978)
Collins   o oo 184134 3
Lions   o oo 6715 19 2
Two collections of punchy, often funny, and subtle short stories about
Asian, Black and white London teenagers. *East End . . .* is set in the East
End of London and the stories tell, for example, how Bhupinder finds that
conventional Indian views about women just don't apply to his lovely sister
Manju ("Dear Manju"), while a white boy on a housing estate finds out
what racist violence is when the Asian family next door is attacked
("KBW"). (*Other Award* winner 1977)
Come to Mecca has stories set in the East End and in South London about
teenagers at school and in their first jobs. In "Free Dinners" a white boy
remembers the mixed race girl at school he fancied and what became of
her, while "Go Play Butterfly" takes the preparations for the Notting Hill
Carnival as its background. (*Other Award* winner 1979)

Trip Trap (1982)
Gollancz   o 575 03193 x
Lions   o oo 6724 28 o
Eight short stories about young Londoners, Asian and white, and which

include fables and fantasy. In "The Bride", for example, Jaswinder makes Tony into her "brother" and comes back to find him after her death, while "The Fifth Gospel" has a search for an isolated band of Christians whose version of Christ's death is significantly and mysteriously different from that in the other Gospels. 12 years and upwards.

EMECHETA Buchi
Titch the Cat (1979)
illus. by Thomas Joseph   0 85031 252 3
Nowhere to Play (1980)
illus. by Peter Archer   0 85031 266 X
Allison & Busby
Nigerian writer Emecheta who lives in London (and is well known for her adult novels) wrote her first children's books basing them on stories by her eleven year old daughter.

In *Titch the Cat* a Black London family panic when their kitten goes missing and then seems very ill when found. Narrated by eleven-year-old June, the story builds up a lively family portrait.

In *Nowhere to Play* a multi-ethnic group of children have "nowhere to play" during their school holidays and get into a series of scrapes and escapades. 8–10 years.

GAVIN Jamila
The Orange Tree (1979)
illus. by Ossie Murray
Methuen Read Aloud Books   0 416 86240 3
A collection of short stories from an Anglo-Indian writer set in an English city and featuring children from many different ethnic minority families (Polish, Irish, Chinese etc).
Kamla and Kate (1983)
illus. by Thelma Lambert
Methuen "Read Aloud" Books   0 416 22780 5
Six-year-old Kate longs for a friend so she is delighted when six-year-old Kamla's family move into her road. Kamla and Kate share many adventures and also make discoveries about each other's ethnic identities and ways of life. 6–8 years.

JOHNSON Linton Kwesi
Dread Beat and Blood (1975)
Bogle L'Ouverture   0 904 521 060
Born in Jamaica in 1952, Linton Kwesi Johnson came to join his parents in London when he was eleven and he went to Tulse Hill comprehensive. His poetry began to be published in the magazine *Race Today* and gave expression to the experiences of the first generation of West Indian youth to be educated in Britain. Johnson's first major collection of poems, *Dread Beat and Blood* was written in "London Jamaican" and became

immediately popular with young white as well as young Black Londoners, with its powerful treatment of the themes of confrontation and resistance to oppression. 12 years and upwards.

KHAN Hassina
Tariq Learns to Swim (1983)
illus. by Bal Athalye
Bodley Head   0 370 30530 2
Hassina Khan is an Englishwoman married to an Asian but *Tariq Learns to Swim* is included in this section of books by Black British writers and illustrators by virtue of its fine illustrations from a new children's book illustrator, Bal Athalye, who is an Indian living in Manchester. In this story Tariq feels excluded at school because he is no good at football. His father suggests that he learn to swim instead and Tariq soon gains confidence. Athalye's strong, atmospheric illustrations convey feelings as well as capturing well domestic interiors, playground and swimming pool. 6–8 years.

LLOYD Errol
Nandy's Bedtime (1982)
Bodley Head   0 370 30395 4
A picture book for very young children which tells how a small Black girl, Nandy, spends her evening – helping with the dinner, having a bath and getting into bed. Nandy's mother and father are seen sharing tasks in this warm, simply told domestic story. Under 6.

Nini at Carnival (1978)
Bodley Head   0 370 30023 8
Nini on Time (1981)
Bodley Head   0 370 30301 6
Two brightly illustrated picture books about a small Black British girl, Nini. In *Nini at Carnival*, Nini (who looks about six) feels left out of carnival because she has no costume until her friend Betti helps her to improvise one. The crowded pages are filled with children, white as well as Black, parading and dancing in their finery (which incorporates costume detail observed at the Notting Hill carnival).

In *Nini on Time*, Nini (now looking about eight), sets off with her friends to the zoo but they miss the bus. As they walk along hoping for a lift they find they have arrived there without realising it. Lloyd's street scenes (clearly North London's Camden Town) reflect the multi-racial composition of the inner city and present a delightful, bustling mixture of families, couples, groups, young and old, going about their daily business in scenes that convey a strong sense of neighbourhood. Under 6.

MING Tsow
A Day with Ling (1982)
photos by Christopher Cormack
Hamish Hamilton   0 241 10828 4

An English girl, Anne, spends the day with Chinese friend Ling and finds out how to use chopsticks and how to do Chinese writing. The children also visit a Chinese supermarket with Ling's father. Clear, bright photographs help to tell this photo-story. (See discussion of The Crossfield Family's *The Seven of Us*). 6–8 years.

SMITH Rukshana
Sumitra's Story (1982)
Bodley Head   0 370 30466 7
Refugees from Amin's Uganda, eleven-year-old Sumitra's family come to Britain. Life (for a time at a Homeless Families Hostel) is tough as the family settles in. For Sumitra, growing up in Britain may mean breaking away, faced as she is with new possibilities not acceptable to her family. 12 years and upwards.
Rainbows of the Gutter (1983)
Bodley Head   0 370 30526 4
Contradictions and confusions surround Black London teenager Philip who sees himself as a painter without a political perspective. In contrast his sister is a Black militant and her boyfriend a Rastafarian. A naive but angrily written novel of contemporary Black lives. 12 years and upwards.

ZEPHANIAH Benjamin
Pen Rhythm (1980)
    0 907373 00 3
from Page One Books, 53 West Ham Lane, Stratford, London E15
Dedicated to 'the children of the city', Rastafarian poet Benjamin Zephaniah's punchy, often funny poetry is very popular with, and accessible to, teenagers. After comprehensive school in the Midlands, Zephaniah did time in borstal and prison and poems about these experiences, as well as his thoughts on the need for understanding and love, are included in this collection. 12 years and upwards.

Sex Role Presentation in Children's Books

Work on sex role presentation in children's books began in Britain in the early seventies, and the first reviews and lists of non-sexist children's books relied heavily on Scandinavian and North American children's books published in Britain (e.g. Ann-Cath Vestly's *Aurora and the Little Blue Car*, Lila Perl's *That Crazy April*).

Fairy tales in particular came under attack for their presentation of females as "pretty, dutiful and compliant" and in 1972 four Merseyside feminists wrote their own versions of well known traditional tales – their *Red Riding Hood*, for example, kills the wolf herself while Granny helps by brandishing a burning torch. By the end of the seventies, feminist research into folk and fairy tales had also led to the "rediscovery" of traditional tales with "forgotten" heroines who "can fight and hunt as well as any man". Examples of rewritten and rediscovered tales are included here.

Changes in society's expectations of women and men and feminist criticism of sex stereotyping have stimulated a most positive creative response from some children's book writers and illustrators which can be seen in the "domestic" picture book for the very young which now invariably reflects less rigid sex roles within the family (e.g. Shirley Hughes' *Helpers*), in adventure stories for middle age range readers in which girls are now equal protagonists with boys (e.g. Penelope Lively's *The Revenge of Samuel Stokes*) and in teenage novels which treat sensitively the contradictory expectations which confront young people in contemporary society (e.g. Robert Leeson's *It's my Life*). And the challenging of female sex role stereotyping has inevitably led to a reassessment of the way that male characters are depicted in children's books (see, for example, Jean Ure's *A Proper Little Nooryeff*).

Below I list a short selection of non-sexist children's books since other bibliographies in the field are now available – for example Penguin's *Ms Muffet Fights Back* (from Penguin Books, 536 Kings Road, London SW10 OUH) and the updated *Spare Rib List of Non-Sexist Children's Books* (from Spare Rib, 27 Clerkenwell Close, London EC1).

ACKROYD Audrey et al.
Red Riding Hood
The Prince and the Swineherd
Rapunzel
Snow White
illus. by Trevor Skempton
Once and Future Tales (1972)
from 53 Sandown Lane, Liverpool L15 4HU
Four traditional tales rewritten by four Merseyside feminists, "in the belief that our society can never be fundamentally changed while children's imaginations are imprisoned by its myths". The new versions have Red Riding Hood stabbing the wolf through the heart herself and Rapunzel escaping from the tower by climbing down her own plait of hair. 6–8 years.

AHLBERG Allan
Mrs Plug the Plumber (1980)
illus. by Joe Wright
Kestrel 0 7226 5659 9
Puffin 0 14 03.1238 2
One of the "Happy Families" series for beginner readers based on the characters from the card game but jokily updated with non-sexist detail as Mrs Plug the plumber deals with all kinds of plumbing emergencies. 6–8 years.

ANDERSEN Hans Christian
The Snow Queen (1979)

illus. by Errol le Cain
Kestrel 0 72265487 1
Puffin 0 14050.294 7
One of Andersen's most powerful and beautiful tales, *The Snow Queen* is
unusual in that every positive character is female – Gerda, the witch, the
princess, the fierce but kind-hearted Robber Girl – while it is a boy who
must be rescued. This picture book version of the tale has Le Cain's
stylish illustrations. Under 6.

ARDIZZONE Edward
Diana and her Rhinoceros (1964)
Magnet 0 416 45260 4
Diana Effingham-Jones, a small girl in suburban Richmond, befriends the
sick rhinoceros who appears in the family drawing room (bravely
defending it from gun-toting zoo-keepers) and then grows happily in the
course of years into a "comfortable middle-aged lady" with the rhino for
company. Told with Ardizzone's inimitable boldly and clearly drawn
illustrations and a gently satirical text. Under 6.

BURNINGHAM John
Come Away from the Water, Shirley (1977)
Cape 0 224 01372 6
Lions 0 00 662147 3
A picture book for older children with two stories that interweave and
comment on each other, this subtle, witty book has Shirley's Mum and
Dad in their deckchairs on the beach endlessly nagging her (" . . . don't
get any of that filthy tar on your nice new shoes"), while on the opposite
pages Shirley rows out to a galleon, battles with pirates and finds buried
treasure. A fantasy or an allegorical comment on the limitations imposed
on her? 6–8 years.

COLES Diana
The Clever Princess (1983)
illus. by Ros Asquith
Sheba 0 907179 20 7
Arete, the clever princess, is married off by her father to an evil magician
and imprisoned in a dungeon. Granted three wishes by her friend the
witch, Arete uses them to keep herself amused while she plans her escape.
6–8 years.

COOMBS Patricia
Molly Mullet (1977)
World's Work 0 437 32794 9
Molly is dismissed by her father the king as a "sneezly, wheezly, snivelling
girl" but she is the one to take on the local ogre and show him once and
for all that she is as good as his knights, if not better. 6–8 years.

DAHL Roald
Revolting Rhymes (1982)
illus. by Quentin Blake
Cape   0 224 02932 0
Puffin   0 14 050.423 0
This exuberant retelling of six well known folk tales includes Dahl's
version (in verse) of *Little Red Riding Hood* in which Miss Hood acquires a
wolfskin coat. She returns to rescue the third pig in *The Three Pigs* ("once
more the maiden's eyelid flickers/she draws the pistol from her knickers")
but is then seen with a pigskin travelling case . . . 6–8 years.

DE LA MARE Walter(reteller)
Molly Whuppie (1983)
illus. by Errol le Cain
Faber   0 571 11942 5
A picture book version of the traditional tale in which Molly outwits the
giant three times and marries her sisters and herself to a king's sons (who
are not asked if *they* want to get married). Le Cain's decorative full colour
illustrations on the left hand pages are faced with elegant silhouette
drawings that underline or move forward the events of the story. Under 6.

DE PAOLA Tomie
Oliver Button is a Sissy (1979)
Methuen   0 416 89650 2
Magnet   416 24540 4
Oliver Button is a boy who "didn't like to do things that boys are supposed
to do" and he spends his time skipping, reading, dressing up, playing with
dolls and . . . dancing. Tormented at school ("la-de-doo, you gonna dance
for us?"), Oliver finally wins acceptance when he performs a stunning tap
routine at a talent contest. One of the few books for the very young about
male sex-stereotyping. Under 6.

DR SEUSS
Horton Hatches the Egg (1940)
Collins   0 00 195302 8
Mayzie is a lazy, non-maternal mother bird who gets bored with sitting on
her egg and flies off for a vacation to Palm Beach leaving Horton the
elephant in charge. Horton sits dutifully on the egg through thick and thin
and his love and devotion are finally rewarded when the egg hatches. . . . A
funny, touching story about the just deserts of a nurturant male. 6–8 years.

DUMAS Philippe
Laura, Alice's New Puppy (1976)
Gollancz   0 575 02568 9
Lions   0 00 671770 5
Laura and the Bandits (1978)

Gollancz   0 575 02834 3
Lions   0 00 672043 9
With very little text and superb pen and ink drawings, these two
entertaining books tell of the exploits of Alice and that brave and loyal dog
Laura (rescuing the children from drowning, capturing art thieves), ably
supported by their non-sexist family ("Dad made the sandwiches",
"Grandad boiled some eggs".) 6–8 years.

FELL Alison
The Grey Dancer (1981)
Collins   0 00 184267 6
Lions   0 00 671946 5
Set in the fifties in the Highlands of Scotland, past and present
mysteriously interact in this powerfully written novel rooted in women's
history. Eleven-year-old Annie hears the tragic story, from the time of the
Clearances, of Lal and Isobel who married according to the rites of the
Old Religion – of Bride, mother of fire and crops – only to be separated in
death. 10 years and upwards.

FIRMIN Charlotte
Claire's Secret Ambition (1979)
Papermac   0 333 34181 3
Claire's single parent Mum works as a cinema usherette and she is
determined that her daughter Claire will be a star. Claire has acting and
dancing lessons but her secret ambition is to be a vet . . . An entertaining
and well illustrated picture book about a small girl determined to decide
her own future. Under 6.

FITZHUGH Louise
Nobody's Family is Going to Change (1974)
Gollancz   0 7226 6262 9
Lions   00 671109 X
The Sheridans are Black middle class New Yorkers with a conventional
life style. When Emma (11) announces her determination to be a lawyer
and Willie (7) wants to be a dancer, battle is joined. Daddy thinks that
men who dance are sissies and Daddy *and* Mama disapprove of women
lawyers. Full of punchy dialogue and caustic wit, this book glows with life
and humour. (*Other Award* winner 1976). 10 years and upwards.

FOREMAN Michael
All the King's Horses (1976)
Hamish Hamilton   0 241 89291 0 (OP)
The story of a princess who "wasn't the milk-white, golden-haired, pink
little number the way princesses are supposed to be". When suitors come
to vie for her hand they find themselves facing a wrestling match – with
the princess. A witty exploitation of folk tale convention to demonstrate
female autonomy and independence. Under 6.

GOBLE Paul
The Girl Who Loved Wild Horses (1978)
Macmillan   0 333 27107 6
Picturemac   0 333 32176 6
A beautifully told and illustrated picture book about a Native American
girl who loves horses ("people noticed that she understood horses in a
special way".) One day the village horses stampede with the girl and meet
up with the wild horses who roam the hills. The girl returns home to her
parents but misses her new life ("I love to run with the wild horses") and
she returns to live with them. Under 6.

HARPER Anita
How We Work (1977)
illus. by Christine Roche
The Kids Book Group
Puffin   0 14 050.283 1
Together with *How We Live* (now out of print) this book was one of the
first children's books by British feminists to be published by a mainstream
publisher. Wittily illustrated in cartoon style it discusses in images and
simple words complex ideas about the nature and conditions of work,
which kinds of work are paid well, poorly or not at all and who does them.
A double page spread compares the working day of a "traditional"
husband and wife with the caption "some people have one job/some
people have more than one job". Under 7.

HEDLUND Irene
Mighty Mountain and the Three Strong Women (1984)
A & C Black   0 7136 2398 5
A tongue-in-cheek folk tale set in Japan about a mighty male wrestler on
his way to a wrestling match at the Emperor's palace when he meets
Kumiko, her mother and grandmother – all three stronger than he is . . .
6–8 years.

JACKSON Rosalind & JOHNSON Pamela
City Summer and Other Stories (1980)
A & C Black   0 7136 2019 6
A collection of five short stories in which "Match of the Day" deals
directly with the issue of sexism as it affects first years at a multi-racial
urban comprehensive. Georgia gets a girls' football team together only to
find that the referee does not take his responsibilities seriously because it's
"only the girls". How the team overcomes the prejudice against them is
well told in a lively exciting story. 10 years and upwards.

JACOBS Joseph
English Fairy Tales (1890)

Bodley Head   0 370 01023 X
Puffin   0 1403.0466 5
"Molly Whuppie", the story of the girl who outwits the giant three times,
and "Kate Crackernuts" which tells how brave Kate rescues the prince
from the little people, are included in this selection from the tales
collected by Joseph Jacobs in the 1880s. 6–8 years.

HUGHES Shirley
Helpers (1975)
Bodley Head   0 370 10756 X
Lions   0 00 661463–9
Teenager George comes to babysit for Mick, Jenny and baby Sue because
"mother has to go out today". Bright lively pictures of a young man
involved in childcare and housework and all the children helping each
other to get through the day. (*Other Award* winner 1976). Under 6.

KEMP Gene
The Turbulent Term of Tyke Tiler (1977)
Faber   0 571 11405 9
Puffin   0 14 03.1135 1
Told in the first person by Junior school student Tyke, this lively, funny
book chronicles a last term at Cricklepit Junior School packed with
incident and adventure. Comic and unpatronising and written from an
obvious first-hand knowledge of school life, this book has an unexpected
twist to do with sex roles. (*Other Award* winner 1977). 8 years and
upwards.

KLEIN Robin
Thing (1982)
illus. by Alison Lester
Oxford University Press   0 19 554330 0/0 19 554549 4
Pets are not allowed in the flat where Emily and her single parent mother
live, so Emily finds a pet rock – which turns out to be a baby stegosaurus
which keeps on growing. How "Thing" brings the landlady round to
Emily's point of view is told with dead-pan humour and lively line
drawings. 6–8 years.

LEAF Munro
The Story of Ferdinand (1937)
illus. by Robert Lawson
Hamish Hamilton   0 241 90177 4
Puffin   0 1403 0328 6
Ferdinand the bull likes to "sit just quietly and smell the flowers" instead
of fighting with the other bulls. This classic story of the bull who did not
want to fight has been claimed by pacifists but more recently by feminists
who see Ferdinand as a non sex-stereotyped male. 6–8 years.

LEESON Robert
It's My Life (1980)
Lions 0 00 671783 7
When sixteen-year-old Jan's mother inexplicably leaves home, Jan is
expected to take over responsibility for the household. The questions she
begins to ask herself about her mother's life lead her to plan a different
future for herself. A sensitive, searching look at contemporary options for
girls. 12 years and upwards.

LISTER Mary
Princess Polly to the Rescue! (1984)
illus. by Ron Hanna
Methuen 0 416 49890 6
When Haggis the witch carries off Prince Tom to feed to her pet dragon
rather than succulent Princess Polly, the dragon is not amused. Neither is
Princess Polly, who immediately sets out on a complicated and dangerous
quest to rescue Prince Tom. A pacey, amusingly told modern folk tale.
8–10 years.

LIVELY Penelope
The Revenge of Samuel Stokes (1981)
Heinemann 0 434 94899 6
Puffin 0 14 03.1504 7
Jane ("some kind of natural disaster area") and her friend Tim, both ten-
year-olds, move into a new housing estate built on the site of an eighteenth
century garden. The shade of the gardener, Samuel Stokes, is not too
pleased and much entertaining havoc results, especially in relation to the
accident prone Jane ("Jane cracked the other glass of her spectacles").
8–12 years.

LURIE Alison (Ed)
Clever Gretchen and other Forgotten Folk Tales (1980)
Heinemann 0 434 94899 3
A collection of "rediscovered" European folk tales about heroines "who
can fight and hunt as well as any man, heroines who can defeat giants,
answer riddles, outwit the Devil, and rescue their friends and relatives
from all sort of dangers and evil spells. They are not only beautiful and
good, but also strong, brave, clever and resourceful . . .". 6–10 years.

MCNAUGHTON Colin
King Nonn the Wiser (1982)
Heinemann 0 434 94990 6
Methuen Moonlight 0 907144 34 9
A comic, stylishly illustrated picture book treatment of folk tale
expectations of male prowess: "Your people are angry . . . they want a king
who can fight dragons and slay giants", the Prime Minister tells King

Nonn. Nonn sets off obediently and survives his kingly ordeals – by being oblivious to them. Under 6.

MUNSCH Robert N.
The Paper Bag Princess (1982)
illus. by Michael Martchenko
Hippo 0 590 71126 1
When Princess Elizabeth rescues her fiancé Prince Ronald from a fierce dragon, he is shocked at her untidy appearance and she realises that he is a toad . . . A wittily told modern picture book folk tale first published in the U.S. Under 6.

NAMJOSHI Suniti
Feminist Fables (1981)
illus. by Susan Trangmar
Sheba 0 907179 04 5
An elegant, witty yet hard-hitting collection of folk tales transformed into feminist comment – Namjoshi's version of *Bluebeard* allows him "A Room of His Own" while her *Hansel and Gretel* has Gretel electing to stay with the witch. 10 years and upwards.

NESBITT Jo
The Great Escape of Doreen Potts (1981)
Sheba 0 90717907 X
Kidnapped for her resemblance to about-to-be-married Princess Brassica, Doreen Potts turns the tables on the ruling class and exposes their devious deals in this witty, pacily told story. 6–8 years.

OFFEN Hilda
Rita the Rescuer (1981)
Methuen 0 416 21150 X
Rita often feels left out – until the day her Rescuer's outfit arrives and gives her superpowers. Now Rita the Rescuer can save her brother from Basher Briggs the bully, rescue a baby from drowning and mend a car in the nick of time. A jokey picture book told in cartoon strip. Under 6.

PERL Lila
That Crazy April (1974)
Lions 0 00 671228 2
Eleven-year-old Cress has a Women's Movement activist mother who is always pushing her along the feminist path. Cress opts rebelliously for more traditional roles – until the day she discovers that, as a girl, she really is getting the thin end of the stick. A punchy, funny book that deals directly with the ways that the Women's Movement influences the expectations of young people today. 8 years and upwards.

RENIER Elizabeth
The Post Rider (1980)
Hamish Hamilton Antelope   o 241 10335 5
Dora longs to be a post-rider like her brother and her chance comes when
he falls ill and she takes his place, delivering an important letter and
helping an escaped American prisoner of war to safety (it is 1814). Renier
implicitly suggests that her heroine is by no means unusual by having Dora
mention a mail girl written about in the *Torrington Diaries* of 1793 – an
interesting fragment of women's history. 8–12 years.

RIORDAN James
The Woman in the Moon and other tales of forgotten heroines (1984)
illus. by Angela Barratt
Hutchinson   o 09 156760 2
Fourteen stories from round the world with "bold and strong and clever
heroines" – like Nastai the Saami girl, who has all the skills she needs to
survive the winter alone; and Oona the Irishwoman, who outwits the giant
Cuchulain. Some of the tales were gathered by folklorist Riordan on his
travels, others are translated and retold. 6–10 years.

SLEIGH Barbara
Grimblegraw and the Wuthering Witch (1978)
illus. by Glenys Ambrus
Hodder & Stoughton   o 340 22166 6
Puffin   o 14 03.1157 2
A marriage has been arranged between Princess Yolanda and Prince
Benedict but she thinks that boys are "boring, bossy, boastful creatures"
and he thinks that girls are "simpering, giggling, feather-brained
creatures". Both run away but as "Jane" and "John" they find that fate
unites them in defeating the giant Grimblegraw. A wittily told modern folk
tale. 8–12 years.

URE Jean
A Proper Little Nooryeff (1982)
Bodley Head   o 370 30470 5
Puffin   o 14 03.1614 0
" . . . it was alright for girls. If *they* were good at dancing everyone said
'how nice'," thinks ballet dancing working class teenager Jamie who is
worried about "compromising his masculinity". A wittily told story that
tackles male sex-stereotyping head on. 10 years and upwards.

VESTLY Anne-Cath
Aurora and the Little Blue Car (1968)
Puffin   o 1403 1016 9
While Mum goes out to work, Aurora and her baby brother are looked
after by Dad in this Norweigian family story. Aurora's father takes driving

lessons (helped by Aurora who tests him on his highway code) and we learn about a visit to Mum's office. 6–8 years.

WILLIAMS Jay
The Practical Princess and Other Liberating Fairy Tales (1979)
illus. by Rick Schreiter
Chatto & Windus   o 7011 2410 5
Hippo   o 590 72170 4
A collection of six witty tales which turn folk tale conventions on their head. Full of determined, positive princesses (like Petronella who sets out to seek her fortune) and the occasional Prince (Marco who arrives too late to rescue his princess), these stories are freshly written and illustrated with lively silhouette drawings. 6–8 years.

WRIGHTSON Patricia
I Own the Racecourse (1968)
Puffin   o 1403 0452 5
A gang of boys play together in their Australian suburban streets which back onto a racecourse. But Andy cannot distinguish easily between reality and pretence and he believes that the racecourse belongs to him. How his friends protect and rescue him from a situation he cannot understand is warmly told in a story which emphasises the caring, sensitive qualities of its male characters. 10 years and upwards.

YEOMAN John
The Wild Washerwomen (1979)
illus. by Quentin Blake
Hamish Hamilton   o 241 10044 5
Puffin   o 14 050.367 6
Subtitled a "new folk tale" this entertaining picture book has seven exploited washerwomen working from morning till night – until the day their work load is increased. They rush out leaving their employer in a pile of dirty smalls and race off on the rampage. Seven male woodcutters think they can stop them but are sadly mistaken . . . Blake's lively, cartoony illustrations tell the story with great panache. Under 6.

ZALBEN Jane Breskin
Norton's Night-Time (1979)
Lions   o oo 661771 9
Norton, a male raccoon, is afraid of the dark. He tries to comfort himself by imagining what his friends, possum, porcupine and rabbit would do in his place, only to find that they cope with the dark by huddling together: "'We're close by if you need us,' said Rabbit and he put his paw around Norton." A delicate, warmly told picture book of night-time fears. Under 6.

Young People's Own Writing

In 1971 a Stepney teacher, Chris Searle, published a collection of poems written by the children he taught. It was called *Stepney Words* and it served to inspire community publishers, writers' workshops and teachers with the realisation that children and young people have the ability not only to write creatively but to comment objectively on their political and social environment. Many poems, essays, plays and books by young people have now been published, some by community, Black and feminist publishers, some by schools, some by teachers' centres and a few by mainstream publishers:

ABRAHAMS Simon O. & 156 others
Cadbury's First Book of Children's Poetry (1983)
Beaver   0 600 20777 3
From more than 34,000 entries to Cadbury's first children's poetry competition, the judges chose the poems published here, by young poets from seven to seventeen. Themes range from Robert Kaffash's skilful "Rasta Man's Colours" written in Creole to poems about Northern Ireland (Kevin Ward's poignant "Can Johnny Come Out to Play?") and nuclear war (Mark Berry's despairing "Burying the Dead on Plumstead Common"). 8 years and upwards.

ACER PROJECT (Ed.)
Black Youth Annual Penmanship Awards
Winning Essays for 1980, 1981, 1982, 1983
Acer Project
Four collections of the winning stories, poems, short plays and essays by Black people of Afro-Caribbean descent from ten to twenty years of age, which treat the themes of Black identity, racism and roots. As Vera Bell writes in her introduction to the 1982 collection: "I have been greatly stimulated by the self-confidence and sense of group identity being displayed in the writings of a generation of Afro-Caribbean young people in a different and difficult environment." 10 years and upwards.

ASHTON Paul et al. (Eds.)
Our Lives: Young People's Autobiographies (1979)
ILEA English Centre   0 907016 00 6
Nine resilient autobiographical and two semi-fictional accounts of their lives from eleven London teenagers which present the harsh realities of childhood from young people's point of view. The writers, from England, Ireland, Morocco, Hong Kong, Jamaica, India and Uganda, write of separation, war, beatings, immigration, school, home and family. Seven of the pieces were submissions to an English Centre writing competition in 1979 and the editors comment: "When we ran the competition it didn't occur to us that the bulk of the autobiographical writing would come from the children of immigrant families; although on reflection we weren't surprised. Upheavals, adjustments, travel and hardships offer a wealth of

raw material for writing and perhaps encourage self-reflection at an earlier age than usual." 12 years and upwards.

BARHAM Faith et al.
Black Eye Perceptions (1980)
Black Ink Publications   0 9506248 3 7
A collection of mainly autobiographical poems from seven young Black Londoners, one a Rasta ("Killing Me for I"), some written in dialect ("Ridim Skank"). 12 years and upwards.

BENJAMIN Bonnie, MANN Freda & SAMUEL Ann
Bonnie, Freda and Ann (1981)
The English Centre
Two autobiographical, and one semi-fictional, accounts by three teenage girls, one Irish and two of Caribbean origin, which reflect on childhood as they embark on their adult lives. Two of the pieces describe happy, loving families (Freda's recalling the shock and pain of her father's death) while Ann writes of lack of communication and understanding between parent and child. 12 years and upwards.

BLACK INK COLLECTIVE (Eds.)
Black Ink No. 1 (1978)
Black Ink Publications   0 9506248 0 2
An attractive collection of writings by young Black South Londoners including anecdotes, poems (some in dialect) and childhood reminiscences of Africa and the Caribbean. 12 years and upwards.

BLACK INK COLLECTIVE (Eds.)
Wasted Women Friends and Lovers (1978)
Black Ink Publications   0 9506248 2 9
A second collection of writings from young Black South Londoners with plays, poems and prose about a visit to relations in Nigeria, school, carnival, abortion and rape. 12 years and upwards.

BOATSWAIN Hugh et al.
Talking Blues (1976)
illus. by Doffy Weir
Centerprise   0 903738 29 5
A collection of poems by seven teenagers, mostly Black, who used to meet each week at Centerprise community bookshop to read and discuss their poetry. The themes are sexual attraction ("Janet"), late nights and hang-overs ("The Lights are Hazy") and the experience of being Black in Britain ("Cut up Dub"). There is a hard edge to this fine collection – bitterness and anger as well as humour. 12 years and upwards.

BRISTOL BROADSIDES (Ed.)
Fred's People: Young Bristolians Speak Out (1980)
Bristol Broadsides
A collection of accounts of home life, life at school, first jobs, good and
bad, and unemployment from young people, white and Black, who meet at
"Fred's Place". Some of the contributions were written and some taped at
a Rosla literacy unit. 12 years and upwards.

CENTERPRISE YOUNG WRITERS
As Good as We Make It (1982)
Centerprise   0 903738 51 1
A collection of writings (poems, essays, extracts) from young people, Black
and white, who were around the Centerprise bookshop and community
centre at the beginning of the eighties. Some were members of
Centerprise's Young Writers Group, some worked on their own.
Illustrated with photographs by Centerprise Young Photographers' Group.
12 years and upwards.

CHRYSTIE Mara (compiler)
Anna to Zoulla, an ABC colouring book
by infants at a Hackney School (1983)
Centerprise
Created by four- to seven-year-olds at a Hackney school with the help of
their teacher, *Anna to Zoulla* is an ABC colouring book which counters
female and male sex stereotyping by illustrating each letter of the alphabet
with drawings and writing that show girls and boys to be adventurous,
imaginative and caring. Dd, for example, has the caption "Debbie and
Dawn do daring judo" while the Rr page has "Roshan rocks his red
teddy". The young artists' drawings are bold outlines, ideal for colouring
in, and they also reflect positively (as does the use of the names of the
children included for each letter of the alphabet) the multi-racial
composition of our inner-city schools. 6–8 years.

CLAIR Elaine
Elaine's Essays and Poems (1982)
Acer
A brief collection of poems and essays by Black teenager Elaine who died
in 1981 aged fifteen, published here as a tribute to her memory. Forceful,
thoughtful and sensitive, these fragments reveal, as Len Garrison's *Elegy
for Elaine* puts it: "our daughter who sought freedom". 12 years and
upwards.

EXLEY Helen (Ed.)
What It's Like to be Me
written and illus. by disabled children (1981)
Exley   0 905521 44 7

A forceful, moving collection of accounts of their lives from children with many different disabilities (spina bifida, blindness, eczema etc.) from countries all round the world, which speak frankly about their feelings about their disabilities, about the way they are treated by the able-bodied, and about the changes in attitudes and provision that they would like to see. 8 years and upwards.

HEMMINGS Susan (Ed.)
Girls Are Powerful (1982)
Sheba   0 907179 12 6
A collection of challenging pieces by young women from seven to twenty-two (originally published in *Spare Rib* and *Shocking Pink*) about being a girl today, taking in friends and lovers, books, school, work and home. A book of great impact and immediacy, a positive feminist antidote to all those teenage magazines. (*Other Award* winner 1982). 10 years and upwards.

HENSMAN Savitri
Flood at the Door (1979)
illus. by Sarah Moriaty
Centerprise   0 903738 32 3
Of Sri Lankan origin, Savitri Hensman wrote these poems while still at school and experiments boldly with different forms, from haiku to a witty take-off of a Cockney music hall ballad which hits out at the way the "sus" law is used against young Black people. 12 years and upwards.

HORSFORD Marisa
Poems (1981)
illus. by children of Claremont Primary School
Your Own Stuff Press
A very striking and often imaginatively constructed collection of poems about the frustrations of being a young person at the receiving end of adult authority at home and at school, written by a Black Nottingham eleven-year-old. 8 years and upwards.

HUNTLEY Accabre
At School Today (1977)
Bogle L'Ouverture   0 904521 11 7
These poems by the nine-year-old Accabre Huntley, whose parents are from Guyana, range from the private personal ("To mother on mother's day") to the political personal when they express the fighting spirit of young Black Britons ("At School today"; "I am the Best"). 8 years and upwards.
Easter Monday Blues (1983)
Bogle L'Ouverture   0 904521 23 0
Written when she was sixteen, Accabre's second collection of poems demonstrate her poetic development, both technically and in her more

ironic and subtle presentation of the ideas and events that concern teenagers facing up to life in the Britain of the eighties. 12 years and upwards.

IBEKWE Stella
Teenage Encounters (1978)
Centerprise
A collection of witty short stories with a twist written when Stella Ibekwe was still at school in Hackney. In one story she writes from the point of view of a white girl with a racist father, in another about a girl who doesn't want to be old fashioned but then finds that she is pregnant. 12 years and upwards.

LONDON SCHOOL STUDENTS
City Lines (1982)
The English Centre   0 907016 022 2
A selection of poems from London secondary school students submitted to the 1981 English Centre Poetry competition, covering situations and feelings about school friendships, nuclear war, family, future hopes etc. 12 years and upwards.

MCMILLAN Michael
The School Leaver (1978)
Black Ink Publications   0 9506248 1 0
A powerfully written play by a young Black writer in his fifth year at secondary school, *The School Leaver* was performed at the Royal Court theatre. It deals with the predicament of the unemployed school leaver. 12 years and upwards.

MILDINER Leslie & HOUSE Bill
The Gates (1974)
Centerprise   0 903738 13 9
A true story written by two boys who hated school, about how and why they became habitual truants. Full of lively, funny detail, this is a rare account of school life from the school students' point of view. 12 years and upwards.

MILLS Roger
A Comprehensive Education (1978)
Centerprise   0 903738 37 6
The atmosphere of school with its petty tyrannies, teacher eccentricities, playground and corridor life all the seasons round is wittily and vividly recreated in this autobiographical account of life as a school student at a London comprehensive in the second half of the sixties. Only the names have been changed to protect, as Roger Mills puts it, "the innocent and guilty alike". (*Other Award* winner 1979). 12 years and upwards.

NOLAN Christopher
Dam-Burst of Dreams (1981)
Sphere 0 7221 6410 6
Born severely brain damaged, Christopher Nolan is unable to control his
limbs or talk. When he was eleven a new drug gave him enough control to
type, using a unicorn stick, and enabled him to communicate for the first
time a series of powerful and original poems that he had composed in his
head. This book contains Christopher's startlingly exuberant
autobiography, "A Mammy Encomium", ("she was labouring to give birth
to her gelatinous, moaning, dankerous baby boy") as well as poems, short
stories and plays covering the years from eleven to fourteen. 12 years and
upwards.

ST JOHN CASS SCHOOL STUDENTS
Stepney Words I & II (1971)
Centerprise 0 903738 04 X
The now famous collection of poems by children at a Stepney school
whose publication led to the dismissal of Chris Searle, the English teacher
who had published them (because it was felt that they presented a bleak
and despairing view of life in Stepney) followed by many of the children
going on strike in his support. 8 years and upwards.

SHAH Hina
Never Trust a Camel (1982)
illus. by Aneela Shah, Lisa Rice, Yuen Chan & Karen Wharton
Peckham Publishing Project 0 906464 06 4
A lively retelling (with modern touches) of a traditional Asian story about
Ahmed and his good friend Mr Camel who set out on a long journey
through the desert. The night is cold and Ahmet finds that his tent is too
small for both of them. Thirteen-year-old Hina Shah heard this story
from her mother and decided to write it down in English. 6–8 years.

SMITH Kathleen & 37 others
On the Reservation: a second anthology of Gypsy and Traveller children's
writing (1978)
SMITH Charlie & 37 others
Tootsey and the Pups: a third anthology of Gypsy and Traveller children's
writing (1978)
from Traveller Education, 60 Rowley Street, Walsall WS1 2AY
Written by Gypsy and Traveller children aged from five to sixteen, these
stories came together as the result of the 1977 National Gypsy Education
Council's Story Writing Competition for Gypsy Children.
Autobiographical pieces, family history, fantasy and ghost stories make up
these two freshly written, varied collections. Each young writer's
contribution is prefaced by brief autobiographical details. 8 years and
upwards.

USHERWOOD Vivian
Poems (1972)
Centerprise   0 903738 066
Born in Jamaica, Vivian Usherwood wrote these poems when he was
twelve years old at a Hackney school. His view of the world is a pessimistic
one ("Life is playing me up/Spite is having an affair with me") and many
of his poems have a melancholy quality. Vivian died tragically in 1980. His
Poems has now sold over 10,000 copies making him one of Britain's better
selling poets. 10 years and upwards.

Addresses for community publications listed in this section:

Acer Project, 275 Kennington Lane, London SE11 5QZ
ILEA English Centre, Sutherland Street, London SW1
Black Ink, 258 Coldharbour Lane, London SW9
Centerprise, 136 Kingsland High Street, London E8
Bristol Broadsides, 110 Cheltenham Road, Bristol BS6 5RW
Your Own Stuff Press, 13 Mona Road, West Bridgford, Nottingham
Bogle L'Ouverture Publications, 5a Chignell Place, London W13
Peckham Publishing Project, The Bookplace, 13 Peckham High Street,
London SE15 5EB
Traveller Education, 60 Rowley Street, Walsall WS1 2AY

Homosexuality in Books for Young People

It was not until the 1970s that children's books began to reflect, in a handful of
titles, the demand of the Gay Liberation Movement that gay people be positively
presented in cultural forms. As Jean Milloy wrote in 1979 ("Children's Books
Come Out" *Children's Book Bulletin* Autumn 1979): "For young lesbians there
are virtually no books that will tell them anything positive about themselves . . . "
while in the same article John Vincent commented: "We should be seeing gays
both as central characters and as bit parts in novels; not as limp-wristed or ultra-
butch stereotypes, but as real people with a valid lifestyle."

BÖSCHE Susanne
Jenny Lives with Eric and Martin (1983)
photos by Andreas Hansen
Gay Men's Press   0 907040 22 5
First published in Copenhagen, *Jenny* describes five-year-old Jenny and
her family – her father, Martin, and his lover, Eric, with whom she lives,
and her mother, Karen, who often comes to visit. A birthday tea, reading
stories, going to the laundrette and cleaning the house form the routine
domestic background of which Martin and Eric's relationship is a natural
part. Under 7.

239

CHAMBERS Aidan
Dance on My Grave (1982)
Bodley Head   0 370 30366 0
Sixteen-year-old Hal becomes completely besotted with Barry and is
devastated when Barry dies in an accident after they have quarrelled. But
would their relationship have lasted? A perceptive, moving and often funny
account of a love affair between two boys – unusual in that its starting
point is the quality of their relationship rather than the difficulty of
establishing it in a homophobic society. 12 years and upwards.

GUY Rosa
Ruby (1981)
Gollancz   0 575 03052 6
"Bronzie love, we have the whole summer. Whatever happens you are my
Bronzie, the most perfect girl I have ever met." But Daphne, tough,
politically aware and destined for Brandeis, does not promise Ruby that
she will stay. Criticised for its cop-out ending, this novel is nevertheless a
powerful account of a summer love affair between two very different Black
Harlem teenage girls. 12 years and upwards.

HAUTZIG Deborah
Hey, Dollface (1979)
Hamish Hamilton   0 241 89214 7
Lions   00 671964 3
Val and Chlöe, new girls at a smart New York girls' school, stick together
and develop a close friendship – but "how do you separate loving as a
friend and sexual love – or do they cross over sometimes?" A funny,
delicately told story of two teenage girls realising their sexual feelings.
11 years and upwards.

IRELAND Timothy
Who Lies Inside (1984)
Gay Mens Press   0 907040 30 6
About to take his 'A' levels and with plans to do PE at teacher training
college, rugby playing Martin finds himself secretly drawn to brainy
Richard who is hoping to read English at university. Martin starts going
out with Margaret but he cannot get Richard out of his mind . . . A
sensitively told novel of a school student's realisation that he is gay.
(*Other Award* winner 1984). 12 years and upwards.

REES David
In the Tent (1979)
Dobson   0 234 72091 3
Seventeen-year-old Tim is gay but cannot reconcile this realisation with
his Roman Catholicism. He retreats into a fantasy world when an
unexpected crisis forces him to face who he is and to realise that he is not

alone. A complex novel that examines society's view of homosexuality
through a teenager's hard coming-out. 12 years and upwards.

The Third World in Children's Books

In 1971 the Institute of Race Relations published a critical bibliography of
children's books about the Third World, *Books for Children: The Homelands of
Immigrants in Britain*. In the introduction Janet Hill wrote: "Many books are
blatantly biased and prejudiced . . . how is an African child growing up in this
country likely to react to some of the patronizing, insensitive and outmoded tales
of the noble white man and the natives which are still in print? Perhaps saddest
of all is that despite the rich variety of adult novels by African, Indian and West
Indian writers, there are hardly any for children . . ."

In 1985 the situation can be seen to have improved; it is possible to find
children's books from Third World writers of calibre – but only by looking
through the lists of the alternative publishers, the Educational publishers, and
lists designed for the Third World market (Nelson Caribbean, Heinemann
African Writers), or by buying books imported from the Third World by Black
and Asian bookshops or by distributors like Third World Publications. The
mainstream of British children's book publishing has not responded adequately
to the need for books about the Third World from Third World writers and the
number of those published remains pitifully few:

AGARD John
Dig Away Two-Hole Tim (1981)
illus. by Jennifer Northway
Bodley Head   0 370 30421 7
An exuberant picture book about a small boy in Guyana who loves
"digging holes, fixing holes". Sometimes this means that he helps to dig
the garden: "Look how the sun got the earth harden"; sometimes it means
trouble: "at school teacher always got to say, put that karuru seed away".
Northway's bright, lively illustrations reflect the comic situations and
personalities of the story admirably. Under 6.

BENJAMIN Floella
Floella's Fun Book (1984)
illus. by Eileen Browne
Magnet   0 416 46110 7
Three short stories to read aloud about Jason, a small Trinidadian boy,
(making his carnival costume, learning to take photographs, going to the
market for rice for the first time) are included in this cheerful activity
book, full of ideas about things to make and do. Under 7.

BOND Ruskin
Big Business (1979)
illus. by Valerie Littlewood
Hamish Hamilton Gazelle   0 241 10246 4

Ruskin Bond has always lived in and written about India; he writes: "Although my father was British, I grew up an Indian. There has been no division of loyalties; only a double inheritance." Bond writes extremely well for middle age range readers (a rare gift!) and this story about eight-year-old Ranji who spends the day bartering so that he can buy the jalebis he longs for is just one of several fine short novels published in Britain. 6–8 years.
The Road to the Bazaar (1980)
illus. by Valerie Littlewood
Julia MacRae   0 86203 020
A collection of ironic, often funny short stories about young Indians from different backgrounds which present a broad social canvas and in which there are problems that cannot be resolved. In "The Visitor", for example, street seller Mohan, who sleeps rough, studies when he can for an examination which could mean "no more selling combs and buttons at street corners"; but the odds are hopelessly weighted against him and he fails. 8–12 years.

DESAI Anita
The Village by the Sea (1982)
Heinemann   0 434 93436 4
Set in a seaside village near Bombay, this demanding novel tells how thirteen-year-old Lila and eleven-year-old Hari manage, in their different ways, to provide for their family while their mother is away ill and their father escapes into drink. Meanwhile the village's traditional way of life is threatened by plans to build a fertiliser factory. 12 years and upwards.

DHONDY Farrukh
Poona Company (1980)
Gollancz   0 575 02901 3
Lions   0 00 672429 9
A many layered reminiscence of childhood and adolescence in Poona, peopled with school friends, teachers, and the frequenters of the streets, in which Dhondy traces his development into the young man who was to leave Poona for Cambridge. 12 years and upwards.

EMECHETA Buchi
The Moonlight Bride (1980)
Oxford University Press   0 19 271435 X
Set in a Nigerian village, *The Moonlight Bride* tells how Ngbeke and Ogoli, two young girls, make preparations to welcome a new bride into their community – but who is she and who is the groom? A gently humorous story that reaffirms that "the beauty of the heart" matters more than "the colour or superficial beauty of any person". 12 years and upwards.
The Wrestling Match (1980)
Oxford University Press   0 19 271436 8
The young men of Uma aya Biafra (those born around the time of the

Civil War) are making a nuisance of themselves and not finding their place in village life. Then the village elders decide, with the unwitting help of the village girls, to teach them a lesson: "in a good war, nobody wins". 12 years and upwards.

HALWORTH Grace
The Carnival Kite (1980)
illus. by Patrice Aitken
Methuen   o 416 87880 6
A Hertfordshire librarian for many years, Trinidadian Grace Hallworth draws on the tradition of kite-making for carnival in this picture book set in Trinidad about a small boy, Arthur, who longs to have a kite of his own. Full of domestic and neighbourhood detail, this warmly told story reflects positively the dialect speech of Trinidad. (Some commentators have expressed concern about the depiction and nickname of the Chinese boy, Chinky Fat, in this story). 6–8 years.

HIDDEN Norman & HOLLINS Amy
Many People, Many Voices (1978)
Hutchinson   o 09 133661 9
One of the legacies of colonialism is the number of poets round the world who write in English. This collection brings together some of their poetry and arranges it thematically under headings like Love, Animals, Life and Death. The contributors come from Ghana, the West Indies, New Zealand, Cyprus etc. 12 years and upwards.

JONES Jennifer & KNIGHT Penelope
Benji and Carlos (1984)
Arawidi   o 946028 02 8
A small boy, Benji, who lives on the Caribbean island of St Columbus, worries about whom he will play with when he goes to stay with his grandparents. Carlos, a very self-assured and bossy frog who speaks the local dialect, turns out to be an ideal companion. A funny, brightly illustrated story that accords a natural place to dialect speech. 6–8 years.

KURUSA
Nowhere to Play (1981)
illus. by Monica Doppert
A & C Black   o 7136 2236 9
Based on the lives of children in a Venezuelan shanty town, this story tells how they build their own playground when the council fails to keep its promises. (*Other Award* winner 1983). 8–12 years.

MCDOWELL Robert & LAVITT Edward (Eds.)
Third World Voices for Children (1971)
illus. by Barbara Kohn Isaac
Allison & Busby   o 85031 324 4

This excellent book is divided into four sections – Africa, West Indies, United States and Papua, New Guinea – which contain folk tales, poems, snatches of autobiography and modern stories, all stringently selected to add up to a fresh and vigorous taste of the Black experience in these different parts of the world. 8–12 years.

PALMER C. Everard
The Wooing of Beppo Tate (1972)
Deutsch   0 233 95857 6
My Father, Sun-Sun Johnson (1974)
Deutsch   0 233 96454 1
Beppo Tate and Roy Penner: The Runaway Marriage Brokers (1980)
Deutsch   0 233 97258 7
Everard Palmer's birthplace, Kendal, a Jamaican village, is the setting for these warmly told stories of a rural community in the 1950s. *The Wooing of Beppo Tate* is a courtship comedy; *My Father, Sun-Sun Johnson* (Palmer's best book) has a divorced man and his son rebuilding their lives; in *Beppo Tate* two boys find an abandoned baby, while in *The Marriage Brokers* they act as matchmakers in love affairs, even writing one couple's love letters. 10 and upwards.

PEPETELA
Ngunga's Adventures
trans. by Chris Searle
illus. by Steve Lee & by photos.
Young World Books (1980)   0 905405 03 X
This story of a thirteen year old orphan growing up in the midst of the Angolan war of liberation was written by Pepetela while he was actively involved with the M.P.L.A. in the anti-colonialist war against the Portuguese. As Ngunga travels through the war-zone he grasps the extent of the exploitation of colonised Angola and the need to struggle for freedom and independence. As Chris Searle writes in his preface: "Ngunga is . . . the symbol of a young human being who begins his quest to discover the world and its people – as they actually are in the midst of the struggle to build their own new way of living." (The *Other Award* commendation of 1981 went to Young World Books.). 12 years and upwards.

SALKEY Andrew
Hurricane (1964)
Oxford University Press   0 19 277087 X
Puffin   0 1403 0963 2
Drought (1966)
Oxford University Press   0 19 271258 6
Two of Andrew Salkey's Caribbean quartet of novels about natural disasters: in *Hurricane* thirteen-year-old Joe and his family prepare their

Kingston house against an imminent hurricane and come through it safely, while *Drought* tells of the hard conditions endured in a Jamaican village through the adventures of four boys who try to help to make it rain. 8–12 years.

Riot
Oxford University Press (1967)   0 19 277105 1
Kingston, Jamaica; and poverty and unemployment lead to a general strike and riots. Three boys get caught up in the struggle to form trade unions and their growing understanding of the issues at stake is strongly conveyed. 8–12 years.

Joey Tyson (1974)
Bogle L'Ouverture   0 904 52100 1
In 1968 Dr Walter Rodney, the internationally renowned historian and political thinker (murdered in 1980 in Georgetown) was served with an expulsion order when he tried to return to Jamaica. This moving novel based on these actual events, and the demonstrations and police brutality that followed, raises crucial issues for young readers about democracy and state control through its fictional characters. One of the most significant socialist children's books of the 1970s. 12 years and upwards.

THEWLIS et al. (Eds.)
Cuba: An Anthology for Young People (1983)
Young World Books   0 905405 07 2
The story of Cuba's history vividly brought to life through stories, fables, poems and personal accounts illustrating different historical periods. 12 years and upwards.

THOMPSON Roselle
Dreams of a Far-Off Land (1982)
illus. by John Freeman
from Acer Project, 275 Kennington Lane, London SE11 5QZ
Three simply told stories set in the Caribbean which treat the influence of city life on village expectations. In the title story, old Septimus only realises the richness of his rural island life when he has left it behind. In "An Exceptional Boy," the aptly named twelve-year-old Jonathan Smart passes the exam for a new school away from his poor village home – to find that his wealth is "the knowledge in [his] head". Rufus in "Rufus and the Snake" is a restless eighteen-year-old attracted by fast cars and girls although destined to follow his father as village pastor. 12 years and upwards.

Books in First Languages

While Asian and Black bookshops have long been making books in first languages available, mainstream British publishers' few ventures into the field have met with little success (were the books too expensive?). Methuen Educational's publication of texts in various languages on adhesive paper to stick into their Terraced House books is the most flexible and imaginative response so far.

During the 1980s there has also been a spate of locally produced children's books in first languages and with dual language texts to meet the needs of children who have little or no access to books in their first languages. Listed here are examples of this new publishing activity that is emanating from schools, community bookshops, parents' groups and teachers' centres:

AJITSARIA Aruna
The Tiger and the Woodpecker (1984)
illus. by Judy Cobden
Middlesex Polytechnic £1.00 from Jennie Ingham, The Middlesex Polytechnic, All Saints, White Hart Lane, London N17 8HR
The first picture book in what is to be a series of traditional tales collected from British ethnic minority community story-tellers and published in dual language editions. *The Tiger and the Woodpecker* is available in English and Bengali/Urdu/Gujerati/Hindi/Punjabi/Turkish/Greek.

ALI Mahreen & MANN Elizabeth
Mahreen's Secret (1982)
illus. by Amanda Welch
Urdu version by Shaukat Khan (Eng/Urdu text)   0 901974 11 0
from The English Language Centre, London Borough of Waltham Forest, Markhouse Road, London E17 8BD
Mahreen plants the seed of a mango stone and to everyone's surprise it grows into a little tree. (Other titles available.)

DUTTA Krishna
The World of Rani (1983)
Eng/Bengali/Hindi/Gujarati text   0 907615 00 7
from Reading Matters, 10 Lymington Avenue, London N22
A picture book with line drawings and a simple text about how Rani, a small Asian girl, likes to look through the family photograph album. (Other titles available.)

HEASLIP Peter
The Terraced House Books
Methuen Educational
The *texts* of the *Terraced House* books are available in Turkish, Bengali and Urdu on adhesive paper. Details from Schools Promotion Unit, Methuen Educational, Northway, Andover, Hampshire.

MACKAY Karen (Ed.)
Family Books
8 titles to date, from Princess May Junior School, Barretts Grove, Stoke Newington, London N16
A series of lively books written by parents from different cultural

backgrounds about their memories, and illustrated by the children. All the books have been translated and have dual language texts.

NEWHAM WOMEN'S COMMUNITY WRITING GROUP
The Elves and the Shoemaker
Eng/Guj   0 946959 02 1
Eng/Pun   0 946959 01 3
Eng/Urd   0 946959 00 5
Dove Books, from Newham Women's Community Writing Group, 245 Dawlish Drive, Ilford, Essex 1G29EH
A simple version of the traditional tale with illustrations.

RAHMAN Sophia
Galpo Mala (1982)
illus. by Aysha Huda   0 946174 03 2
from Learn Your Language, 38 Umfreville Road, London N4 1SB
A collection of well-known Western traditional tales (e.g. *Goldilocks and the Three Bears*) retold in Bengali for "bilingual children to build a bridge between children's knowledge of mother-tongue and English." For 5–8 year olds. (Other titles available.)

SANDHU Rashpal
The Snake and the Mongoose (1982)
Punjabi version by Alma Singh Bansal (Eng/Punjabi text)
from Newham Language Reading Centre, The Upton Centre, Claude Road, London E13
A traditional tale written by a school student as part of a project to help both Secondary school students and younger children to learn English through traditional tales. (Other titles available.)

Index